RENAISSANCE DRAMA

New Series II ❧ *1969*

Renaissance Drama

New Series II

Essays Principally

on

Dramatic Theory

and Form

Edited by S. Schoenbaum

Northwestern University Press

EVANSTON 1969

THE ILLUSTRATION on the front cover is an engraving of Giangurgolo by F. Joullain in Luigi Riccoboni, *Histoire du théâtre italien* (Paris, 1728). The illustration on the back cover is *Voluptas ærumnosa* from Geoffrey Whitney, *A Choice of Emblemes* (Leyden, 1586), and is reproduced by courtesy of The Newberry Library, Chicago, Illinois.

Editorial Note

RENAISSANCE DRAMA, an annual publication, provides a forum for scholars in various parts of the globe: wherever the drama of the Renaissance is studied. Coverage, so far as subject matter is concerned, is not restricted to any single national theater. The chronological limits of the Renaissance are interpreted liberally, and space is available for essays on precursors, as well as on the utilization of Renaissance themes by later writers. Investigations shedding light on theatrical history and actual stage production are especially welcome, as are comparative studies. Editorial policy favors articles of some scope. Essays that are exploratory in nature, that are concerned with critical or scholarly methodology, that raise new questions or embody fresh approaches to perennial problems are particularly appropriate for a publication which originated from the proceedings of the Modern Language Association Conference on Research Opportunities in Renaissance Drama.

The 1970 volume will be devoted mainly to drama in its intellectual context. Contributions offered for publication should be addressed to the Editor, RENAISSANCE DRAMA, Northwestern University, 2040 Sheridan Road, Evanston, Illinois 60201. Prospective contributors are requested to follow the recommendations of the *MLA Style Sheet* (revised edition) in preparing manuscripts. For quotations from Shakespeare the Alexander edition is used.

Contents

RENAISSANCE DRAMA
New Series II ᔌ *1969*

Three Types of Renaissance Catharsis

O. B. HARDISON

URING THE SIXTEENTH CENTURY theories of catharsis were as abundant and as various as they are today. Some Renaissance theories were academic. They are found in critical treatises but have little or no relation to the living drama of the period. Others, among them the most influential, were not even labeled "theories of catharsis" by the writers who formulated them. If we define catharsis functionally as "the effect of tragedy," the most common Renaissance theories are in this category. Evidently, the academic theories served chiefly to display the learning of their bookish inventors, while the non-academic ones had a vital and direct effect on the work of practicing artists.

Among the practical theories, three are sufficiently well defined and influential to warrant more consideration than they have yet received in studies of Renaissance drama. As it happens, all three are found in English Renaissance criticism, and, perhaps more interesting, all are self-consciously utilized by Shakespeare. For convenience, they can be labeled respectively as the moral, religious, and literal theories of catharsis. Although these labels are not used by sixteenth-century writers, the theories themselves are sufficiently distinctive to be easily identified wherever they

3

appear. Since they are all theories about the effect of tragedy and were formulated during what is generally considered the most vital period of English drama, they should have a lively interest not only for readers of Shakespeare, but also for historians and critics of tragedy as a literary genre.

I

The first of the three theories appears in its most obvious form in Thomas Heywood's *An Apology for Actors,* written around 1604. In the course of demonstrating the social utility of plays, Heywood remarks on their capacity for "attaching the consciences of the spectators, finding themselues toucht in presenting the vices of others." [1]

What Heywood means is that tragedies can so move individual spectators that they voluntarily divulge, as he says, "notorious murders, long conceald from the eyes of the world." He is so taken with this effect that he devotes some three pages to illustrating it.

The most lurid of his instances concerns a townswoman of Lynn in Norfolk who attended a play titled *Fair Frances.* It seems that the heroine of this Elizabethan soap opera had "mischieuously and secretely" murdered her husband and was thereafter harassed by his ghost, which appeared "at diuers times . . . in most horrid and fearefull shapes." While watching the avenging ghost, the townswoman of Lynn "suddenly skritched and cryd out Oh my husband, my husband! I see the ghost of my husband fiercely threatning and menacing me." Questioned by other members of the audience, she confessed "vn-urged" that she had murdered her own "real-life" husband. Later, she repeated her confession before a magistrate, by whom she was promptly sent to the scaffold. Heywood adds, "That this is true, as well by the report of the Actors as the records of the Towne, there are many eye-witnesses of this accident yet liuing, vocally to confirme it." [2]

Although Heywood is content to tell the story, the psychology underlying it is plain enough. The perpetrator of an undiscovered crime is troubled by a guilty conscience. He is in torment. Confession, the only

1. Thomas Heywood, *An Apology for Actors,* ed. Richard H. Perkinson, Scholars' Facsimiles & Reprints # 27 (New York, 1941), F3^r.
2. *Ibid.,* G1^r–2^r.

way to relieve the pain, is prevented by his fear of the consequences. Seeing the crime enacted on the stage can make the pangs of conscience so intense that the need for relief via confession becomes stronger than the fear of exposure. The confession has two beneficial results. First, a crime is solved and a criminal punished. Society is strengthened, if only minutely, by the clearing up of an injustice. In fact, this is one of Heywood's chief arguments for the social utility of drama. Second, and equally important, confession brings relief to the criminal (or sinner). It is the first step toward moral regeneration. The cathartic value of such a step—the purgation of guilt and fear—is obvious. Confession, as the divines say, is good for the soul. Psychology merely underwrites the religious formula. The criminal who confesses after seeing his crime reenacted on the stage is in the same position as the mental patient relieved of guilt symptoms by recalling (and reliving) the experiences that caused them—a technique that Sigmund Freud aptly called "the cathartic method" when he first began using it in the 1880's. Of course, Freud's method was anticipated by Dostoevsky in *Crime and Punishment* as well as by Heywood.

The idea of moral catharsis presented in *An Apology For Actors* may seem rather crude and simplistic to a modern reader. It is used, however, with remarkable effectiveness in Shakespeare's *Hamlet*. After Act I, it will be recalled, Hamlet suspects Claudius of having murdered his father but is also worried that the ghost who has revealed the murder to him may be lying. At the end of Act II Hamlet devises a plan to test the ghost's veracity. He explains the plan as follows:

> I have heard
> That guilty creatures sitting at a play,
> Have by the very cunning of the scene
> Been struck so to the soul that presently
> They have proclaim'd their malefactions;
> For murder, though it have no tongue, will speak
> With most miraculous organ. I'll have these players
> Play something like the murder of my father
> Before mine uncle. I'll observe his looks;
> I'll tent him to the quick. If 'a but blench,
> I know my course.
>
> (II. ii. 584–594)

Hamlet is referring to the play titled *The Murder of Gonzago,* which he has modified to bring out its parallels with the story told him by the ghost, and which is actually presented before the Danish court in Act III.

Note that Claudius may respond to it in three ways. First, he may simply enjoy it, showing no signs of discomfort. If so, Hamlet evidently plans to delay his revenge or abandon it on the assumption that the ghost lied. Second, Claudius may behave like the townswoman of Lynn and "proclaim his malefactions." Third, he may be strong enough to endure the play without confessing, but his behavior may betray his guilt: "if 'a but blench, I know my course."

In the context of Shakespeare's play, the most desirable of the three possibilities is the second, public confession. The Danish court and people accept the legitimacy of Claudius' rule. Unlike Hamlet and the theater audience, they are not aware that a crime has been committed. They may, in fact, share the suspicion of Claudius, suggested in at least two places (I. ii. 108–109; II. ii. 248–266), that Hamlet is "ambitious" for his father's crown. If Claudius does not "proclaim his malefactions"—that is, if the court and people are not made aware of the King's guilt—Hamlet's revenge will appear to be a brutal political assassination and the kingdom may be plunged into turmoil. As Rosencrantz remarks, "The cease of majesty / Dies not alone, but like a gulf doth draw / What's near it with it" (III. iii. 15–17). Denmark, then, desperately needs the sort of social purification that Heywood (and Hamlet) feel tragedy can provide. The point is neatly underscored by Shakespeare's use of the imagery of disease to characterize Denmark's condition. A confession by Claudius would literally purge the kingdom of the sickness that is destroying it.

Unfortunately, as we all know, Claudius does not confess. This may be because Hamlet lacks faith in his own strategy and spoils the play's effect by his interruptions. At any rate, instead of confessing, Claudius abruptly leaves the hall. To Hamlet this is a clear admission of guilt, and most producers of the play accept his interpretation. On the other hand, the precise way in which Claudius should behave when leaving is ambiguous in Shakespeare's text. The only characters who do not know of the murder and who comment on the King's departure are Guildenstern and Gertrude, and both of them believe that he left in a rage as a result of Hamlet's tactless insults. The fact is that no matter what Hamlet may think and Shakespeare's audience may know, to the members of the court Claudius seems in the right and Hamlet in the wrong. The possibility of a public redress of justice has been lost. We are vividly reminded of this fact during the last scene of the play, when the reaction of the courtiers to

Hamlet's attack on the King is the horrified cry, "Treason! treason!" (V. ii. 315). Even at the end they are unaware of Claudius' guilt.

But seeing one's crimes enacted in the theater has personal as well as public significance. When Guildenstern informs Hamlet of the King's "choler," Hamlet replies with the brutal pun, "for me to put him to his purgation would perhaps plunge him into far more choler" (III. ii. 297–299). Whatever sense we attribute to Hamlet's word "purgation," he has just made an attempt to "put Claudius to it," and in spite of his momentarily triumphant mood, he has failed. There has been no confession, not even an unambiguous sign of guilt. We may assume that Heywood's gentlewoman of Lynn went to the scaffold with an easy conscience, even as Mistress Anne Frankford in his play *A Woman Killed with Kindness* died in the odor of sanctity. Claudius, on the other hand, feels intensified torment, which vents itself publicly as rage.

The anguish of conscience which the courtiers interpret as rage is movingly revealed in the soliloquy that Claudius utters in the scene following the play-within-a-play. As Claudius attempts to pray, he expresses himself in images of horror and self-revulsion. His offense has the stench of a decaying animal: it is "rank, it smells to heaven!" He, himself, is as vile as Cain, the archetypal criminal: "It hath the primal eldest curse upon't / A brother's murder" (III. iii. 37–39). Because the impulse to repent is blocked by the desire to retain the crown, the soliloquy develops as a series of paradoxes expressing bafflement, frustration, and entrapment:

> My stronger guilt defeats my strong intent,
> And, like a man to double business bound,
> I stand in pause where I shall first begin,
> And both neglect.
>
> (III. iii. 40–43)

And:

> Try what repentance can. What can it not?
> Yet what can it when one cannot repent?
> O wretched state! O bosom black as death!
> O limed soul, that, struggling to be free,
> Art more engag'd.
>
> (III. iii. 65–69)

In short, instead of cooperating with the tragic therapy like the townswoman of Lynn, Claudius resists it. The result is not catharsis—not a calming of the mind—but, as we might say, an anti-catharsis, an intensification of the perturbations associated with guilt.

II

A second, rather more complex, theory about the effect of tragedy is found in Elizabethan discussions of the requirement that drama observe poetic justice. It is a commonplace of the period that at the end of a drama the characters should be rewarded and punished according to their virtues and vices. William Baldwin wrote of the "tragedies" in the 1559 edition of *A Mirror for Magistrates:* ". . . here, as in a loking-glas, you shall see (if any vice be in you) howe the like hath bene punished in other heretofore, whereby admonished, I trust it will be a good occasion to move you the soner to amendment."[3] And in his *Apology* Heywood applies the same theory to the formal drama that had come into being since *A Mirror for Magistrates:*

If we present a Tragedy, we include the fatall and abortiue ends of such as commit notorious murders, which is aggrauated and acted with all the Art that may be, to terrifie men from the like abhorred practises. If wee present a forreigne History, the subject is so intended, that in the liues of *Romans, Grecians,* or others, either the vertues of our Country-men are extolled, or their vices reproued, as thus, by the example of *Caesar* to stir souldiers to valour, & magnanimity: by the fall of *Pompey,* that no man trust in his owne strength: we present *Alexander,* killing his friend in his rage, to reproue rashnesse: *Midas,* choked with gold, to taxe couetousnesse. . . .[4]

The belief that the aim of literature is moral instruction—and that it achieves this aim by making the punishment fit the crime—underlies a vast (and often rather tedious) body of homiletic writing from Aesop's *Fables* through the morality plays to *Uncle Tom's Cabin* and beyond. The surprising fact about this belief is that, on the one hand, it is almost universal in Elizabethan criticism, while, on the other, it is often hard to discern in the tragedies of the major Elizabethan playwrights. Marlowe, Shakespeare, Chapman, Webster, and Ford, to name only the most ob-

---

3. "Preface" to *A Mirror for Magistrates,* ed. Lily B. Campbell (Cambridge, Eng., 1938), pp. 65–66.
4. Heywood, *Apology,* F3ᵛ.

vious, simply do not write tragedies like those described by Heywood, in which the protagonist exemplifies a neatly labeled moral flaw that the audience is taught to "abhor" by the catastrophe.

Let us file this fact away for future reference. For now, we will merely observe that poetic justice has—like moral catharsis—both social and personal significance. The social aspect is easy to define. Society is obviously strengthened if its members learn, when they visit the theater, to cultivate virtue and shun vice.

The personal aspect is more difficult. Literary history, not to mention countless Grade B movies and television serials, teaches us that poetic justice is a standard formula for popular entertainment. In fact, one of the distinguishing features of much of what has been considered "serious literature" since the Victorian period is that it self-consciously *rejects* poetic justice. Since very few people learn their morality from the theater, the enduring appeal of poetic justice must come from the fact that it satisfies needs that go much deeper than simple moral improvement.

We can begin to get an insight into these needs by recognizing that poetic justice is a conscious or unconscious imitation of ideal justice. Ideal justice, however, is not a legal but a religious concept. It is defined not by jury trials and rules of evidence but by eschatology, and its two defining characteristics are a judge who is omniscient and a judgment perfectly suited to the offense. Shakespeare's Claudius makes the contrast nicely. Having observed that in the real world justice is often imperfect, since "the wicked prize itself buys out the law," he adds:

> But 'tis not so above:
> There is no shuffling; there the action lies
> In his true nature; and we ourselves compell'd
> Even to the teeth and forehead of our faults,
> To give in evidence.
>
> (III. iii. 60–64)

The fact that plays emphasizing poetic justice are modeled on—or symbolic of—ideal justice is perhaps sufficiently evident from the quite inhuman assurance with which rewards and punishments are parceled out at their conclusions. It also helps to explain the curious tendency of such plays to end with trials in which the judge is either supernatural, or has supernatural powers, or, at the very least, possesses an unrealistic fullness of knowledge concerning the issues. In the *Eumenides* of Aeschylus, to take an example from Greek drama, the judgment is guaranteed by the fact that the judge is no less a figure than the Goddess Athene herself. Shakespeare's *Measure for Measure* is more typical of modern practice, which likes to cover the supernatural with a veneer of rational "explanation." Shakespeare's Duke of Vienna is definitely human, but he spends most of the play disguised as a friar who is able to share the most private thoughts of the other characters. The result is that when he acts as judge in Act V he has acquired a quite un-judicial omniscience that enables him to deal out perfect justice, tempered with mercy. Among less sophisticated examples of the arraignment play are Shakespeare's *Merchant of Venice* and Ben Jonson's *Every Man in His Humour*. That such resolutions are universal is shown by almost every episode of the Perry Mason television series. Indeed, the typical ending of a Perry Mason episode exactly parallels what Claudius imagines about the Last Judgment. Each episode ends with a trial, and at the end of every trial, with monotonous regularity, the criminal is overwhelmed by a nightmarish impulse to confess—to "give in evidence, even to the teeth and forehead of his faults."

If poetic justice can be understood as an attempt to imitate or symbolize dramatically the ideal of perfect justice, the satisfaction that it provides is best understood in the same context. Evidently, the satisfaction comes from having one's deepest feelings about what is right confirmed by the action on the stage. Life is imperfect, mysterious, frustrating; it seldom works out as we feel it should. A drama based on poetic justice, on the other hand, offers what life cannot. One says of the villains that "they got what they deserved" and of the hero and heroine, "they were married and lived happily ever after."

Like poetic justice, this reaction is sharply defined in traditional thought about divine Judgment. For better or for worse, the most authoritative version of Judgment in the Christian tradition is the Book of Revelation. In chapter 16, St. John has a vision of angels pouring God's vials of wrath onto the sinful earth. As the third angel empties his vial, he exclaims, "Thou art righteous, O Lord . . . because thou hast judged thus. For they have shed the blood of saints and prophets, and thou hast given them blood to drink; for they are worthy" (Rev. 16: 5–6). In other words, instead of arousing pity, the terrible judgment brings righteous satisfaction. One assumes, of course, that St. John's angels do not take a sadistic delight in suffering. Rather, their satisfaction is a by-product of their vision of the completion of God's plan for measuring out to the wicked exactly what they have merited. As the angel observes, "they are worthy" —they have gotten what they deserved.

This is logically understandable, but it does seem a trifle grim. Therefore we turn with relief to the much more congenial expression of the same idea in Dante's *Divine Comedy*. Here again the poet examines human affairs from a transcendent vantage point, but his presentation of this perspective develops only gradually. As Dante passes through the Inferno, he is as troubled as his reader by the suffering that he encounters. Ironically, the pagan Virgil, his guide, often has to reprove him for excessive pity toward the victims of Christian justice. Gradually, as he ascends toward Paradise, his vision clears. On the third level of Paradise he meets the nun Piccarda, who perfectly expresses the lesson that he— and his readers—are to have learned from the preceding journey, with the single line "In His will is our peace" (*Paradiso,* III, 85). That is, in life, where we see through (or in) a glass darkly, pity is a virtue. If we could see truly, however, the pity would be replaced by the deep peace that comes from knowing the perfection of the whole.

To return now to drama, the spectator watching a play based on poetic justice stands in the same relation to the action on the stage as St. John's angel and Dante's saints stand to the world of experience. The spectator sees the dramatic world as these beings see the human world looking down on it from Paradise. This explains, incidentally, why so little pity is elicited for the villains of melodrama: we know of them all that there is to know, and we enjoy seeing them get their comeuppance just as surely as St. John's angel is pleased by the sight of the wicked being punished. But this implies something about the way in which the dramatic world is presented. If the salient characteristic of everyday experience is mystery, the salient characteristic of drama shaped according to poetic justice is clarity. The playwright obviously cannot make his spectators into angels or saints. Instead, he achieves his goal by making the dramatic world simpler than the world of experience. It is life, as it were, purified—the world as it might appear if we could for once penetrate its obscurity. The result is a sense of satisfaction—a catharsis—that meets a deeply felt, inarticulate, but essentially religious, need.

To follow these ideas in Elizabethan criticism we need go no further than Sir Philip Sidney's *Apology for Poetry,* the most eloquent critical statement of the age. Throughout the *Apology* the idea that poetry should conform to poetic justice is central. Frequently poetry is contrasted with history, which, because it lacks poetic justice, can be confusing and morally injurious. In tragedy, Sidney says,

. . . if euill men come to the stage, they euer goe out (as the Tragedie Writer answered to one that misliked the shew of such persons) so manacled as they little animate folkes to followe them. But the Historian, beeing captiued to the trueth of a foolish world, is many times a terror from well dooing, and an incouragement to vnbrideled wickednes.

For see wee not valiant *Milciades* rot in his fetters? The iust *Phocion* and the accomplished *Socrates* put to death like Traytors? The cruell *Seuerus* liue prosperously? The excellent *Seuerus* miserably murthered? [5]

Sidney is not content simply to assert the moral superiority of the poet's world to the historian's. He is interested in the nature of this world, and the burden of his comments is that the poet's world has the quality of transcendence. The maker who creates it is momentarily lifted out of himself by divine inspiration. He sees, as it were, with the vision of St. John's angels or Dante's saints. Our world, says Sidney, is "brasen," but the poet's is "golden." History is "captiued to the trueth of a foolish world," but the poet "disdaning to be tied to any such subiection, lifted vp with the vigor of his owne inuention, dooth growe in effect another nature." And in perhaps the best known passage in the *Apology* Sidney urges his readers to

. . . giue right honor to the heauenly Maker of that maker, who, hauing made man to his owne likenes, set him beyond and ouer all the workes of that second nature, which in nothing hee sheweth so much as in Poetrie, when with the force of a diuine breath he bringeth things forth far surpassing her dooings, with no small argument to the incredulous of that first accursed fall of *Adam:* sith our erected wit maketh vs know what perfection is, and yet our infected will keepeth vs from reaching vnto it. [6]

Here the religious basis of the idea of poetic justice is made explicit. The poet is godlike—a maker—in creating his work. As he composes, his wit is "erected" and a "divine breath" inspires him. The work that results has a "perfection" that in some way parallels the vision of Adam before the fall —that is, before the darkness of sin closed around man's mind. [7]

5. *An Apology for Poetry,* in *Elizabethan Critical Essays,* ed. G. Gregory Smith (Oxford, 1904), I, 170.

6. *Ibid.,* I, 157.

7. The comparison between the poet's vision and that of Adam before the Fall is apt. In *Paradise Lost* Adam (although fallen) is accorded one last ideal vision of

Sidney's ideal is noble, but—crude dramatic homilies like Heywood's *Fair Frances* aside—it seems to have little application to major Elizabethan tragedies. Attempts have been made to read Shakespeare's tragedies as homiletic—*Romeo and Juliet* a warning against disobeying parents (the moral of Shakespeare's source); *Macbeth* a warning against ambition; *Hamlet* a warning against vacillation; *Lear* a warning against ingratitude or wrath; and so forth. A serious effort to apply this approach in depth and in terms of Elizabethan psychology was made by Miss Lily Bess Campbell in *Shakespeare's Tragic Heroes: Slaves of Passion.*[8] But all of these efforts, from naïve to sophisticated, seem rather inadequate beside the plays themselves. The problem seems to be that poetic justice as conceived by Heywood and Sidney is the wrong formula for tragedy. It leads to melodrama, and its typical result is not "in His will is our peace" but the smug satisfaction of St. John's angels: "they got what they deserved." Although there is some parceling out of rewards and punishments at the end of *King Lear*, "they got what they deserved" is probably the last thought that Shakespeare wanted to induce in his audience. Indeed, the chief effect of Albany's pious comment at the end of the play—

> All Friends shall taste
> The wages of their virtue, and all foes
> The cup of their deservings
>
> (V. iii. 302–304)

is to make him look slightly ridiculous.

The most obvious place for poetic justice and the sort of catharsis

---

history before being expelled from Eden. This vision includes two moments that illustrate the ways of absolute justice. At the end of Book XI (ll. 810–880) Adam learns of the Flood, which will sweep away all mankind but Noah and his family. Adam's response is joyous: "Far less I now lament for one whole World / Of wicked Sons destroyed, than I rejoice / For one Man found so perfect and so just" (ll. 874–876). In Book XII Adam learns of the Last Judgment, when Christ will come "to judge both quick and dead, / To judge th' unfaithful dead, but to reward / His faithful" (ll. 460–462). Again his response is not pity but joy: "O goodness infinite, goodness immense! / That all this good of evil shall produce" (ll. 470–471). Such undeviating righteousness would be amiss in the real world, where the limitations of human knowledge make judgments fallible and contingent. It is perfectly appropriate in context, however, since Adam is seeing absolute truth–the world as it really is–just as St. John's angel, Dante's Piccarda, and Sidney's poet see it.

8. (New York, 1952).

associated with it is comedy. As explained by Elizabethan critics, poetic
justice requires that no truly good or noble person suffer irrevocable harm
and that all but the most villainous be redeemed after chastisement. This
is in accord with the religious view of which poetic justice is a symbol.
Even the Fall of Man, according to theologians from St. Augustine to
Milton, was fortunate—a *felix culpa*—and the classic expression of religious catharsis is spoken by a Christian nun in Paradise in a poem
conspicuously labeled "comedy." It is only natural, then, that Sidney's
golden world should be most evident in comic dramas. *The Merchant of
Venice, Twelfth Night,* and *As You Like It* all depend for their effect on
unexpected but inspired solutions to the problems of their characters. The
qualities of the golden world emerge most explicitly, however, in Shakespeare's romances, which provide the supreme instances of religious
catharsis in English drama. It seems quite possible, moreover, that Shakespeare understood both the effect and its religious basis, for in the romances he consistently emphasizes the interplay between supernatural or
divine forces and the destinies of the characters. At the end of *The
Tempest* Prospero is so much the *deus ex machina* that he has been
equated with God by at least one allegorizing critic; and if this interpretation commits the error of converting a symbol into a sign, it remains true
that Prospero resolves the problems of *The Tempest* in the manner of the
deus ex machina—with magic and the assistance of a supernatural agent.
But perhaps the most explicit statement of the point is at the end of
Pericles, when Gower steps forth to interpret the outcome of the play as
the completion of poetic justice by providential means:

> In Antiochus and his daughter you have heard
> Of monstrous lust the due and just reward:
> In Pericles, his queen, and daughter; seen,
> Although assail'd with fortune fierce and keen,
> Virtue preserv'd from fell destruction's blast,
> Led on by heaven, and crown'd with joy at last.
>
> (V. iii. 86–91)

III

Heywood's moral and Sidney's religious catharsis lead to worthwhile
insights into Elizabethan concepts of drama, but they do not, as we have

seen, tell us much about the concepts underlying the major Elizabethan tragedies. Fortunately, we have some extremely suggestive hints on this subject from no less an authority than Shakespeare himself.

Before considering these hints, it will be useful to summarize a recent article on Aristotle's *Poetics* by Professor Leon Golden.[9] According to Golden, Aristotle introduces his theory of catharsis in Chapter IV (not Chapter VI) of the *Poetics,* where he asserts that the cause of imitative art is the pleasure it provides. Imitative pleasure, moreover, is not a generalized emotion but a quite specialized one associated with learning. As Aristotle says, "The reason for the delight in seeing a picture is that one is at the same time learning—gathering the meaning of things; e.g., that the man there is such and such [a type]" (1448^b 9–12). What he evidently has in mind is that when seeing a properly constructed work of art, the viewer gains a sense of the generic nature of the object represented. This explains why objects that are unpleasant when encountered directly—Aristotle mentions the lower animals and corpses—can bring pleasure when presented in a work of art. Aristotle applies this theory to tragedy in Chapter IX of the *Poetics,* where he differentiates poetry from history. An artistic plot, he says, should be constructed along lines of probability and necessity; and therefore "poetry is something more philosophic and of graver import than history, since its statements are of the nature rather of universals, whereas those of history are singulars" (1451^b 5–7).

Tragic catharsis, then, is the result of learning something about the events forming the tragic plot. What we learn is the way the events happened according to necessity and probability, rather than the way they may be set down by the historian, whose job is to record, not necessarily to explain, them. Golden argues that the best translation of Greek *katharsis* is "clarification" rather than "purgation." It occurs at the end of a proper tragedy, and it is enjoyable because it is a form of learning. It is analogous, perhaps, to the pleasure that accompanies the solution of a puzzle; but in tragedy it is much more significant, for it involves the discovery of coherence in a world that usually seems dark and chaotic.

The reason for this foray into the *Poetics* is not to solve the problem of what Aristotle meant, although Golden is undeniably persuasive. It is, rather, to establish a background of ideas sufficient to cope with the sort of

9. "Catharsis," *Transactions of the American Philological Association,* XCIII (1962), 51–60.

catharsis that Shakespeare seems to present in *Hamlet*. Since the first two kinds of catharsis have been labeled moral and religious, the present one can be called "literal" catharsis. It does not require a happy (or sad) ending, a spontaneous confession, or the completion of poetic justice. It requires only that the play be experienced exactly as presented and asserts only that when the play is experienced in this way the spectator emerges with a deepened—and hence pleasurable—understanding of its events.

Let us now turn to the final scene of *Hamlet*. Claudius is dead, but Hamlet, too, is mortally wounded. He forgives Laertes and then turns to the Danish court:

> You that look pale and tremble at this chance,
> That are but mutes or audience to this act,
> Had I but time as this fell sergeant, Death,
> Is strict in his arrest, O, I could tell you—
> But let it be. Horatio, I am dead:
> Thou livest; report me and my cause aright
> To the unsatisfied.
>
> (V. ii. 326–332)

We learn several things from these words. First, that the courtiers are terrified by what they have seen. Within a few minutes they have witnessed the murder of the man they considered the rightful king (recall their cry of "Treason! treason!" (l. 315) and have also heard accusations of dire treachery by Laertes and Hamlet. They are "audience to this act" in the sense of having been present while it occurred, but they are not audience to the action of the play as it has unfolded before the spectators in the theater. They are dumb with fear precisely because they do not understand what has happened.

Hamlet makes no effort to console the courtiers. Instead, his chief desire is to tell his story. "Had I but time" is followed by "O, I could tell you" and then, as he feels his life ebbing, his request to Horatio, "report me and my cause aright / To the unsatisfied" (ll. 328–332).

Although untouched by the fear that overcomes the courtiers, Horatio is so shaken by Hamlet's words that he threatens to commit suicide. Hamlet stops him with a second petition:

> O God! Horatio, what a wounded name,
> Things standing thus unknown, shall live behind me!
>
> (V. ii. 336–337)

With his dying breath Hamlet repeats the petition a third time:

> So tell him, with th' occurrents, more and less,
> Which have solicited—the rest is silence.
>
> (V. ii. 349–350)

Even though Hamlet is now dead, the theme of "telling his story" continues to dominate the dialogue. As soon as the ambassadors have reported, Horatio requests,

> give order that these bodies
> High on a stage be placed to the view;
> And let me speak to th' yet unknowing world
> How these things came about.
>
> (V. ii. 369–372)

The theme is repeated in Fortinbras' reply:

> Let us haste to hear it,
> And call the noblest to the audience.
>
> (V. ii. 378–379)

This is followed by a last comment from Horatio:

> But let this same be presently perform'd
> Even while men's minds are wild, lest more mischance
> Or plots and errors happen.
>
> (V. ii. 385–387)

We need consider only the essentials of the preceding lines, but we should take them seriously. A terrible and incomprehensible event has taken place. It has made the courtiers dumb with fear (l. 326); it has induced Horatio to threaten suicide (l. 334); it has filled Fortinbras with "woe or wonder" (l. 355); and it has left men's minds "wild" and ripe for "plots and errors" (ll. 386–387); one strategy and one strategy only is offered to remedy this situation. First Hamlet, then Horatio, then Fortinbras insists that Hamlet's "story" must be told. Furthermore, it must be told "aright" (l. 331) and "with the occurrents, more and less, / Which have solicited" (ll. 349–350)–a statement that may be paraphrased, "with all the circumstances, great and small, that have contributed." Although there is no need to insist on the parallel between telling Hamlet's story "on a stage" before "an audience of the noblest" and producing the play *Hamlet,* the ambiguity of the language points to a fact that is of prime importance. If Horatio tells Hamlet's story "aright" and "with the occurrents, more and less" he can only tell it one way: that is, as closely as possible to the way Shakespeare told it. The fact is that Shakespeare's play is absolute truth as far as our knowledge of the affairs of Denmark is concerned. Given the contract between the dramatist and his audience to make every scene and line count, we must assume that everything in the play is relevant or seemed so to Shakespeare when he wrote it. To omit or change part of the story as Shakespeare told it would be to falsify it by omitting "occurrents," no matter how small, that in some way "solicited" the final result.

Let us pursue this train of thought one step further. What is the anticipated result of telling the story? Hamlet wishes his reputation to be cleared, but Hamlet's reputation is of minor concern to the terrified courtiers. Horatio informs us quite explicitly what the telling of his story is intended to accomplish. It will have two effects. In the first place, it will calm men's "wild" minds. In the second, it will prevent new "plots and errors"—i.e., social upheavals such as the treason of Claudius or the rebellion of Laertes. This is, I take it, a concise and authoritative description of the catharsis to be anticipated from telling the story of Hamlet "with the occurrents, more and less, / Which have solicited."

Furthermore, because Shakespeare places his statements in a context which is fully known, we can understand a good deal about how the effect is created. It is lack of understanding that has made the minds of the Danish courtiers "wild" and ripe for "plots and errors." Terrible events have occurred. Evil seems rife, and the Danish state seems on the verge of plunging into chaos. Telling Hamlet's story will not make up for Hamlet's death (or for that matter for the deaths of Polonius or Ophelia or Laertes), but, to quote Horatio, it will show "how these things came about" (l. 372). Hearing Hamlet's story will therefore be learning in the most literal sense for the "audience of the noblest" assembled before the stage on which Horatio speaks. Its effect will be to alleviate their fear—fear of the present and even greater fear of the future.

If we step back now we can perhaps catch a glimpse of the kind of catharsis that *Hamlet* offers the spectators in the theater. A tragedy, Aristotle reminds us, is more universal and more philosophical than history. The Danish courtiers confronting the bodies of Gertrude, Laertes, Claudius, and Hamlet stand in the same relation to the dramatic event as do members of the theater audience to human experience as recorded in history or what they accept as history. In good Renaissance fashion, Shakespeare regularly used historical or legendary sources for his trage- dies. Sometimes he drew on formal history (*Julius Caesar*), sometimes on legendary history (*Lear*), and sometimes, as in *Hamlet,* he drew on stories from legendary history that had already been embellished by previous artists. Yet Shakespeare was always free with his sources. To say that his changes "made better plays" is, I think, to refer impressionistically to what Aristotle considered an essential characteristic of poetic art and explained in detail. The events presented in the sources are insufficiently clear. They are "singulars" which the poet must reshape in terms of "the universal." This is true even for sources that were already dramatic like the *Ur-Hamlet,* since by definition Shakespeare would not have reworked an earlier play if he had felt that it already said everything necessary.

In moving from source to finished drama, Shakespeare added, com- pressed, combined, and invented. The result in the great tragedies is an almost perfect coherence of parts. If catharsis can be understood in Gold- en's sense as "clarification," the theater audience that has attentively followed Shakespeare's version of the Hamlet story is surely experiencing catharsis. Their experience is similar to what the Danish courtiers will feel when they have heard Horatio tell "how these things came about" and the wildness of their minds is calmed. For both groups, the disturbing and frightening singulars of history have been replaced by the universals of poetry.

IV

We have, then, three types of catharsis recognized by Elizabethan critics and embodied significantly in Elizabethan plays. Obviously these types are not entirely unrelated. They all involve calming of mental perturbations, and all of them depend on various ways of using or expressing truth. Moral catharsis achieves purgation of guilt and fear through the device of presenting a dramatic imitation of truth to the guilty party, who then reveals truth itself *via* a confession. As a literary convention, this confes- sion can be (and is) taken as absolute. Goethe's knowledge that the best we can hope for when we try to confess is *Dichtung und Wahrheit*—truth mixed with poetry—is simply irrelevant to the literary convention. The strategy of moral catharsis is neatly summed up in Polonius' advice to Reynaldo: "Your bait of falsehood take[s] this carp of truth."

Religious catharsis also depends on the dramatic use of truth. As we have noted, it has the effect of putting the spectator in the position of one of St. John's angels, and the play in the position of "the world seen as it is." Exposure to this world is therapeutic. That is, the spectator may harbor doubts about the possibility of justice in the actual world and may even fall into the kind of despair illustrated by King Lear's speech on justice:

> Robes and furr'd gowns hide all. Plate sin with gold,
> And the strong lance of justice hurtless breaks;
> Arm it in rags, a pigmy's straw does pierce it.
>
> (IV. ii. 165–167)

Such perturbations are dissipated by the dramatic experience of poetic justice. To say this is to say that poetic justice operates as a form of reassurance. To see valiant Milciades released from his fetters and the cruel Severus put to death violates our knowledge of the singulars of history, but it refurbishes our faith that God does not play dice with the world. Moreover, this is not necessarily escapism. The morally coherent world is not a fiction but an imitation of a world that faith tells us actually exists. Unless we dismiss eschatology as pure superstition (which Renaissance humanists most certainly did not) we must admit with Sidney that it is truer than history. In other words, to a Christian humanist, the play based on poetic justice is not the world as we would like it to be (sentimentalism) but the world as it is or would be if we could penetrate the dark glass that clouds the vision of all but inspired makers.

Recalling Heywood's gentlewoman of Lynn, we can say that moral catharsis restores harmony between the sinful individual and the Divine. Religious catharsis is the satisfaction that comes from experiencing this harmony and sharing in it. Clearly the two are complementary, the negative and positive aspects of a single experience. The individual whose affections are not "in right tune" must experience moral catharsis first. Only after he has set them "in right tune" can he affirm the angelic view provided by poetic justice. Tragedy, as we have seen, tends to emphasize moral rather than religious catharsis. This is because the tragic hero is more likely to be a sinner than a saint, to stand with Claudius at the first stage of the cathartic process. Indeed, Francis Fergusson's much-admired formula for the tragic rhythm—purpose, passion, perception—makes it almost mandatory that the tragic hero begin "out of joint" with the true order of things, suffer because of this, and finally discover (and affirm) this order as a result of his suffering. Comedy, on the other hand, is lighter in tone, and its lightness comes from our secure sense that no matter how bad things may seem, we are sure to approve of their resolution. This is simply to say that we view the comic world in terms of its end, which we know will be justice tempered with mercy.[10]

If we try to relate religious to literal catharsis, we seem to encounter the impasse mapped out by Allen Tate in his distinction between the angelic and the symbolic kinds of imagination. What relation, if any, can there be between the world seen as absolute truth and the world seen as world? Religious catharsis operates in terms of the first perspective, literal catharsis in terms of the second. The first seems to demand a turning away from experience to eschatology; the second gives a detailed treatment of experience "with the occurrents, more and less, / Which have solicited." One demands poetic justice; the other merely offers a clarification, an object lesson in "how these things came about."

The easy solution would be to say that religious and literal catharsis are not relatives but antitheses: that one operates as drama aspires to eschatology, the other as it stubbornly remains tied to history. To take this option would, however, be to miss the implications of the concepts which we have been examining in such detail. The fact is that poetic justice claims to be a clarified vision of reality, not an escape from it, while—by the same token—the literal level of drama is not a copy of history but something more universal and more philosophical. We are dealing not with antitheses but with ideas that converge.

Poetic justice and "the world as world" are only antagonistic in a Platonic or Manichean frame of reference. They are not antagonistic in terms of the Christianity of Renaissance humanists. The possibility of

---

10. Critics who argue that "Christian tragedy" is a contradiction in terms usually seem to be making the assumption that Christian tragedy is necessarily eschatological. Comedy *does* tend in this direction, but tragedy—as distinguished from melodrama—does not. It is written from the (limited) human point of view—hence its use of moral and literal catharsis and its avoidance of poetic justice. Tragedy is stubbornly grounded in this world and only looks toward the eschatological to the degree that the poet "universalizes" the data of experience.

their convergence is no more difficult (though, by the same token, no easier) than Pope's "whatever is is right." From the point of view of Christian humanist poetics, it is our inability to see, our own imperfection, which encourages us to turn away from what is, in our search for what is right. If this is so, then the ultimate function of the dramatist is to make clear the presence of the absolute ("what is right") in the actual ("what is"). In doing this the dramatist provides a clarification that might also be called an illumination. To put it another way, the courtiers assembled to hear Horatio's tale at the end of *Hamlet* will not learn that the characters "got what they deserved." They may, however, learn that things as they are, understood according to probability and necessity, are identical with things as they would be if we could see them clearly. It is the erected wit of the poet that grants this vision. As Milton wrote in his Elegy VI:

> Diis etenim sacer est vates, divumque sacerdos,
> Spirat et occultum pectus et ora Iovem.

The Elizabethan "Three-Level" Play

RICHARD LEVIN

S INCE THE PIONEERING INVESTIGATIONS of William Empson and Muriel Bradbrook back in the thirties, we have grown so accustomed to discussions of Elizabethan "double-plot" plays that we may have to be reminded that many of the works now tagged with this label are literally "two-and-one-half-plot" plays. These are the dramas, found throughout the period, which include in addition to the standard main plot and subplot a third distinct set of characters, usually of the clownish sort, who sometimes figure in one of these two major plots but are also elaborated independently to produce a kind of effect that is quite different from either. This elaboration, however, typically occurs in more or less isolated episodes, rather than in a sequential line of action, and so might be conceived of more meaningfully not as another plot, or fractional equivalent, but as another level of emotional tone or sensibility. And since in most of these plays the main plot and the subplot are sharply differentiated from each other, similarly, in terms of the modes of sensibility they embody— in the characters themselves, and in the response these characters evoke in the audience—the result is a dramatic structure that can be called, with some precision, a "three-level" play. Such a conception of emotional levels, in fact, implying as it does a vertically articulated relationship, seems to be particularly useful here, for while the nature of the three components

23

varies considerably from play to play, they very frequently are ordered in
a hierarchy of descending magnitude and seriousness which can be reduced to a simple formula: a main plot consisting of characters deliberately elevated above the others, usually in heroic or romantic terms; a
subplot of more ordinary people viewed from a realistic and often satiric
perspective; and a third set of characters who are debased to the level of
farce.

This hierarchy can be seen very easily, for example, in one of Middleton's earliest city comedies, *The Family of Love* (*c.* 1602),[1] where these
separate levels give us three different, and complementary, treatments of
the sexual relationship. The main action depicts a pair of true lovers,
Gerardine and Maria, whose idealized passion (rendered in some very
lofty and frigid blank verse) ultimately triumphs over the opposition of
Doctor Glister, the girl's uncle. The subplot satirizes the hypocritical and
venal kind of "love" practiced by the Puritan sect named in the title,
centering about Rebecca Purge, an elder in the Family, and her clandes-
tine affair with Glister. And, finally, there are a pair of avowed libertines,
Lipsalve and Gudgeon, who are driven by sheer physical lust into a series
of slapstick misadventures. The three-level gradient here is certainly obvious enough (and is even confirmed by a comic pecking order—Gerardine makes a fool of Glister, as Glister does of Lipsalve and Gudgeon); it
is, in fact, one of the crudest and most straightforward applications of this
basic structural formula in the entire period.[2]

A more complex and interesting deployment of this structure can be
found in *Eastward Ho* (1605), the joint effort of Jonson, Chapman, and
Marston, which is built on very similar affective levels: in the main plot
we observe the success of Touchstone, Mildred, and Golding, the model
parent, child, and apprentice; in the subplot, the downfall and penance of
their erring counterparts, Mistress Touchstone, daughter Gertrude, and
Quicksilver, Golding's fellow apprentice; and in a third farcical episode,
loosely connected to the subplot, the cuckolding of an old usurer by

1. Dates are those given in Alfred Harbage, *Annals of English Drama, 975-1700,*
rev. S. Schoenbaum (London, 1964).

2. I discuss this play at length in "The Family of Lust and *The Family of Love,*"
SEL, VI (1966), 309-322, and two of the other three-level plays in "The Three
Quarrels of *A Fair Quarrel,*" *SP,* LXI (1964), 219-231; and "The Subplot of *The
Atheist's Tragedy,*" *HLQ,* XXIX (1965), 17-33.

Gertrude's husband, Sir Petronel Flash. Much of the special comic flavor of this play derives, it is true, from an added dimension of irony which serves to qualify the virtue of the paragons in the first plot and the reformation of the prodigals in the second, but a sophistication of this sort is necessarily posterior to, and dependent upon, the original "straight" formula itself.

It is a formula, moreover, which is by no means limited to comedy. It appears again in a very obvious form in *The Old Law* (c. 1618), a tragicomedy ascribed to Middleton, Rowley, and Massinger, where the same three levels are generated out of the various reactions, on the part of potential beneficiaries, to a fantastic law that condemns to death all persons reaching a certain age. The first is an exercise in heroics, portraying the scheme of Cleanthes and his wife, Hippolita, to save Cleanthes' father by circumventing the law at the risk of their own lives. The second depicts the ignoble exploitation of the law by two of their peers—Simonides, who rejoices in his father's death and proceeds to squander his inheritance, and Eugenia, who eagerly anticipates the execution of her aged husband by entertaining a group of gallants seeking to supplant him. (These situations are linked by making Simonides one of Eugenia's suitors and by having her use him in her plot against Cleanthes.) And the third is a low-comedy sequence dealing with the maneuvers of the clown, Gnotho, and his cronies to dispose of their ancient wives. It is clear that here the three-part formula operates to exhaust the possible family relationships affected by the law; the victims are female in the third level and male in the first two, and these two are differentiated by the contrasts established between the good and bad son, and the good and bad wife. The emotional tone of each level, moreover, is defined in terms of these relationships, the two situations of the subplot being balanced at an intermediate pitch—in Simonides' family the old victim approaches the seriousness of the main action, and his young beneficiary approaches the farce of the Gnotho-scenes, whereas in the marriage of Eugenia these feelings are just reversed. The whole conception is very neat and simple, much like our first example, and demonstrates how readily this formula can be adapted to the tragicomic effect.

Another Middleton-Rowley tragicomedy, *A Fair Quarrel* (c. 1617), is also developed out of this same formula, but in a somewhat more subtle fashion. The main plot here is, again, a heroic exercise, centering in the duel between Captain Ager and the Colonel; the subplot is based on the conventional theme of romantic comedy—the success of two young lovers, Jane and Fitzallen, in overcoming a series of obstacles to their marriage; and the sub-subplot follows the adventures of Jane's foolish suitor, Chough, and his servant among the Roarers. These three components are related to each other and arranged on a single scale of value through the nature of their commitment to the ideal of "honor." The major action turns upon the strict imperative of the military "fellowship of honor" that precipitates Ager's excruciating crisis of conscience during the duel and is finally satisfied by the exalted contest of magnanimity reconciling him to the Colonel. In the underplot the problem is feminine honor, or chastity, presented in Jane's dilemma as an unwed mother, which is resolved at the end by a clever contest of wits wherein her father is tricked into paying Fitzallen to marry her. And at the Roaring School the noble cult of "manhood" of the main action is translated into a fantastic and meaning-less ritual, which is further debased, through Chough's earthy perspective, into a version of the Cornish hug. Thus the standard formula emerges in this drama as three distinct levels of moral sensibility that determine the course of the respective actions and their relative seriousness, descending from the soldiers' rarified and exacting code of conduct, through the lovers' more relaxed and practical accommodation to circumstance, down to the clowns' grossly physical buffoonery.

A number of examples could also be cited of the use of this formula in the tragic genre. *The Atheist's Tragedy* (*c.* 1611) of Tourneur, for in-stance, is based on it: the main plot is a conflict between absolute vice (in D'Amville, the "atheist") and absolute virtue (in his intended victims, Charlemont and Castabella), in which the gravest theological issues are explicitly implicated; the more realistic subplot, however, scales down these polar extremes in the fatal liaison between D'Amville's milder counterpart, the lustful Levidulcia, and his son, the good-natured Sebas-tian; while developing out of this is an episode of bawdy burlesque in which Languebeau Snuffe, the Puritan chaplain, attempts to seduce a complaisant servant girl in a graveyard. And Ford's *'Tis Pity She's a Whore* (*c.* 1632) is constructed on roughly similar lines. The incestuous union of Giovanni and Annabella is elevated, by the intensity and extraor-dinary nature of their passion, and, again, by the heavy ideological burden it carries, far above the subplot centering upon Hippolita, where the same ingredients of illicit love and jealousy appear in a more mundane and sordid form, which is still much more serious than the sequence involving Bergetto, Annabella's clownish suitor, and his servant Poggio. In both of these plays, it should be noted, the subplot is also technically a "tragedy," insofar as it terminates in the death of the protagonist; but in all important respects—the quality of the action, the characters themselves, the moral issues, and the emotional effect—it seems to be deliberately and consistently deflated in order to establish a contrast to, and thereby enhance, the tragic significance of the main plot.[3]

This sort of functional contrast would also seem to be the principal purpose of the subplots in the other plays cited here (making allowance, of course, for the various kinds of responses aimed at in each genre), and the same can be said, in general, of the "clown" episodes, although their role is sometimes more complicated. Clearly, in this mode of construction dramatic unity is achieved not despite, but because of, the marked difference in tone of the separate components. That point has not always been grasped by the critics, who have been known to complain of the inappropriateness of the realistic or satirical emphasis in these subplots, implying that the only legitimate subplot is one which reproduces the mood of the main action.[4] And a similar assumption apparently underlies the defenses of these plays which stop short after pointing out some parallelism between the plots, as if that itself proved they were properly unified. But such arguments, pro or con, treat artistic unity as a simple aggregate of homogeneous parts, such as is found in the most primitive multicellular bodies, and in very few Elizabethan plays.[5] The type of unity developed in these three-level dramas is much more like that of the higher organisms where the components are heterogeneous and complementary, each contributing in its own unique way to the total living process. It is true that the multiplication of plots has an accumulative effect, as Empson indi-

3. The same is true of the most famous tragic subplot of them all, in *King Lear* (1605–6). Gloucester's tragedy is obviously meant to parallel Lear's but on a lower level.

4. See, for instance, Swinburne on *A Fair Quarrel*, in *The Age of Shakespeare* (London, 1908), pp. 163–164; or Richard Barker on *The Family of Love*, in *Thomas Middleton* (New York, 1958), pp. 30–31; or Inga-Stina Ekeblad on *The Atheist's Tragedy*, in *ES*, XLI (1960), 234.

5. One example is Yarington's *Two Lamentable Tragedies* (c. 1594) which, as its running title acknowledges, is merely "Two Tragedies in One."

cates, in suggesting that the work deals with life as a whole, and in satisfying a wider range of the audience's natural impulses,[6] although even that depends upon meaningful differences in subject and perspective among the various actions. Beyond that, however, is the organic integration achieved through these differences, for all the analogical parallels between the plots (as well as the causal connections, which have been passed over here) do not function as ends in themselves, but as means for bringing the plots to bear upon one another, so that our response to any line of action conditions, and is conditioned by, our responses to the others. In this way each level, with its distinctive tone, operates to "place" those above and below it in the hierarchic scheme and to reinforce and circumscribe their effect; and all three levels combined establish what amounts to a structured "contextual" definition of their specific emotional and intellectual significance.

The terms of this argument may well sound needlessly complex, since the rationale behind the three-level composite is after all quite simple. It is so simple, in fact, and so relatively easy to implement in practice, that there would seem to be little point in searching for a special source of this dramatic structure, which presumably evolved, through the normal artistic processes of elaboration and sophistication, out of the naïve combinations of serious and comic action inherited from the native tradition of the Mystery cycles and Moralities. Nor is our knowledge of the roles played by this tradition during the formative period of the secular theater—or, for that matter, of the possible influence of Roman comedy upon this process [7] —sufficiently detailed to allow us to trace the exact stages of such an evolution building up to the more or less mature exemplars of the formula discussed above. But one can hypothesize a "model" genesis of the formula, provided that no actual historical claim is made for it. A model of this sort might be discovered, for instance, in the conception of the

---

6. See *Some Versions of Pastoral* (London, 1935), pp. 27, 29, 53–54. What Empson claims here for the double plot would apply a fortiori to the three-level structure.

7. Although the relevance of such an influence has been regularly ignored in statements about the origins of the Elizabethan double plot, it is worth noting that the *Heauton Timorumenos, Eunuchus, Phormio,* and *Adelphoe* of Terence all have two complete plots that form a pattern roughly analogous to the first two levels of our formula, and that the third level of the formula may owe something to the slaves of Plautus' *Stichus, Trinummus,* and *Truculentus,* who are portrayed imitating their masters in episodes of low comedy.

Psychomachia underlying the early Morality dramas. These were all single-plot constructs, to be sure, but the very nature of this plot required agents of three completely different orders of "reality": the allegorical virtues necessary for salvation; below them the protagonist, representative man (Humanity, Humanum Genus, Mankind), who by definition occupied an intermediate place in this hierarchy; and below him the vices who tempted him to damnation and also, even in these early plays, indulged in their own semi-independent, episodic sequences of slapstick buffoonery. It is not difficult to see how with the secularization of the drama these theological categories could reappear as the characters "better than us," "like us," and "worse than us" (to adopt the Aristotelian terminology[8]) who were to figure, respectively, in the heroic, realistic, and farcical levels of the formula. This analogy could be extended still further, since in these plays the virtues and vices typically appear in alternating scenes,[9] much like the separate plots of the three-level structure; yet it breaks down at one important point—the "real" man in the middle level of the Psychomachia does not act in a sequence of his own, but only in conjunction with these forces above and below who are battling for his soul. For this reason, it might be argued that there is an even closer analogue to the formula in such relatively late Moralities as *Nice Wanton,* Wager's *Enough Is as Good as a Feast, The Trial of Treasure,* and Fulwell's *Like Will to Like,* written during the 1550's and 1560's, where the good and evil aspects of the universal protagonist separate into two different men (Heavenly Man and Worldly Man, Just and Lust, etc.) whose lives are presented in contrasting and alternating episodes, the virtues leading one man to his reward, and the vices the other to his punishment. We have only to carry this process one step further, segregating the comic component of the vices from the more serious career of the man they accompany (or, again using Aristotle's terms, subdividing the agents "worse than us" into the vicious and the ridiculous[10]), and this becomes one possible model of the three-level formula.

8. *Poetics* ii.1448ᵃ1–6.

9. David Bevington asserts that this alternation is related to the "doubling" of roles required in the small repertory companies (*From* Mankind *to* Marlowe [Cambridge, Mass., 1962], chap. 8).

10. *Poetics* v.1449ᵃ31–36. In the Morality itself these categories were combined, particularly through the figure of the Vice, in what has been aptly called "the comedy of evil."

It is, in fact, almost a paradigm of the earliest example of this formula known to me, Richard Edwards' *Damon and Pithias* (1565?), which may actually have preceded some of these Moralities in time. The main plot here portrays the ultimate triumph of the true friendship of the titular characters; the underplot, the downfall of a pair of false friends, Aristippus and Carisophus; and the third level, the ludicrous escapades of their equally false servants, Will and Jack.[11] And this same mode of differentiation of the three components, in which the first deals with moral activity, the second with immoral, and the third with amoral mischief, is also basic to the structure of *The Family of Love, Eastward Ho,* and *The Old Law.* But it is by no means the only form that the three-level drama takes, since the comic characters of the lowest group may range from the Vice-like rogues of *Damon and Pithias* to the simple fools of *Wit at Several Weapons* (1609), with many intermediate combinations, and the ethical relationship of main to subplot shows even greater variation. In some plays, such as *A Fair Quarrel, Much Ado about Nothing* (c. 1598), or *The Shoemakers' Holiday* (1599), both of these plots center on virtuous characters, but those in the second are clearly less serious and less elevated. And in *The Atheist's Tragedy, 'Tis Pity She's a Whore, The Witch of Edmonton* (1621), *Women Beware Women* (c. 1621), and other tragedies of this sort, the main plot depicts an evil action which is more terrible or "grander" than the comparable deeds of the underplot. There are even cases—*The Insatiate Countess* (c. 1610), for example—where these values are completely reversed, the major action showing the punishment of vice, and the minor one the reward of virtue. It seems, then, that what is most constant in this formula is not the ethical quality of its three levels, but the relative seriousness of their emotional tone.

The regularity with which this same emotional scale reappears may suggest another kind of source of the three-level drama, not in some theatrical tradition, but in the society that produced it. For one might reasonably suppose that, with the secularization of the stage, the theological hierarchy of the Morality would be translated into the class hierarchy

---

11. The contrast of plots one and two has been shown to derive from the distinction between "friendships of virtue" and "friendships of utility" in the *Nicomachean Ethics,* Book VIII. Perhaps the relationship of Will and Jack, especially in their scene with Grim, is meant to exemplify Aristotle's third type, "friendships of pleasure."

of the actual world, especially since it seems so appropriate to relate the idealized, heroic main plot to aristocratic characters and values, the realistic subplot to the bourgeoisie, and the farcical sub-subplot to the urban or rural proletariat. What is surprising is how relatively seldom such an equation is in fact made. In most of these plays, when the third-level characters are menials, as in *Damon and Pithias* or *The Old Law,* the agents of the two major actions belong to a single class; and where there is a significant social distinction between main and subplot, in such plays as *A Fair Quarrel,* the protagonist of the third level usually is not differentiated in the same manner.[12] Apparently the class division of Elizabethan society speaks more insistently to us, with our post-Marxist perspectives, than it did to them; when they wished to dramatize a systematic cross section of their nation, it was much more likely to emerge as a survey, not of classes, but of vocations or "estates,"[13] which do not readily fit into the kind of fixed hierarchy suitable for our formula. There are, however, a few three-level plays which do correspond to this class structure. One early example is Lodge and Greene's *A Looking Glass for London and England,* which very methodically sets about to expose and castigate the representative vices of the entire social scene. The main plot concentrates upon the court of King Rasni, where the sins—adultery, incest, murder, and an overweening arrogance and defiance of divine law—are most heinous and require the miraculous intervention of an avenging God; the subplot of the Usurer and his two victims, a young gentleman and an old farmer, is limited to the more venial offenses of the economic realm—

12. As the drama develops there seems to be a general tendency to elevate the social status of this third level, often by pairing off a silly gentleman and his manservant, whose relationship may remind us of Don Quixote and Sancho Panza —cf. Lapet and Galoshio in *The Nice Valor* (c. 1616), Chough and Trimtram in *A Fair Quarrel,* the Ward and Sordido in *Women Beware Women,* Sancho and Soto in *The Spanish Gypsy* (1623), Bergetto and Poggio in *'Tis Pity She's a Whore,* Freshwater and Gudgeon in *The Ball* (1632), Young Barnacle and Dwindle in *The Gamester* (1633), etc.

13. See Alan Dessen, "The 'Estates' Morality Play," *SP,* LXII (1965), 121–136. He includes *A Looking Glass for London and England* (c. 1590) in this category, along with such late Moralities or semi-Moralities as *The Three Ladies of London* (c. 1581), *The Cobbler's Prophecy* (c. 1590), *A Knack to Know a Knave* (1592), and *Nobody and Somebody* (c. 1605); and elsewhere he tries to show the influence of this tradition on *The Phoenix* (c. 1604) and *The Alchemist* (1610).

usury, bribery, and theft—and has a substantial comic element (even here the class gradient applies, since the farmer is the source of most of this comedy, rather than his fellow victim who is socially above him); and in the third level a servant, called the Clown, reenacts some of the crimes of the royal court in a broad, drunken burlesque which is placed below the didactic scheme of repentance and punishment of the two major actions.[14] A roughly similar arrangement can be seen in Dekker's *The Shoemakers' Holiday,* although the treatment of all three castes is basically sympathetic: the first action concerns the problem of young Lacy, a nobleman, in marrying Rose; the second the rise of Simon Eyre, the shoemaker, to the height of "citizen" aspiration, the mayoralty of London; and the third the trials of Eyre's journeyman, Ralph Damport, and his wife Jane, which form a kind of mirror image of the Lacy-Rose plot. In this case, however, the class system is the actual "subject" of the play, and that introduces a new dimension of complexity which would require a separate discussion.

Social classes also figure significantly in another well known three-level drama, Heywood's *A Woman Killed with Kindness* (1603), but here the hierarchy is strikingly reversed. The titular action of Frankford and Anne is saturated with middle-class domesticity, while the subplot of Sir Charles Mountford and Sir Francis Acton deals with a higher class, in terms not only of the participants' rank but also of their characteristic activities and preoccupations—the sporting wager, the resultant duel, the role of the ancestral estate, and so on. Even the servants of the third level contribute to this inversion, since they are an integral part of Frankford's household and, through their intimate relationship with him, impart a homely and genre-like quality to the portrayal of his world, which contrasts very sharply with the more rarified atmosphere of the subplot. For the reversal of the class hierarchy in these two plots accompanies a reversal in the scale of sensibility of the standard three-level formula. Here it is the primary action, with its characters "like ourselves," that is clearly meant to be realistic, while the secondary action is conceived of as an exercise in extraordinary heroics, based upon a thoroughly patrician obsession with

---

14. There is also a "divine" level above these three, represented not by another plot but by the choric prophets, Oseas and Jonas. In *The Shoemakers' Holiday,* analogously, the entrance of King Henry adds a higher level which caps the class hierarchy of the three plots.

debts of honor. And the purpose of this reordering also seems reasonably clear: it incorporates the avowedly naturalistic program of the "Poet's dull and earthy Muse," announced in the Prologue, by deliberately subordinating the conventional artificialities of the "glorious" contest between the two knightly foes to the humbler verisimilitude of the Frankfords' "bare scene"; and, as a necessary corollary to this, it underscores the crucial transvaluation of values here that elevates Frankford's middle-class morality, with its restraint, prudence, and respect for religious and legal sanction, over the aristocratic code of private honor exemplified by the sub-plot.[15] Therefore the transposition of the first two levels in this drama serves the ethical as well as the esthetic purposes of the author and is probably in large part responsible for the impression, recorded in most of our literary histories, that it is the outstanding "domestic" or "bourgeois" tragedy of the entire period.

A few of James Shirley's comedies of manners invert these two levels in a similar fashion, although the effect of this inversion is certainly very different. In *Hyde Park* (1632), *The Ball,* and *The Lady of Pleasure* (1635) the two principal actions are both versions of the battle of the sexes and are constructed symmetrically. In the major plot of the first two plays a man defeats and reforms a "scornful lady" who is too cruel to the opposite sex, while in the minor plot a woman does the same to a man

---

15. Sir Francis himself makes this clear in the closing scene:

> My brother Frankford show'd too mild a spirit
> In the revenge of such a loathed crime;
> Less than he did, no man of spirit could do.
> I am so far from blaming his revenge
> That I commend it; had it been my case,
> Their souls at once had from their breasts been freed;
>
> (xvii. 16–21; [The Revels Plays; London, 1961], ed. R. W. Fossen)

For a fuller discussion of this point, see Herbert Coursen, "The Subplot of *A Woman Killed with Kindness,*" *ELN,* II (1965), 180–185. Muriel Bradbrook notes the similarity between Heywood's subplot and the main plot of *A Fair Quarrel* (*The Growth and Structure of Elizabethan Comedy* [Berkeley, 1956], p. 232), which gives some indication of the extent of his departure from the standard three-level formula found in that play. (In both works members of the main and subplots are siblings, even though they inhabit separate social worlds; this seems to reflect a conflict between the need to connect the two plots and to differentiate their modes of sensibility.)

who is too free with his love; in the third play these vices have changed gender—the hero of the main plot converts a philandering lady, and the heroine of the subplot converts a male misogamist. But in all three comedies the "battle" of the first level is a clever contest of wits, observed realistically and even satirically, whereas that of the second level tends to be more sentimental and more serious (and we also have the usual third level of farce, provided by a separate episodic sequence and by the rejected clownish suitors of the heroine of the main action). Moreover, the characters of the subplot are socially superior—the hero in each case is a Lord, the only one in the play, and the manners are somewhat more elaborate and refined. Yet class differences are much less significant here than in *A Woman Killed with Kindness,* and the intention is obviously not to recommend the more realistic attitudes of the main plot, which does not set up another code of conduct and is, it was seen, less serious than the subplot. Indeed, it is his innocence of any such didactic impulse that makes Shirley's intention in transposing these levels more difficult to pin down than Heywood's. The best hypothesis I can suggest is that the romantic emphasis of the subplots is meant to drain off any potentially serious response to the main action by separating it structurally from the arena of genuine moral concern. Thus we are left free to enjoy the essentially amoral play of wit between the two principal contestants, and are at the same time reassured, in the background, of this more meaningful dimension of emotional attachment which establishes the real point of all their tactical maneuvering and validates their happy union at the end.[16]

Still more interesting are the reversals of the standard formula in two works of Shakespeare generally held to be his greatest achievements in the genres of romantic comedy and historical drama. The "romance" in *As*

16. This must be qualified in the case of *The Lady of Pleasure,* where Shirley does contrast the true and false sophistication of the ladies in his two plots. The main action of *Hyde Park* resembles the subplot of *Much Ado about Nothing*—again, an indication of Shirley's reversal of the standard formula. Coursen, however, would deny that *Much Ado* follows this formula, since he tries to equate it with *A Woman Killed with Kindness,* arguing that Shakespeare intended a "contrast of the puppet-like figures of Claudio and Hero against the full-bodied personalities of Beatrice and Benedick" (p. 185). But one must then ask why their story was made the subplot, and why it attains a new level of seriousness, necessary for its resolution, through the Claudio-Hero action.

You Like It (*c*. 1599)—leaving aside Oliver's courtship of Celia, which is handled quite perfunctorily and does not really add a new element to this scheme—inheres in three separate couples, each enacting a different conception of the sexual relationship. The Touchstone-Audrey sequence involves the sort of earthy, burlesque treatment that one might expect at the lowest level of such a structure. But here it is the secondary pair, Silvius and Phebe, who represent an idealized and sentimentalized view of love, while the tone of the primary action—or, more strictly, of Rosalind's role, which dominates it—is much more realistic, ironical, and witty. The consequence of this arrangement, as has been noted by various critics,[17] is to impart a special value to the main-plot romance by having it synthesize and transcend the attitudes of these other two. With her clear vision and buoyant sense of humor, Rosalind can comprehend, and see through, both the Petrarchan posturing of Silvius and Touchstone's bawdy cynicism, so that her own love seems to maintain a kind of miraculous balance between the spiritual and carnal, between illusion and mere pragmatism. This romantic hierarchy, moreover, also involves something very much like a class angle. The Forest of Arden, despite its egalitarian associations with "old Robin Hood" and "the golden world," is actually a very rigidly stratified society of three distinct castes which, before the arrival of Rosalind, Orlando, and their companions, apparently had not even made contact with each other: the "real" peasants, Audrey, William, and Sir Oliver Martext; the shepherds of pastoral convention, Phebe, Silvius, and Corin; and the exiled Duke and his court, engaged in such aristocratic pastimes as hunting deer, feasting, and philosophizing.[18] And while there is no simple one-to-one relationship between these castes and the pairs of lovers (this would not account, for instance, for the part played by Jaques, or for the fact that Rosalind, the Duke's daughter, takes up residence with

---

17. See especially Harold Jenkins, *"As You Like It," ShS*, VIII (1955), 40–51.

18. Each caste has its own nomenclature (French names for the nobility, classical for the shepherds, and English for the peasants), as well as its own animal emblem or "totem" (deer, sheep, goat). The castes also seem to recapitulate the progress—or, more likely, the degeneration, since the movement proceeds downward—of man from a hunting to a pastoral to an agrarian economy, where Audrey and William become contemporaries of Shakespeare's audience (although even in their own English countryside the deer park, sheep enclosure, and farm were competing for the land).

the shepherds), the general correspondence is clear enough and tends to reinforce the scale of values established by the three-level plot structure.[19]

The relationship of social class to dramatic structure is even clearer in *1 Henry IV* (*c.* 1597), which is built on a hierarchical arrangement of the three worlds of the royal court, the rebel nobility, and the tavern, and of their principal representatives—Prince Hal, Hotspur, and Falstaff. And this hierarchy dramatizes a range of perspectives and values analogous to those found in *As You Like It,* given the necessary translation from an amorous to a martial subject. Falstaff's practical and cynical view of honor, argued out in his famous catechism, can be seen as the equivalent of Touchstone's view of love; Hotspur's enraptured deification of "bright honor" is comparable to Silvius' own infatuation; and Hal, like Rosalind, is able to recognize the absurdity of the extremes embraced by each of these men and yet to encompass them both, ultimately, in the kind of honor that he achieves at Shrewsbury where, in an emblematic rendering of this triadic opposition, he stands triumphant with their prostrate bodies at his feet.[20]

In dealing with dramas of such richness and complexity, one is all too conscious of the pitiful bareness of the bones yielded up by schematic analyses of this sort. But if this analysis has been correct, it would suggest that these poor bones constitute the actual skeleton upon which Shakespeare built his two masterpieces, and in terms of which it should be possible to explicate and appreciate them. It would also suggest, I believe,

19. It is possible to see a foreshadowing of this structure in some of Shakespeare's earlier comedies. The nobles in the main action of *Love's Labor's Lost* (*c.* 1595) are certainly no Rosalinds, but their courtships are made to seem less artificial when compared to Don Armado's, which is so much more fantastically elevated above reality than their own, while Costard acts on the same principle as Touchstone: "Such is the simplicity of man to hearken after the flesh." In *A Midsummer-Night's Dream* (*c.* 1595) Theseus and Hippolyta, at the top of the hierarchy, represent a realistic norm of mature love, in contrast to the romantic "madness" of the young couples in the wood, and to the imperturbable concentration on eating and scratching exhibited by Bottom (whose name states his place on this scale) during his great love scene with Titania.

20. Harry Levin presents a very interesting three-level analysis of this play from a different point of view in "The Shakespearean Overplot," *RD,* VIII (1965), 63–71; compare also Empson, *Some Versions of Pastoral,* pp. 43–46.

that the conception of the three-level formula advanced here could provide a useful tool for examining other plays of the period—both those based upon it, and those deviating from it in various ways—and may therefore contribute something to our understanding of Elizabethan dramaturgy in general and its relationship to the work of its greatest practitioner.

Emblems in English Renaissance Drama

DIETER MEHL

D URING THE LAST TWENTY YEARS or so it has become a critical commonplace to assume a significant and deeply rooted connection between the emblem books of the sixteenth and seventeenth centuries and the poetry of that period.[1] Whereas earlier emblem specialists often collected their material independent of any literary scholarship and treated the links between emblems and literature rather as an interesting sideline,[2] there are a considerable number of recent studies in which such links are investigated in greater detail and with interesting results. Curiously enough, Elizabethan and Jacobean drama has received comparatively little attention in this connection. Apart from an unpublished American dissertation, there is, as far as I am aware, no comprehensive study of the

1. A lecture given at the Universities of Munich and Erlangen. The text has been slightly expanded in translation and the notes added. The German version will appear in *Anglia.*

2. This applies even to the indispensable study by Mario Praz, *Studies in Seventeenth-Century Imagery,* Sussidi Eruditi, 16 (Rome, 1964), with its invaluable bibliography of emblem books.

39

subject.[3] Above all, there has been no adequate methodical assessment of the possibilities and limitations of such an approach. Valuable suggestions can be found in some studies on German Baroque tragedy,[4] but their results can only be applied to English Renaissance drama with several reservations, and the same has to be said, of course, about studies of the emblematic elements in the lyric poetry of the period.[5]

The difficulties of the subject begin even with the definitions. What, for the purposes of our study, do we mean by an emblem, and what kind of interrelation between drama and emblem can be reasonably expected and usefully explored?

In Henry Green's often criticized but little read book *Shakespeare and the Emblem Writers*,[6] practically any illustrated work is considered as an emblem book: Sebastian Brant's *Ship of Fools,* Holbein's *Dance of Death,* illustrated bibles as well as collections of devices (impreses), and emblem books proper. Now it is certainly true—and this has to be emphasized in view of some definitions which are sometimes given that are all too narrow—that the forms mentioned above and others as well have contributed to the emblem tradition and helped to shape it. It is also important to remember that even Andrea Alciati's collection, the earliest and most influential emblem book, contains a surprising diversity of emblems; their subjects are taken from classical mythology and the Greek Anthology, from the observation of nature, popular superstition, and allegorical traditions. Often Alciati's pictures are little more than illustrations of moral aphorisms and fables. These, however, should be considered as exceptions or spurious forms of emblems. The history and the theory of emblems provide ample proof that more than mere pictorial

3. Cf. Arthur O. Lewis, *Emblem Books and English Drama: A Preliminary Survey, 1581–1600* (Unpublished Dissertation, Pennsylvania State College, 1951).

4. Cf. the seminal study by Walter Benjamin, *Ursprung des deutschen Trauerspiels,* rev. ed. (Frankfurt, 1963), and the particularly useful account by Albrecht Schöne, *Emblematik und Drama im Zeitalter des Barock* (Munich, 1964).

5. There is a great deal of perceptive criticism of lyric poetry in the light of the emblem books in Rosemary Freeman's study *English Emblem Books* (London, 1948), which contains some of the most helpful definitions of the emblematic method.

6. *Shakespeare and the Emblem Writers: An Exposition of their Similarities of Thought and Expression* (London, 1870). The book contains a wealth of material that is useful though rather uncritically collected and assorted.

illustration was intended. The well-known tract *Dialogo dell'Imprese Militari et Amorose* by Paolo Giovio of 1555, which was translated into English by Samuel Daniel as early as 1585, insists that in a proper imprese neither the picture nor the motto must be in itself sufficient to indicate the full meaning of the whole device: "As when the figure of it selfe or the mot of it selfe, suffice to declare the meaning, wherfore either the one or the other is superfluous."[7] He is quoted with approval by Abraham Fraunce in his Latin dissertation *Insignium, Armorum, Emblematum, Hieroglyphicorum, et Symbolorum, quae ab Italis Imprese nominantur, explicatio,* which was printed in London in 1588.[8] Fraunce, too, lays great emphasis on the fact that it is the combination of word and picture that provides the full meaning of an emblematic device and that it is this mutual illumination which distinguishes the emblem and the imprese from every other form of art. The soul of an emblem, he claims, is more than the sum of its parts, just as in a human being, *forma* is more than the mere addition of *corpus* and *anima,* though on the whole he allows greater latitude for an emblem than for an imprese and is particularly insistent that emblems should not be obscure.

This is why it must be said that the connection between picture and explanation in a successful emblem is anything but arbitrary, though it may in fact seem so in some cases, especially in the more popular emblem books.[9] In England, in particular, there was an evident awareness of the deeper, far more than merely illustrative, possibilities of pictorial representation. This was due not only to the popular tradition of al-legorical pageants and moralities but also to the influence of the Italian Neo-Platonists and their ideas concerning symbols and their powers of illumination.[10] It is probably the fascinating figure of Giordano Bruno

7. *The Worthy Tract of Paulus Iovius . . . ,* trans. Samuel Daniel (London, 1585), A 7.

8. See especially M 2ʳ ff. I have used the edition in the British Museum.

9. I differ slightly from Praz and Freeman on this point.

10. There are some fascinating studies on this subject. See especially E. H. Gombrich, *"ICONES SYMBOLICAE:* The Visual Image in Neo-Platonic Thought," *JWCI,* XI (1948), 163–192; and Erwin Panofsky, *Studies in Iconology: Humanistic Themes in the Art of the Renaissance* (New York, 1939). Cf. also Samuel C. Chew, *The Virtues Reconciled: An Iconographic Study* (Toronto, 1947); and Walter J. Ong, "From Allegory to Diagram in the Renaissance Mind: A Study in the Significance of the Allegorical Tableau," *JAAC,* XVII (1959), 423–440.

and his famous visit to England that provide the most interesting and concrete link between Italian Neo-Platonism and Elizabethan poetry. His dialogue *De Gl'Eroici Furori,* published in 1585 in London during his sojourn in England and dedicated to Philip Sidney, suggests a most interesting connection between Neo-Platonic thought, the emblems, and the Elizabethan "conceit."[11] It is true to say that the emblem tradition became sterile and irrelevant as soon as this organic and by no means arbitrary interrelation between word and picture, which constitutes the essence of a true emblem, was lost. This can be seen clearly enough in some devotional emblem books of the nineteenth century where the illustrations have become quite unnecessary and the whole concept of emblem has degenerated into a homiletic gimmick.[12]

It is perhaps clear from all this that not too much importance should be attached to the subject matter of the emblems which has often been unduly overestimated and used as the basis for some studies. Many of the most common and best-loved emblems can be traced back to literary *topoi* that enjoyed great popularity long before the first emblem books appeared and were still used after the vogue for emblems had come to an end. One example of this adaptability is the famous motif of elm and vine of which Peter Demetz has made a most illuminating study,[13] but the same could be applied to many other emblems, such as the pelican, the phoenix, and others drawn from the whole field of classical mythology.

The problem of definition is closely related to the question of the

---

11. See the interesting studies by Frances A. Yates: "The Emblematic Conceit in Giordano Bruno's *De Gli Eroici Furori* and in the Elizabethan Sonnet Sequences," *JWCI,* VI (1943), 101–121; and *Giordano Bruno and the Hermetic Tradition* (London, 1964), especially the chapter "Giordano Bruno: Heroic Enthusiast and Elizabethan," pp. 275–290.

12. Cf. G. S. Cautley, *A Century of Emblems* (London, 1878), for a rather amusing example. The introductory poem bears the characteristic title "Emblems Everywhere" and contains the following lines (which might serve as a warning to emblem enthusiasts):

> Nor blame thou this simplicity,
>   For love is at the core,
> Which only sees what others see
>   But feels a little more (p. 4).

13. "The Elm and the Vine: Notes toward the History of a Marriage Topos," *PMLA,* LXXIII (1958), 521–532.

precise kind of connection we should look for between emblem and drama. The majority of previous studies touching on this subject are based on a rather vague concept of literary influence. From similarities in the use of subject matter or verbal agreements it is often concluded that there was direct imitation of certain emblem books by dramatists. This may well have been the case occasionally, but such a conclusion tells us only about the popularity of the emblem books and nothing about the specific character of a given play. Instead, it seems more rewarding to discuss the form and function of emblematic methods as used by Elizabethan dramatists. It is not very important for our purpose to establish indisputable links between particular collections of emblems and individual plays. For instance, it would be very difficult to define exactly the influence of Geoffrey Whitney's popular collection *A Choice of Emblemes* (1586) on Elizabethan literature, but it is surely more to the point to treat the emblem books not as the starting point, but as symptoms of an attitude that found its equally pronounced expression in the drama of the time.

There are, it appears to me, three ways of looking for emblematic elements in English Renaissance drama, and I should like to discuss them briefly in turn.

1. The most obvious manner in which emblems can be used within plays is by direct borrowing or quotation, as scholars such as Henry Green have endeavored to point out. In this respect, however, there is a great difference between English drama and the German Baroque tragedies whose authors obviously made extensive use of certain emblem books and even quoted them in the notes on their own plays.[14] In English plays of the period, we do indeed find a great number of emblematic images and similes as well, but they are for the most part so closely integrated in the dramatic movement of the scene that they lose their static and pictorial character and are hardly recognizable as emblems at first sight. An example of this form of "veiled emblem," as I would call it, can be found in the first scene of Shakespeare's *Twelfth Night* where Orsino is languishing in his romantic infatuation with Olivia:

> O, when mine eyes did see Olivia first,
> Methought she purg'd the air of pestilence!
> That instant was I turn'd into a hart,

---

14. Examples are given by Schöne, *Emblematik und Drama,* pp. 3 ff.

And my desires, like fell and cruel hounds,
E'er since pursue me.

(I. i. 19–23) [15]

It is obvious that this image is more than a picturesque metaphor and that its full meaning is only intelligible if we see the allusion to the unhappy Actaeon who was torn to pieces by his own hounds and who, as an embodiment of blind desire or foolish curiosity, was one of the commonplaces of Renaissance literature. He appears, for instance, in Whitney's *Choice of Emblemes* under the heading *Voluptas aerumnosa* (p. 15) and with the warning moral:

And as his houndes, soe theire affections base,
Shall them deuowre, and all their deedes deface.

In Giordano Bruno's *De Gl'Eroici Furori,* on the other hand, the story of Actaeon is used to illustrate man's innate desire for the divine beauty. In *Twelfth Night,* then, the allusion does much more than merely illustrate a sentiment; it adds a new dimension and places Orsino in a context which at first sight seems almost too large for him. By such means, Shakespeare achieves what Benjamin has, most appropriately, called the *Unscheinbarkeit des Allegorischen* (perhaps "unobtrusiveness of the allegorical" would do for a translation).[16] In this instance, however, little is gained by a reference to emblem books, because neither is the use of the Actaeon story confined to them nor is there anything distinctly emblematic in the way it is employed here.

This, of course, raises the general question whether an emblem that is merely quoted in the text can be called an emblem in the true sense any more, a question that applies to many of the "emblems" in Elizabethan drama that have been listed by scholars. It is certainly important to train one's ear to discover emblematic associations in the imagery of Elizabethan plays, but it is even more essential to recognize their dramatic function within their particular context.

15. The allusion to Actaeon is, of course, pointed out by most commentators. There is also some useful material in John M. Steadman's article, "Falstaff as Actaeon: A Dramatic Emblem," *SQ,* XIV (1963), 230–244.

16. See *Ursprung des deutschen Trauerspiels,* p. 214 ("Dem deutschen Trauerspiel blieb die Unscheinbarkeit des Allegorischen dank der Vergaffung in den Ernst versagt").

Thus, the quoting of emblems can often serve to characterize a certain situation or an individual speaker. The lines quoted from *Twelfth Night* are a typical instance of such linguistic characterization. Orsino's artificial pose of romantic love, not yet touched by any real experience of human partnership, finds expression in his stylized and slightly pretentious imagery. Similarly, in *As You Like It,* the gloomy Jaques, enjoying his own melancholy, is characterized by his habit of emblematizing the everyday world, as it is described in his somewhat absurd reflections on the wounded stag.[17] There are many scenes in Elizabethan drama where emblems and impreses are used with comic effect. For example, the ignorance of characters can be exposed by their foolish misapplication of Latin mottoes, as in Middleton's comedy *Your Five Gallants,*[18] or the whole tradition of sophisticated emblems and "devices" is parodied by the invention of ridiculous and absurdly inappropriate emblems, as in Marston's *Antonio and Mellida,* where the madcap Balurdo gives the following instructions to a painter:

I would have you paint me for my device a good fat leg of ewe mutton swimming in stew'd broth of plums—boy, keel your mouth; it runs over—and the word shall be: "Hold my dish whilst I spill my pottage." Sure, in my conscience, 'twould be the most sweet device now.

(V. i. 19–24)[19]

The comic effect of the scene derives above all from the significant contrast between this misplaced realism and the sickly and degenerate court atmosphere in the main plot.

There is also a more serious manner in which emblems can be used to indicate artificial and decadent court societies, especially in Jacobean drama, where emblems, like masques, often appear as the characteristic mode of expression of a corrupt and unnatural mentality. This can be suggested in a rather superficial way, as when in Webster's *White Devil* Camillo is informed by an emblem, thrown into his window by some

17. See II. i. 29–66.

18. Cf. William Stanley Hoole, "Thomas Middleton's Use of *Imprese* in *Your Five Gallants,*" *SP,* XXXI (1934), 215–223.

19. I quote from the edition by G. K. Hunter (Regents Renaissance Drama Series; Lincoln, Nebr., 1965). The passage is also mentioned by Praz, *Studies in Seventeenth-Century Imagery,* p. 216.

anonymous calumniator, that he is cuckolded by his wife.[20] There is a much more elaborate scene in Tourneur's *Atheist's Tragedy;* it takes place in the house of the bawd Cataplasma who employs herself and her maid with the embroidering of emblems. The profligate Sebastian joins them and attempts to explain the devices.[21] All the corruption and wickedness of the aristocratic world, as portrayed in this play, seems to be depicted in that emblematic embroidery and its highly ambiguous interpretation. Similarly, Vindice *(The Revenger's Tragedy)* and Flamineo *(The White Devil),* both typical specimens of the sinister version of the Jacobean malcontent, are distinguished from the other characters by their emblematic manner of speech.[22]

Thus, in the English drama of the period, as in the German, we find an abundant use of emblems in dramatic speech, but they are nearly always subordinated to the dramatic movement of the play. It is only perhaps in Chapman's tragedies that the quotation of emblems often seems to be a merely rhetorical device, used for the purposes of stylistic embellishment as well as moral argumentation and example.[23]

2. Another form of the emblematic in drama is the insertion of allegorical scenes or tabeaux providing a pictorial commentary on the action of the play, thus creating that mutually illuminating combination of word and picture which is central to the emblematic method. Of course, the primary source of this technique has to be sought not in the emblem books but mainly in those popular allegorical and emblematic pageants and civic entertainments that were often devised by well-known dramatists, such as Thomas Dekker, Thomas Heywood, Thomas Middleton, and Ben Jonson. These men worked from conceptions similar to those of the authors of emblem books. Thus, Thomas Dekker, describing the preparations for his *Magnificent Entertainment,* intended for the recep-

20. See II. i. 323–331, and Praz, *Studies in Seventeenth-Century Imagery,* p. 224. See also the note on the passage in the edition of J. R. Brown (The Revels Plays; London, 1960).

21. See IV. i. 1–43, in Irving Ribner's edition (The Revels Plays; London, 1964).

22. Thus Vindice recommends himself to Lussurioso by an emblematic conceit. See IV. ii. 85–107, in the edition by R. A. Foakes (The Revels Plays; London, 1966). Lussurioso concludes from it that Vindice must have "wit enough to murder any man" (ll. 106–107).

23. This applies particularly to the Byron tragedies, where numerous emblems are quoted, but very often without any obvious relation to the action on the stage.

tion of James I in London, 1603, says: "By this time Imagine, that *Poets* (who drawe speaking Pictures) and *Painters* (who make dumbe Poesie) had their heads and hands full." [24] He is, of course, referring to a critical commonplace frequently quoted during the Renaissance and applied with particular appropriateness to the emblem books. [25] This awareness of the fascinating possibilities for the mutual interpretation of word and picture which the theater provided, has from the very beginning strongly influenced the style and scenic technique of English drama and is perhaps the most important reason for the significant part played by emblematic elements in Elizabethan drama.

The earliest and most striking examples are the dumb shows between the acts of the first classical tragedies that were produced at the Inns of Court. It has not, as far as I know, been remarked that here the tableaux and the dramatic text stand in the same relation to each other as the picture and its explanation in an emblem. [26] A completely new dimension is added to the static and almost purely rhetorical tragedies by these accompanying emblematic shows. The largely exemplary and didactic content of the play is presented visibly to the eye, and the allegorical connotations of the characters are thus conveyed to the audience. Such moralizing and allegorizing of classical tragedy, which can be seen even in Fulke Greville's very untheatrical plays, is very characteristic of English Renaissance drama. Thus, some plays, consisting in effect of five pictures (one before each act) and their dramatic explication, form a kind of dramatized Mirror for Magistrates and seem distinctly related to some emblem books that are also intended as guides for princes and are chiefly devoted to the political virtues and the art of governing. [27] *Gorboduc* is

24. See *The Dramatic Works of Thomas Dekker,* ed. Fredson Bowers (Cambridge, Eng., 1953–1961), II, 257.

25. See the useful study by Robert J. Clements, *Picta Poesis: Literary and Humanistic Theory in Renaissance Emblem Books,* Temi e Testi, 6 (Rome, 1960), especially pp. 173 ff.

26. See my *The Elizabethan Dumb Show: The History of a Dramatic Convention* (London, 1965). I feel that I paid too little attention to the emblematic aspect of the dumb-show tradition in this study.

27. See, for example, Henry Peacham's *Basilikon Doron,* a collection of emblems based on the *Basilikon Doron* of James I and preserved in three manuscript versions. For details of the manuscripts see Freeman, *English Emblem Books,* pp. 236–237.

perhaps the most obvious example, and there are clear links between some
of its dumb shows and the emblem books.[28]

The close relationship between the Elizabethan dumb shows and the
popular emblem books is nowhere more evident than in the anonymous
university play *Locrine*. In this rather crude tragedy, every act is preceded
by a proper emblem, and even Latin mottoes are provided. Thus, before
the third act, a crocodile appears on the stage, bitten by a snake until both
tumble into the water. The motto, which does not quite fit the picture, is:
Scelera in authorem cadunt, and the events of the following act are
presented as an exact illustration of this sentence.[29] Again we can say that
each act forms a complete emblem, with the picture and its explanation
visibly enacted on the stage. The fact, often recognized, that this play has
taken over whole lines from some likewise rather emblematic poems by
Spenser,[30] suggests that the author was not unaware of his own particular
method. Like several of Spenser's complaints, this play presents a series of
Visions of the World's Vanity in the form of emblems and pageants.

A more elaborate and sophisticated example of the use of emblematic
dumb shows can be found in Thomas Hughes's tragedy *The Misfortunes
of Arthur* which was composed as part of an entertainment for Queen
Elizabeth by the gentlemen of Gray's Inn. Several members seem to have
collaborated, especially in devising the dumb shows.[31] These elaborate
allegorical pageants are just as important a part of the whole tragedy as
the formal dialogue. There is, for instance, a whole series of living
emblems in the dumb show before the last act. One of them shows a
pelican pecking his own breast, with the motto *Qua foui, perii,* and the
descriptive text tells us that this is "signifying *Arthurs* too much indulgen-

28. For instance, the story that underlies the first dumb show is also used in *The
Heroicall Devises of M. Claudius Paradin Canon of Beauieu. Translated out of Latin
into English by* P.S. (London, 1591), p. 240; and again in George Wither's *A
Collection of Emblemes* (London, 1635), pp. 177 and 220.

29. I have used the edition in The Malone Society Reprints (Oxford, 1908). See
also my *The Elizabethan Dumb Show,* pp. 72–76, for further comments.

30. Cf. Baldwin Maxwell, *Studies in the Shakespeare Apocrypha* (New York,
1956), pp. 22 ff. On Spenser's emblematic imagery see Freeman, *English Emblem
Books,* pp. 101 ff.

31. See the edition of the play in *Early English Classical Tragedies,* ed. John W.
Cunliffe (Oxford, 1912); and for some helpful criticism, Ribner, *The English
History Play in the Age of Shakespeare,* 2d ed. (London, 1965), pp. 229–235.

cie of *Mordred,* the cause of his death." The pelican was, of course, a particularly well-known emblem; its usual motto was: *Pro lege et pro grege.*[32] Here, the application of the pantomime is left to the spectator, that is to say, it is contained in the following act. Again drama and dumb show explain each other: the action of the play serves as an illustration of the general truths presented in the allegorical tableaux, and these, in turn, can be said to add a timeless meaning to the history of Arthur which is the subject of the play.

It is certainly a coincidence that in the same year (1588) another member of Gray's Inn, Abraham Fraunce, published his Latin tract on emblems and devices, but it suggests, nevertheless, that the new fashion of emblems was cultivated by the same sort of men who also produced the allegorical dumb shows, and there is no doubt that the same mental attitude lies behind both these conventions.

Apart from this rather direct method, Elizabethan drama developed a variety of other techniques to bring home the exemplary nature of characters and actions, such as the allegorical frame, the inclusion of personifications among the dramatis personae, the masque within the play, supernatural apparitions, and many others.[33] They all function as direct pointers to the deeper significance of the action, and they all give an emblematic quality to the events presented on the stage.

It might be worthwhile discussing in this connection the intriguing and not adequately explored problem of the double plot in Elizabethan and Jacobean drama.[34] Whereas Shakespeare developed his own brilliant mode of intricately fusing two or more plots by themes, images, and recurring motifs, his contemporaries often juxtaposed different plots in a more abrupt way; sometimes the subplot seems to be a literal application of themes and images suggested in the main plot. This is the case in

32. See, for instance, Nikolaus Reusner's popular collection *Emblemata* (Frankfurt, 1581), II, 14; and Wither's *Collection of Emblemes,* p. 154.

33. I have commented briefly on some of these techniques in my article "Forms and Functions of the Play within a Play," *RD,* VIII (1965), 41–61.

34. I have not been able to see Norman Rabkin's unpublished Harvard Dissertation "The Double Plot in Elizabethan Drama" (1959). Cf. his article "The Double Plot: Notes on the History of a Convention," *RD,* VII (1964), 55–69. The subject has been very helpfully reopened by Richard Levin. See his important article "The Unity of Elizabethan Multiple-Plot Drama," *ELH,* XXXIV (1967), 425–446, and "Elizabethan 'Clown' Subplots," *EC,* XVI (1966), 84–91.

Middleton and Rowley's tragedy *The Changeling,* where the main action shows the moral perversion of human beings by the ungoverned passion of love while the subplot introduces the realistic comedy of a mental asylum. The notion of love as a kind of madness, implied in the action and imagery of the main plot, is here acted out in a literal way,[35] and the relationship between the two plots can thus be compared to that of an emblem and its explanation. A very similar relationship exists between the two plots in *The Two Noble Kinsmen,* probably by Shakespeare and Fletcher.[36] Of course, the parallel between double plots and emblems should not be pressed too far, and it certainly does not apply to all plays with double plots, but it can perhaps contribute to a more precise understanding of the many-sided and long-lived double-plot tradition in Elizabethan and Jacobean drama.

A curious and rather unusual method of combining drama and emblem can be seen in Thomas Dekker's somewhat neglected play *The Whore of Babylon* (1606). The action of this strange play takes us into an allegorical fairy world, like that of Spenser's great epic, among personifications and fairy-tale characters, but the spectator soon realizes that behind this allegorical guise a patriotic history play is being acted in which contemporary events are described and interpreted in terms of a moral conflict. The emblematic method is here carried to an extreme form; there are also interesting links between this play, Queen Elizabeth's coronation pageant, and Whitney's *Choice of Emblemes.*[37]

From here it is only a little step to the elaborate masques of Ben Jonson where an original and highly sophisticated fusion of emblem and theatrical entertainment is achieved. These masques take their material not so much from the popular emblem books, however, as from such learned

35. See the excellent introduction to N. W. Bawcutt's edition of the play (The Revels Plays; London, 1958), pp. lxii–lxviii, with further bibliographical references.

36. Cf. the edition by Clifford Leech, The Signet Classic Shakespeare (New York, 1966), and Philip Edwards, "On the Design of 'The Two Noble Kinsmen,'" *REL,* V (1964), 89–105. This excellent article is also reprinted in Leech's edition of the play.

37. See Samuel C. Chew, *The Pilgrimage of Life* (New Haven, 1962), pp. 19–21. This book is a rich mine of valuable information about emblems and their relation to literature as well as the visual arts. For some comments on *The Whore of Babylon* see Ribner, *The English History Play,* pp. 283–287.

compilations as those of Valeriano Bolzani and Cesare Ripa.[38] This esoteric form of emblematism was fortunately never adopted in Elizabethan drama proper.

3. Apart from the quoted emblems and the emblematic shows, there was also a less obtrusive manner in which emblems were incorporated into English Renaissance drama—as emblematic images in the course of a scene, as a significant combination of verbal and pictorial expression. It is in this field that I feel the most interesting and rewarding studies could still be made because here we are discussing not just external influences but the very nature of Elizabethan drama.

Glynne Wickham, in his history of the early English theater, rightly stresses the fact that the emblematic mode of dramatic representation persisted longer in England than on the continent and was superseded by a more realistic style of staging only at a rather late date.[39] If we look at the dramatic texts of the period, it is easy to see what a large share in this development the playwrights had and to what extent many plays reflect this tendency to portray events on the stage in such a manner that they form significant and often emblematic images of the play's meaning. Just as the dialogue illuminates the dramatic story, the visible action can add a deeper and more general meaning to the spoken word, and this is akin to the characteristic method of an emblem book. This mutual interaction as it is demonstrated in the plays of Christopher Marlowe has been discussed in a very valuable article recently written by Jocelyn Powell. His main thesis seems to me to apply, though in varying degree, to almost the whole of Elizabethan and earlier Jacobean drama: "Marlowe illustrates his theme with living 'emblems,' which continually develop one into another to create concrete dramatic images of the spiritual action they describe." [40]

The use of stage properties is particularly illuminating in this connec-

38. See Don Cameron Allen, "Ben Jonson and the Hieroglyphics," *PQ*, XVIII (1939), 290–300; D. J. Gordon, "The Imagery of Ben Jonson's *The Masque of Blacknesse* and *The Masque of Beautie*," *JWCI*, VI (1943), 122–141; and Allan H. Gilbert, *The Symbolic Persons in the Masques of Ben Jonson* (Durham, N.C., 1948).

39. See *Early English Stages 1300–1660* (London, 1963), Vol. II, Part I, especially pp. 206–244 ("The Emblematic Tradition").

40. See "Marlowe's Spectacle," *Tulane Drama Review*, VIII (1964), 195–210. The passage quoted is on page 197.

tion because they often serve as means of underlining the significance of a certain scene. An obvious example is the frequent appearance of torches and candles which could serve a number of symbolic as well as practical purposes. In the emblem books, torches and tapers are often used as images of life and death. They are employed with very similar intention in Chapman's *Bussy D'Ambois,* where Montsurry explains to his adulterous wife the extinction of his love by a practical demonstration. The taper in front of him is turned into an emblem, illustrating and generalizing what is going on in the scene:

> And as this Taper, though it upwards look,
> Downwards must needs consume, so let our love;
> As having lost his honey, the sweet taste
> Runs into savour, and will needs retain
> A spice of his first parents, till (like life)
> It sees and dies; so let our love: and lastly,
> As when the flame is suffer'd to look up
> It keeps his lustre: but, being thus turn'd down
> (His natural course of useful light inverted)
> His own stuff puts it out: so let our love
> Now turn from me, as here I turn from thee . . .[41]

Thus, the whole scene, by virtue of its emblematic significance, helps to make the play far more than a presentation of individual suffering. It also proves, like many other similar scenes in the play, that Chapman was anything but a mere rhetorician and that his plays could reveal their full meaning only in performance.

Even more frequent, especially since the gravedigger scene in *Hamlet,* is the use of a skull as an emblematic *memento mori* within the action of a scene. At the beginning of *The Revenger's Tragedy,* Vindice appears with the skull of his murdered mistress, holding it up against the degenerate pomp of the court marching past him, a particularly effective dramatic emblem. In a later scene, the same skull moves him to a gloomy reflection on the theme of *vanitas vanitatum*; it is then dressed up as a living person and presented as a death-giving mistress to the same Duke

---

41. V. iii. 252–262, in Nicholas Brooke's excellent edition (The Revels Plays; London, 1964). A very similar emblem can be found in Otto Vaenius' *Amorum Emblemata* (Antwerp, 1608), pp. 190–191 ("Loue killeth by his owne nouriture"); in Paradin's *Heroicall Devises,* p. 357; and in Whitney's *Choice of Emblemes,* p. 183, where the motto is (as in Paradin): *Qui me alit me extinguit.*

who once seduced her while she was still alive. It is difficult to imagine that any but a Jacobean dramatist could have devised such scenes, but it should also be clear that this has nothing to do with any kind of sensational and macabre realism, as is often suggested, but implies a concept of dramatic representation which is completely different from our own and for which "emblematic" is perhaps the most accurate term.[42] Again it is the concrete visualization of a spiritual and moral experience that the dramatist is striving for, not a realistic imitation of actual events and characters.

Even more literal and striking is the use of stage properties in Tourneur's *Atheist's Tragedy*; here, this technique leads to some almost grotesque situations, as when Charlemont and Castabella lie down to sleep in a churchyard with skulls for their pillows. This sight convinces the atheist that "Sure there is some other happiness within the freedom of the conscience than my knowledge e'er attained to" (IV. iii. 286–287). Charlemont, in particular, is never at a loss to give emblematic interpretations to natural phenomena. An example, bordering on the absurd, is the following passage:

To get into the charnel house he takes hold of a death's head; it slips and staggers him.

CHARLEMONT

Death's head, deceiv'st my hold?
Such is the trust to all mortality.

(IV.iii.77.1–79)

Later, when he is about to be executed, he asks for a glass of water, addressing it as "thou clear emblem of cool temperance" (V. ii. 210).[43] Such symbolism appears rather forced, but its naïve simplicity should make us more perceptive to emblematic elements even where they do not obtrude themselves as unmistakably as here. What the authors of the early classical tragedies tried to achieve by their juxtaposition of allegorical show and sententious dialogue is in many later plays conveyed by the

---

42. See the useful introduction to the Revels Plays edition by R. A. Foakes, with further bibliographical references. I feel that the emblematic method used in *The Revenger's Tragedy* links the play very strongly with *The Atheist's Tragedy*.

43. The emblematic aspect of Tourneur's imagery would repay closer study. See Inga-Stina Ekeblad, "An Approach to Tourneur's Imagery," *MLR*, LIV (1959), 489–498, for some suggestive comments.

emblematic associations of certain properties, without the play turning into an allegorical morality. With this tendency to exploit the emblematic possibilities of the surrounding world, some Jacobean dramatists almost anticipate the method of the Puritan emblem writers which culminates in the ubiquitous allegory of Bunyan.[44]

Even without the use of stage properties, however, single scenes can be turned into emblems by the interaction of word and gesture. This technique can be found even in early Elizabethan drama where, as in the early emblem books, emblems are used not so much for moral and didactic purposes, but as rhetorical devices and a kind of stylistic embellishment. The well-known *topos* of elm and vine (or ivy) can serve as an example. It occurs as early as *The Spanish Tragedy* where the meeting of the lovers shortly before the murder of Horatio is, by the use of this image, presented as an emblem of marriage, and the tragic irony of the scene is effectively underlined:

> HORATIO
> Nay then, my arms are large and strong withal:
> Thus elms by vines are compass'd till they fall.[45]

The same image is used with particularly pointed effect in Shakespeare's *Midsummer-Night's Dream* when Titania embraces Bottom's ass's head:

> So doth the woodbine the sweet honeysuckle
> Gently entwist; the female ivy so
> Enrings the barky fingers of the elm.
>
> (IV.i. 39–42)

The comedy of the scene is greatly heightened by the absurdly inappropriate use of a marriage emblem in word and action, a fact usually overlooked by commentators.

---

44. On Bunyan and the emblematic tradition see Freeman, *English Emblem Books,* pp. 204–228; and Roger Sharrock, "Bunyan and the English Emblem Writers," *RES,* XXI (1945), 105–116.

45. See the edition by Philip Edwards (The Revels Plays; London, 1959), II. iv. 44–45. For some valuable comments on the emblematic aspect of Shakespeare's imagery see Horst Oppel, *Titus Andronicus: Studien zur dramengeschichtlichen Stellung von Shakespeares früher Tragödie,* Schriftenreihe der deutschen Shakespeare-Gesellschaft, Neue Folge, IX (Heidelberg, 1961), 67–83.

More dramatic is the appearance of the same emblem in Shakespeare's *Comedy of Errors,* where Adriana tries to win back her supposed husband and her possessive jealousy finds expression in a suggestive elaboration of the image:

> Come, I will fasten on this sleeve of thine;
> Thou art an elm, my husband, I a vine,
> Whose weakness, married to thy stronger state,
> Makes me with thy strength to communicate.
> If aught possess thee from me, it is dross,
> Usurping ivy, briar, or idle moss;
> Who all, for want of pruning, with intrusion
> Infect thy sap, and live on thy confusion.
>
> (II.ii.172–179)

Again the comic effect is produced by the misapplication of the emblem because, as the spectator knows, it is not her husband whom she embraces but his brother, whom she has never seen before. In this instance, too, the emblematic significance of the image is underlined by the stage action. Passages like those quoted show again and again the close relationship between Elizabethan dramatic imagery and the method of the emblem writers.[46] In plays of the early seventeenth century, this relationship becomes even more marked, and the emblematic implications of character groupings and gestures often help to bring home the moral lesson which the action is meant to exemplify. One example has to suffice.

In Jacobean drama, as later in German Baroque tragedy, suffering and death are often presented in the form of an emblematic spectacle. Death scenes are frequently not only rhetorical climaxes but are also staged as tableaux that are intended to serve as warnings to the spectators. The adulterous Levidulcia (*The Atheist's Tragedy,* IV. v. 68–86), kneeling at the side of her husband's corpse, points at herself as a warning example of the "hatefulness of lust." Her reflections bear some resemblance to Donne's emblematic imagery,[47] and her observation that now she is

---

46. There are many valuable comments on this in M. C. Bradbrook's *Shakespeare and Elizabethan Poetry* (Peregrine Books; Harmondsworth, 1964). See also the studies by Praz, Freeman, and Chew.

47. Cf. the image of her tears and Donne's "A Valediction: of weeping." See also Josef Lederer, "John Donne and the Emblematic Practice," *RES,* XXII (1946), 182–200.

embracing the dead body of him whom she avoided while he was still
alive, sounds very like the subscription of an emblem. In Chapman's *Bussy
D'Ambois,* the enraged Montsurry declares that he wants to make a
visible image of Adultery out of Tamyra by stabbing her. The whole
passage turns on the imagery of emblems:[48]

> MONTSURRY
> I'll write in wounds (my wrongs' fit characters)
> Thy right of sufferance. Write.
>
> TAMYRA
> O kill me, kill me:
> Dear husband be not crueller than death;
> You have beheld some Gorgon; feel, O feel
> How you are turn'd to stone; with my heart blood
> Dissolve yourself again, or you will grow
> Into the image of all Tyranny.
>
> MONTSURRY
> As thou art of Adultery, I will still
> Prove thee my like in ill, being most a monster:
> Thus I express thee yet.   *Stabs her again.*
>
> TAMYRA
> And yet I live.
>
> MONTSURRY
> Ay, for thy monstrous idol is not done yet:
> This tool hath wrought enough. . . .
>
> (V.i.125–136)

A similar, though less dramatic example can be found in *The Revenger's
Tragedy,* where Antonio's wife, a kind of new Lucrece, is shown dead on
a bier, with her finger pointing to the lines in a prayer book: *Melius
virtute mori, quam per dedecus vivere* (I. iv. 17). This tableau, together
with Antonio's narrative and the choric comments of the other characters
on the stage, is a particularly memorable dramatic emblem, and the whole
scene is typical of the unrealistic and morality-like technique of this play,
in which there are several such stylized emblematic scenes.

There is no need to multiply examples, but I hope that enough has been
said to show that the relationship between drama and emblem is not
simply a matter of superficial influences or straightforward imitation. It is

---

48. Cf. the notes on this passage in Brooke's edition. Throughout his excellent
introduction, Brooke rightly stresses the emblematic elements in the staging as well
as in the rhetoric of the play. Bussy's death (V. iii. 141 ff.) provides another example.

a characteristic part of the dramatic style of the period and has to be continually borne in mind, whether we try to define the moral vision of these plays or their dramatic technique, their characters or their imagery.

It would be unwise, on the other hand, to generalize too much about the function of emblematic elements in English Renaissance drama or to see this as an indiscriminately applicable method of interpretation. Although it is probably true to say that there are very few plays of this period in which emblematic techniques cannot be detected in some form or other, so many traditions have contributed to the shaping of these plays, and the methods of individual playwrights differ so greatly from each other that it would be misleading to attach undue importance to one particular aspect. Indeed, this very diversity and experimental vitality of English Renaissance drama can perhaps explain why its exemplary and emblematic features have attracted comparatively little notice. A closer consideration of some of the points briefly outlined here, however, could help to combine literary and dramaturgic criticism more effectively and also remind us of the fact, which seems sometimes forgotten, that all these plays reveal their full significance only in performance.

The Persuasiveness of Violence in Elizabethan Plays

MAURICE CHARNEY

W E USED TO BE TOLD, with a good deal of authority, that "No author exercised a wider or deeper influence upon the Elizabethan mind or upon the Elizabethan form of tragedy than did Seneca."[1] Those are T. S. Eliot's words in an influential essay, but it now seems as if Elizabethan "Senecanism" might have come from diverse, non-Senecan sources, including medieval narrative poems. One striking difference between Seneca and the Elizabethans is in their treatment of violence. Seneca delights in powerful and abnormal emotions, frenzies, hysterias, schizophrenic fantasies, if not actual madness. The violence of his plots is rarely shown directly, but rather is described and commented on in full psychological detail. Seneca is a master of morbid rhetoric, so that the narration of horrors gives him an occasion for thrills—real *frissons*—that would not be possible in a direct presentation. Everything depends upon the heightened style, and we are willing to accept the most minutely gory details from the anonymous but omniscient messenger.

1. T. S. Eliot, Introd. to *Seneca His Tenne Tragedies,* ed. Thomas Newton (1581) (Bloomington, Ind., n.d.), p. v. First published in the Tudor Translations series, 1927.

In *Thyestes,* for example, the messenger relates the exact preparations that Atreus made for the bloody banquet of his brother. We are practically given the recipe for the pasty in which Thyestes' children are the principal ingredient; I quote from the fourteeners of Jasper Heywood's Elizabethan translation:

> From bosomes yet alive out drawne the trembling bowels shake,
> The vaynes yet breath, the feareful hart doth yet both pant and quake:
> But he the stringes doth turne in hand, and destenies beholde,
> And of the guttes the sygnes each one doth vewe not fully cold.
> When him the sacrifyce had pleasd, his diligence he puttes
> To dresse his brothers banquet now: and streight a sonder cuttes
> The bodyes into quarters all, and by the stoompes anone
> The shoulders wyde, and brawnes of armes he strikes of everychone.
> He layes abroad their naked lims, and cuts away the bones:
> The onely heads he kepes and handes to him committed once.
> Some of the guttes are broacht, and in the fyres that burne
>   full sloe
> They drop, the boyling licour fome doth tomble to and froe
> In moorning cawderne: from the flesh that overstandes aloft
> The fyre doth flye, and skatter out and into chimney ofte
> Up heapt agayne, and there constraynd by force to tary yet
> Unwilling burnes: the liver makes great noyse upon the spit,
> Nor easely wot I, if the flesh, or flames they be that cry,
> But crye they do: the fyre like pitch it fumeth by and by:
> Nor yet the smoke it selfe so sad, like flithy miste in sight
> Ascendeth up as wont it is, nor takes his way upright,
> But even the Gods and house it doth with fylthy fume defile.[2]

The culinary details are so precisely rendered that our natural impulse of terror is mitigated by our admiration for Seneca's art. There is, after all, a difference between representation and presentation, between narration and dramatization. As an impartial and eloquent observer, Seneca's messenger protects the audience from the rude shock of what has actually happened.

Although they may have been influenced by Seneca, the Elizabethan dramatists agreed almost unanimously to get rid of the messenger and to show violence directly on stage. I would not want to suggest that there were only literary reasons for this tough point of view, since some

2. Seneca, *Thyestes,* trans. Jasper Heywood, in *Seneca His Tenne Tragedies,* pp. 81–82.

members of the audience would have preferred the spectacle of a good hanging—with some drawing, quartering, and disemboweling—to just about anything the stage had to offer. There was a good deal of gratuitous violence in Elizabethan plays, the sort of Grand Guignol that could only arouse either laughter or admiration for its ingenuity—and if the drama really does teach anything, some members of the audience must have learned many practical details of Machiavellian villainy. But the direct presentation of violence on stage could also powerfully evoke the emotions of pity and fear that Aristotle tells us are the proper effects of tragedy. The rawness and the cruelty of these scenes do not allow for any mitigating effects, so that violence on stage may be persuasive and emotionally convincing in a way no narration could aspire to. The events may be crude, bloody, offensive to good taste, perhaps even disgusting, but we cannot escape what we see in the stage action. It is actually happening before our eyes, and no degree of rhetoric can make it more or less credible or temper its outrage.

We may test these assertions in what is probably the cruelest scene in Elizabethan drama: the blinding of Gloucester in *King Lear*.[3] Samuel Johnson could explain the cruelty of Lear's daughters by historical fact, but he was not able "to apologize with equal plausibility for the extrusion of Gloucester's eyes, which seems an act too horrid to be endured in dramatic exhibition, and such as must always compel the mind to relieve its distress by incredulity." [4] The "extrusion of Gloucester's eyes" is an odd way of putting it, almost as odd as the coinage of an immortal graduate student, who, at a Ph. D. oral examination, is reputed to have spoken of the "deocularization" of Gloucester. Johnson's "incredulity" relieves the mind of its unendurable horror; it is not a natural effect of the dramatic exhibition. Despite Johnson's repulsion, he is testifying to the ability of this scene to arouse strong emotions.

The blinding of Gloucester is presented with a fidelity to detail very different from anything else in the play. As the production of Peter Brook so powerfully demonstrated, *King Lear* does not depend upon any sense of actuality for its tragic effect. The story is drawn from a remote and

3. There are striking similarities between this scene and the attempted blinding of Prince Arthur in *King John* (Act IV, scene i).

4. *Samuel Johnson on Shakespeare,* ed. W. K. Wimsatt, Jr. (New York, 1960), p. 97.

legendary period of British history, and King Lear himself is immeasur-
ably old and archetypically paternal. Yet the scene of the blinding of
Gloucester is painfully realistic; its cruelty has all the immediate horror of
everyday life. Shakespeare seems as interested in showing us the passion
of Gloucester (combined with the recognition of his tragic blindness
towards his sons) as in demonstrating beyond any contradiction the
fiendish and inhuman nature of Cornwall and Regan.

The scene turns particularly on Regan, who is made to show her
"tiger's heart wrapp'd in a woman's hide" (*3 Henry VI* I. iv. 137). She is
the setter-on, who advises her husband to bind Gloucester's "corky arms"
"Hard, hard" (*King Lear* III. vii. 28, 31), and she begins the interrogation
by plucking a few hairs from Gloucester's beard. It is also Regan who
insists sardonically that Cornwall have both eyes: "One side will mock
another; th' other too" (l. 70), who stabs the First Servant from behind,
and who bids farewell to Gloucester with savage sarcasm: "Go thrust him
out at gates and let him smell / His way to Dover" (ll. 92–93). The scene
leaves us no possibility of doubt about the nature of Regan or of
Cornwall, and from this we may draw appropriate conclusions about
Goneril, Cordelia, and King Lear. We have seen Regan and Cornwall in
action, so that we will not be able to wonder why they are unmitigatingly
excluded from any possibility of redemption, when even the villain
Edmund is allowed a change of heart.

One of the effects of this scene that may not be noticed in reading is
that each eye of Gloucester is blinded separately and differently. For the
first eye, the staging is rather elaborate. Gloucester is tied to a chair, which
is held by servants, who presumably turn the chair over when Cornwall
says: "Upon these eyes of thine I'll set my foot" (l. 67). We see Cornwall
stamping out Gloucester's eye with his military boot. The method is so
unusual and so shocking that the First Servant risks his life in order to
stop Cornwall. The blinding of the second eye follows directly from the
words of the dying servant: "O, I am slain! My lord, you have one eye
left / To see some mischief on him. O!" (ll. 80–81). Cornwall answers
with sarcastic decorum in word and deed: "Lest it see more, prevent it.
Out vile jelly! / Where is thy lustre now?" (ll. 82–83). The swiftness and
finality of "Out vile jelly" seems to mean that Cornwall plucks out
Gloucester's second eye by thrusting his finger in it.

The different blinding of the second eye gives the impression of the same scene being played over twice, but it more than doubles the feeling of physical revulsion. By showing us directly this scene of almost unbearable cruelty, Shakespeare is insisting that the evil at the heart of the play is real and unmetaphoric. Through Cornwall and Regan we come to understand the farthest limit of human depravity, although the blinded Gloucester emerges from this scene with a new possibility of tragic insight. As witnesses to this frightening spectacle, we are not allowed to disbelieve what we see with our own eyes. This is what I mean by the persuasiveness of violence.

Violent scenes in Elizabethan drama have a shock effect that forces us to draw immediate conclusions. Murders on stage, for example, are often used to shift our sympathies toward the victim, even if he has consistently alienated our sympathies during the play. Thus the murder of Richard II in Pomfret Castle finishes a careful progression by which the frivolous and euphuistic King becomes a "sweet lovely rose" (*1 Henry IV* I. iii. 175) and Christlike martyr. The agony of suffering, visibly portrayed, cannot fail to evoke our commiseration, and even sometimes persuade us that, if the murderers are irrevocably damned, then their victims must necessarily have been beatific innocents.

There is an impressive array of child murders in Elizabethan drama which are meant to play upon our emotions, since the children are always represented as guiltless victims in an adult world. We should probably begin with the plays of the medieval craft cycles, especially the sacrifice of Isaac and Herod's slaughter of the innocents, but we may more conveniently start with *Cambises,* an old-fashioned tragedy in fourteeners from the middle of the sixteenth century. Praxaspes, a true counselor of the King, advises Cambises to amend his vice of drunkenness, but the King takes offense and proposes a sardonic test. If he can pierce the heart of Praxaspes' youngest son with an arrow, then this will be proof that he is not in any way disabled by drink. The child speaks six touching lines before he is shot through the heart by the King:

> O father, father, wipe your face;
>   I see the teares run from your eye.
> My mother is at home sowing of a band.
>   Alas! deere father, why doo you cry?

And:

> Alas, alas, father, wil you me kill?
> Good Master king, doo not shoot at me;
> my mother loves me best of all.[5]

In a few lines the child's heart is brought on stage as evidence of a direct hit, and the King wallows in drunken self-praise.

If *Cambises* is a tragedy at all, it is, as its title suggests, "A Lamentable Tragedie Mixed Full of Plesant Mirth." The stage directions give us some graphic insight into the sort of impression *Cambises* must have made on its original audience. The punishment of the false judge Sisamnes, for example, is described in full pantomimic detail: *"Smite him in the neck with a sword to signifie his death,"* and, more spectacularly, *"Flea* [i.e., flay] *him with a false skin."* Whatever feeling of tragedy there may be is certainly mitigated by Ambidexter, the Vice, who "with both hands finely can play," and who dominates the action. At one point, *"Let the Vice fetch a dish of nuts, and let them fall in the bringing of them in,"* and at another, Marian-may-be-good fights with Ambidexter: *"she gets him down, and he her down,—thus one on the top of another make pastime."* In the midst of all this rollicking farce, deaths do occur, and Cambises shows himself to be a capricious tyrant on the model of Herod. Yet the murder of Praxaspes' son by the drunken king does offer a moment of real horror—perhaps the only one—in this ranting and frolicsome old play. It is difficult to avoid such a strong emotional reaction to an aimless and insolent child murder.

In *A Yorkshire Tragedy,* the murder is also aimless, as the enraged and despairing bankrupt father sets out to destroy his family. The stage direction for the entrance of the first son begins the pathos: *"Enters his little sonne with a top and a scourge."* [6] In his unthinking innocence, the boy cannot comprehend why his father should want to kill him. He protests that he is his father's "white boie," or darling, but the father insists that he shall be his "red boie" and strikes him a blow on the head. With schoolboy's wordplay, the son asks: "How shall I learne now my heads broke?" The father answers: "Bleed, bleed rather than beg, beg!"

5. Thomas Preston, *Cambises,* in *Chief Pre-Shakespearean Dramas,* ed. Joseph Quincy Adams (Boston, 1924).

6. *A Yorkshire Tragedy,* in *The Shakespeare Apocrypha,* ed. C. F. Tucker Brooke (Oxford, 1908), IV, 110 s.d.

and proceeds to stab him to death. *A Yorkshire Tragedy* is based on a series of lurid murders of the early seventeenth century. It is a crude play, and it seems difficult to believe that it was once attributed to Shakespeare, but the murder scenes are frightening in their directness. We cannot believe in the characters, but the events have their own veracity.

The brutal slaying of Macduff's children in *Macbeth* is the most convincing of these child murders in Elizabethan drama, since it carries with it the sense of a world turning to chaos. Like the blinding of Gloucester, the scene is presented directly, without any mitigation of its cruel details. Actually, we see only Macduff's son, a "poor monkey" and "Poor prattler" (IV. ii. 58, 63), as his mother calls him, who, now that his father is gone, must learn to live "As birds do" (l. 32). The son's extended dialogue with his mother prepares us for the sudden shock of the entrance of the Murderers. When one of them calls Macduff a traitor, the son defends his father's honor: "Thou liest, thou shag-ear'd villain" (l. 82). This is the cue for the stabbing of the son, and the insults of the Murderer intensify our sense of savagery: "What, you egg? / Young fry of treachery!" (ll. 82–83). The son's dying lines conclude the sweetness and innocence of his part: "He has kill'd me, mother. / Run away, I pray you" (ll. 83–84). This murder in all of its anguish seals the fate of Macbeth. It outrages our sensibilities in a way that the murder of Duncan could not, since the one is presented in the dramatic action and the other is only narrated.

The Elizabethan dramatists loved violence, and they loved to show it on stage because it had an emotional impact that could not be achieved in any other way. There is a harsh verity about murders that we see with our own eyes. The spectacle can release a tremendous energy of pity and fear and also persuade us of certain bitter, metaphysical truths about the world of the play. The staging of scenes of violence tended to be very realistic. Animal blood in concealed bladders was used freely, and all of the swordplay and executions were presented with precise, technical details. Actual instruments of torture were sometimes brought on stage, and one of Henslowe's properties was a severed head, which could be made up to resemble a variety of male characters. The stage properties of violence are not, of course, persuasive in themselves, but they were used by the Elizabethans as part of a determined dramatic effort to excite and even to terrify the audience.

The moral force of violence in Elizabethan drama should not be exaggerated. There is a sense that the violence is performed for its own sake and is to be judged by esthetic rather than moral criteria. That is why revengers are always boasting about the quaintness, cunning, originality, complication, and appropriateness of their plots, as if they were dramatists themselves, preparing their own kinds of plays. There is an ironic doubleness in the fact that the murders are so often accomplished in a play within the play, the so-called "killing masque," in which the revenger is indeed the author, director, and stage manager of his own show. Hamlet's *Mousetrap* is kin to these "killing masques."

In the usual version, however, the Players do not "poison in jest; no offence i' th' world" (*Hamlet* III. ii. 229–230), but commit real murders under the guise of histrionic illusion. The "killing masques" are generally written in an artful style set apart from that of the main play. Hieronimo's show in *The Spanish Tragedy* offers the additional extravagance of polyglotism:

> Each one of us must act his part
> In unknown languages,
> That it may breed the more variety.
>
> (IV.i.172–174) [7]

Kyd apologizes to his readers for this exotic touch: *"Gentlemen, this play of* HIERONIMO *in sundry languages, was thought good to be set down in English more largely, for the easier understanding to every public reader"* (IV. iv. 10 s.d.).

At the end of the masque, Hieronimo explicates the true nature of mimesis for his appreciative but uncomprehending audience:

> Haply you think, but bootless are your thoughts,
> That this is fabulously counterfeit,
> And that we do as all tragedians do:
> To die today, for fashioning our scene,
> The death of Ajax, or some Roman peer,
> And in a minute starting up again,
> Revive to please tomorrow's audience.
> No, princes, know I am Hieronimo,
> The hopeless father of a hapless son,

7. Thomas Kyd, *The Spanish Tragedy,* ed. Philip Edward (The Revels Plays; London, 1959).

> Whose tongue is tun'd to tell his latest tale,
> Not to excuse gross errors in the play.
>
> (IV.iv.76–86)

He then *"Shows his dead son"* (l. 88 s.d.), just as Antony shows the corpse of Caesar to the mob in order to demonstrate his oratorical points. Hieronimo is still to bite out his own tongue and kill the Duke and himself with a convenient penknife. He ends his life and his part with a brilliant flourish that satisfies all possible requirements for an esthetically and morally complete revenge. It is, in fact, more than complete, with an inventiveness and dramatic energy that go far beyond any minimum requirements. The whole notion of esthetic villainy is a complex one, since the murdering villain is so often a *persona* for the creating author, and they both seem to be accomplices in some forbidden but magically potent act.

The best description I know of the esthetics of villainy is in Dryden's praise of Jack Ketch, the great seventeenth-century executioner. With malicious understatement, Dryden draws a distinction between

the slovenly butchering of a man, and the fineness of a stroke that separates the head from the body, and leaves it standing in its place. A man may be capable, as Jack Ketch's wife said of his servant, of a plain piece of work, a bare hanging; but to make a malefactor die sweetly was only belonging to her husband.[8]

Just as in satire there is a difference between "fine raillery" and a brutal lampoon, so in Elizabethan drama one may distinguish between clumsy skulduggery and the fine artistic stroke of a graduate Machiavel.

The esthetic sense of violence is very strong in *The Revenger's Tragedy,* a play that is a curious mixture of crude formulas and sophisticated poetry. Vindice enunciates two of the principles on which the action is based: "When the bad bleeds, then is the tragedy good" (III. v. 205), and "When thunder claps, heaven likes the tragedy" (V. iii. 47).[9] Both are full of artifice, since Vindice is claiming moral support from the gods as audience to his play, an audience applauding enthusiastically "When the bad bleeds." Like most revengers, Vindice loses sight of his original

8. John Dryden, "A Discourse Concerning the Origin and Progress of Satire," *Essays of John Dryden,* ed. W. P. Ker (Oxford, 1926), II, 93.

9. Cyril Tourneur, *The Revenger's Tragedy,* ed. R. A. Foakes (The Revels Plays; London, 1966).

purpose, which is caught up in a grandiose vision of artistic omnipotence. He dresses up the skull of his "bony lady" with frantic relish, and when he puts the poison on her lips to destroy the lecherous old Duke, we are meant to believe that Vindice nows loves her more fervently than he did during her lifetime. His brother Hippolito fittingly praises "The quaintness of thy malice, above thought" (III. v. 109). At the very end of the play, after a lethal masque, Vindice cannot keep back a boastful confession of his deeds: " 'twas somewhat witty carried, though we say it" (V. iii. 97). He and his brother are immediately condemned to death, but Vindice seems only concerned with having rescued their brilliant exploits from oblivion: "This murder might have slept in tongueless brass, / But for ourselves" (ll. 113–114), and "This work was ours, which else might have been slipp'd" (l. 120). He is only echoing the noble sentiments of Shakespeare's sonnets:

> Since brass, nor stone, nor earth, nor boundless sea,
> But sad mortality o'ersways their power. . . .
>
> (Sonnet 65)

Vindice has tried heroically to conquer time by making his revenge into a work of art.

The Revenger's Tragedy is a puzzling play, whose meanings are sometimes too simple and sometimes too complex. Marlowe's *Jew of Malta* is much more of a piece throughout and much more direct in its presentation. Barabas takes an innocent pride in his work, so that his wit combat with Ithamore seems to be the sort of self-magnifying talk one hears at professional conventions:

> As for myself, I walk abroad a-nights
> And kill sick people groaning under walls:
> Sometimes I go about and poison wells. . . .
>
> (II.iii.180–182)[10]

Barabas concludes by asking Ithamore: "But tell me now, how hast thou spent thy time?" (l. 207). Ithamore answers in a way that can only delight his new master:

> Faith, master,
> In setting Christian villages on fire,

10. Christopher Marlowe, *The Jew of Malta,* in *The Plays of Christopher Marlowe,* ed. Leo Kirschbaum (Cleveland, 1962).

Chaining of eunuchs, binding galley-slaves:
One time I was an ostler in an inn,
And in the nighttime secretly would I steal
To travellers' chambers and there cut their throats:
Once at Jerusalem where the pilgrims kneel'd
I strowed powder on the marble stones
And therewithal their knees would rankle so
That I have laugh'd a-good to see the cripples
Go limping home to Christendom on stilts!

(II.iii.208–218)

There is something hearty and inventive in all this, and the actual violence of the play is also "cunningly perform'd." In Barabas' preparations to entertain Calymath, we see him characteristically *"Enter with a hammer above, very busy"* (V. v. s.d.). He has become the theatrical engineer, testing the worthiness of his device: "How stand the cords? How hang these hinges? Fast? / Are all the cranes and pulleys sure?" (ll. 1–2). Everything is perfect in this intricate mechanism, and we cannot help feeling sorry for Barabas that he himself should fall through the trap door of the upper stage and tumble into his own cauldron. Our sense of evil is exacerbated by the fact that Barabas is made to deliver his death speech from this same steaming cauldron, a type image for the pit of hell.[11]

The violence in *The Jew of Malta* does not seem very terrifying, but it is persuasive in the sense that its ingenuity and its esthetic artifice engage our attention. Barabas forces us to notice how the pulleys work and which rope releases the fatal trap door. All of these mechanical effects that so delighted popular audiences are used with ironic intent in Webster's *Duchess of Malfi*. By a series of stage tricks, Ferdinand is attempting to drive his sister to despair. He appears to her in darkness, and he gives her what purports to be the hand of her dead husband. But it is all only waxwork horrors, as is the spectacle Bosola discovers of her husband and children *"appearing as if they were dead"* (IV. i. 55 s.d.).[12] But the Duchess will not despair; the theatrical shows only strengthen her forti-

11. See G. K. Hunter, "The Theology of Marlowe's *The Jew of Malta,*" *JWCI*, XXVII (1964), 233–235 and Plate 28. One of Henslowe's properties was "j cauderm for the Jewe."

12. John Webster, *The Duchess of Malfi*, ed. John Russell Brown (The Revels Plays; London, 1964).

tude and define her tragic stature. She is surrounded by a chorus of contentious, shrieking madmen, and Bosola appears to her in the guise of tomb maker and bellman, but in the midst of all these histrionic trials, she can assert: "I am Duchess of Malfi still" (IV. ii. 142). All of her brother's quaint and cunning stage effects are made to seem like mere parlor magic in the face of the Duchess' moral courage, and she forces her adversaries to strangle her to death with open and direct brutality.

I have not tried to answer the question why violence, both in the subject matter and in the staging, should have been so attractive to Elizabethan dramatists. Admittedly, they preferred bold and striking effects to more rational and orderly ones, and violence tends to produce an extreme situation in which ideas, values, and styles may be confronted and tested. It creates the existentialist moment of truth that we have recently encountered in the "Theater of Cruelty," most notably in Peter Brook's production of *Marat-Sade*. There is no direct link between Peter Weiss's play and the Elizabethans, yet both are trying to present a kind of metaphysical "action" drama that is intended to disturb and shock its audiences.

Even in those Elizabethan plays with the quaintest and most ingenious sort of violence, we still have a sense that the will and being of the characters are both displayed and put to the proof. If we cannot speak of many plays in terms of their morality, we can, nevertheless, speak of degrees of intensity, or the relative success or failure of powerful effects. Violence directly presented on stage is exciting. At its best, it can engage our pity and terror with an immediacy not possible in narrations. There is, of course, a world of difference between Shakespeare and the author of *A Yorkshire Tragedy*, even though the play was confidently attributed to Shakespeare and printed with his works, but both are not afraid to make their plays a radical imitation of life, and neither attempts to escape from his responsibilities by the pusillanimity of rhetoric.

The Weak King History Play
of the Early 1590's

MICHAEL MANHEIM

I N A RECENT REVIEW, M. C. Bradbrook observes that "Shakespeare's
dramatizing of English history provided a reflection of men's hopes
and fears. The 'Tudor myth' reflected the national anxiety; not only pure
doctrine but contemporary social pressures supply the background to these
plays."[1] Without attempting to identify all the "social pressures" in
question, I think it can be shown that a group of plays in the early 1590's,
by Shakespeare and others, involve dilemmas about the crown which
reflect the public anxiety of which Miss Bradbrook speaks, and further
that these dilemmas are integral to the construction of these plays. The
plays are the anonymous *Woodstock,* Marlowe's *Edward II,* the King
John plays, Shakespeare's Henry VI plays, and his *Richard II,* all works
dealing with the reigns of kings so weak that they ultimately lost their
thrones or perished (or both).

Irving Ribner states the problem which shapes the weak king plays

1. M. C. Bradbrook, review of Irving Ribner's *The English History Play in the
Age of Shakespeare,* rev. ed. (New York, 1965), in *SQ,* XVIII (Spring, 1967),
188–189.

when he asks: "Which is more important. . . , the divine sanction of hereditary right or proven ability to govern, combined with a *de facto* possession of the crown?"[2] He later expands the question: "The dominant political question of the England which produced the history plays . . . was . . . the terms of political obedience. Under what conditions, if ever, was rebellion against a lawful monarch justified?"[3] The contradictions implicit in *de facto* possession are not explicitly debated in the plays I am considering, but they may provide a means of understanding vacillation or sudden shifts heretofore seen only as weak construction. Some of these plays have been compared in the past, and a variety of similarities among them have been observed.[4] No one, however, has looked at the weak king history plays as a group. My aim is to show how these plays represented in their construction the audience's anxiety over the questions implicit in them.

In his preface to the anonymous *Woodstock,* A. P. Rossiter sees the central issue of that play in similar terms:

On the one hand he [the anonymous author] accepts the commonplaces about God's deputy, the celestial omens which naturally foreboded "change and fall of states," the condemnation of upstarts as symptoms of "corrupted blood" necessitating political phlebotomy (as in I. i. 142–150). But on the other he shows a revolt succeeding, against a king who is himself in arms, all without a line of condemnation from anyone for whom his audience could feel much sympathy. . . . The political-moral interest of *Woodstock* . . . seems to verge on controversial ground, since to question the duty of full obedience, even to the wickedest king (sent by God for His own good reasons), was to risk the dangerous association with those who upheld the doctrine of Tyrannicide: the theory that the Subject had, in certain circumstances, the right to rebel for conscience' sake.[5]

Through the strong morality-play construction of *Woodstock,* we clearly see the struggle between the two opposing and irreconcilable

2. *The English History Play in the Age of Shakespeare,* rev. ed. (New York, 1965), p. 166.

3. *Ibid.,* p. 312.

4. See, for example, *Woodstock: A Moral History,* ed. A. P. Rossiter (London, 1946), pp. 47–65; Ribner, *English History Play,* pp. 152–153; F. P. Wilson, *Marlowe and the Early Shakespeare* (Oxford, 1953), pp. 94–103; F. E. Schelling, *The English Chronicle Play* (New York, 1964), pp. 98–114.

5. *Woodstock,* pp. 14–15.

concepts of the Tudor myth. On the one hand, we have the King's chief critic, good Thomas of Woodstock, repeatedly avowing adherence to the divine authority of the crown, and on the other we have the King irresponsibly "farming out" the kingdom to Bushy, Bagot, and Green, and making a corrupt, ambitious upstart (Tresilian) Lord Chief Justice of the realm. Richard is represented throughout as "God's deputy" and "not all the water in the rough rude sea" quite washes "the balm off from his anointed head." Nevertheless, despite Woodstock's loyalty to the crown, he is murdered on the King's orders for seeking reforms; while the less-restrained Lancaster ultimately leads a successful rebellion. The case for opposing a king seems almost justified. The lost ending of the play certainly involves a reconciliation of some kind between Richard and his rebellious uncles, but any treatment of Richard's reign also assumes audience knowledge that he would one day be deposed, and the possibility of deposition hardly seems unwelcome in *Woodstock*.

Nevertheless, in going along with Rossiter, one must be careful not to go too far. The play does not absolutely assert "the right to rebel for conscience' sake." Richard's sacred position is never denied, and the orthodox attitudes of Woodstock himself represent one of the two opposing poles of right in the play. The play makes no attempt to assert which right is transcendent. *Woodstock* is art, not political tract. It represents in dramatic form the clash of awful opposites; it does not suggest how those opposites may be reconciled. It articulates for its audience the terror that underlies the prospect of totally irresponsible rule side by side an ethos in which rebellion cannot be sanctioned. I believe the same holds true for the other plays with which I am concerned. The construction of *Woodstock* can be better viewed after a look at Marlowe's *Edward II*.

While *Woodstock* suggests the common theme of these plays, *Edward II* better suggests their similar construction. On the one hand, again, is the King's special and divine position, and on the other is his willingness to sacrifice the good of his kingdom and forsake his royal responsibilities for the sake of a debauched favorite. In construction, moreover, the play seems built around a sudden and unexpected shift in appeal to audience sympathy following the murder of Gaveston in Act III, scene i. So long as Edward's power is secure and there is little threat of unified insurrection, so long as Edward is lost in his sensual preoccupations with Gaveston, our sympathies are with the incensed lords of the realm. But the minute

Gaveston is murdered as part of a conspiracy unknown even to most of
the rebels, our sympathies shift—and the shift is not gradual. Up until
Gaveston's death, Young Mortimer is an energetic and admirable spokes-
man for responsible lords who see the kingdom going to ruin because of
the King's refusal to do his job. The Queen, too, later to be Young
Mortimer's lover, is highly sympathetic throughout the first part of the
play, seeking pathetically to win her husband's love and consistently
abused for her efforts. Yet following Gaveston's death, Young Mortimer
is immediately seen as an ambitious cutthroat who will stop at nothing to
gain power and the Queen, his willing accomplice and trull. The King,
who is a most unsympathetic figure during his courtship of Gaveston,
throughout the latter part of the play is a tragic figure; he does not
become one; he *is* one from the moment of Gaveston's death. Such
sudden shifts in character are completely in the nature of Elizabethan
drama; they are sometimes important in a play's construction. Character
exists to serve theme, and the theme here is the ambiguity, implicit in the
Tudor myth, between the king as God's deputy and the inadequacies of a
particular monarch.

Marlowe almost seems to be inviting audience analysis of their own
responses in *Edward II*. While the ruler is in a relatively secure position,
they are asked as subjects to judge him, condemn him for his faults, and
sympathize with those who would rebel "for conscience' sake"; but the
moment he is on the run, when his enemies, despite all the justice that
seems so clear and apparent on their side, gain the upper hand, the sense
of the King's divine position and all the prohibitions against rebellion
become dominant. The latter half of the play evokes guilt toward the
very responses which were invited in the first half, when Young Mortimer, the Queen, and the incensed nobility seemed to be such attractive
figures—and Edward seemed so weak and unstable. Marlowe concentrates on developing this sense of guilt until it culminates in our response
to the terrible demise of Edward, so that we as audience have moved from
one pole, represented by the just complaints of the lords, to the other pole,
represented by Edward's awful death. The reversals of the well-meaning
but confused Earl of Kent mirror our own shift in sympathies. It must be
reemphasized, however, that the image of a tragic Edward left with us at
the end of the play represents but a single pole. The reactions of the lords
early in the play, like our own, are just as real and defensible as the

reactions of Edward and Kent—and again our own—late in the play. Because Edward dies in so lamentable a fashion, we must not forget the miserable image of royal authority he created at the start, putting his lust for Gaveston before even the minor responsibilities of his office. In the final analysis the play articulates, through its stark shift in appeal to our sympathies, the helplessness in which we find ourselves when God's deputy acts in disgustingly irresponsible fashion. Young Mortimer and his followers are not wrong early in the play. They are wrong later in the play because they threaten to, and finally do, depose a king. Their earlier complaints were valid; but such complaints, unchecked, lead to the usurpation of power. Yet if they are not acted upon in some way, the kingdom rots. Such is the dilemma, and the play evokes feelings of anxiety and frustration toward that dilemma.

To look briefly back to *Woodstock,* there is a point in that play when its author seems to be working for something of the same shift in audience sympathies as exists in *Edward II.* Early in the play our sympathies are with the nobles, against whom the King and his favorites conspire. With the death of the Queen late in the play, however, a change takes place comparable to that in Marlowe's play. Richard suddenly becomes aware of his past sins and abruptly seeks to save Woodstock's life, though the favorites see to it that his injunction comes too late. His sudden attack of conscience makes us recall that he is still God's deputy and that our hatred for him, like that of his uncles, is treasonable. Thus in *Woodstock,* as in *Edward II,* the contradictory responses of the audience have been evoked.

The basic arrangement of characters in Shakespeare's *Richard II,* of course, is not unlike that in *Woodstock.* Arrayed against the sober, conservative uncles, upholders of tradition, are the same irresponsible young lords whom the author of *Woodstock* put to death at the end of his play but whom Shakespeare, working more directly with the chronicles, resurrected. In general, however, the similarity between the two plays stops there. Richard's favorites are a match for their *Woodstock* counterparts only in a single scene in Shakespeare's play; the harassment of Gaunt, paralleling that of Woodstock, is quickly ended with his death early in the second act. Shakespeare's play, of course, is also vastly superior to its predecessor in its language and its much-discussed insight into character. What the plays significantly hold in common with one another and with *Edward II* is the sudden shift in appeal to audience sympathies.

Despite all the praise given *Richard II* in twentieth-century criticism, a few commentators still dislike it. Rossiter finds it something of a patched-up job, with totally unprepared-for events and changes in attitude on the part of its central characters.[6] These "flaws," of course, may result from the shifting appeal to our sympathies I have been talking about. Like Edward early in the Marlowe play, Richard is at first presented in most unattractive colors. His handling of the Bolingbroke-Mowbray feud is whimsical, and his treatment of John of Gaunt is as paltry as any action of Marlowe's Edward or the Richard in *Woodstock*. But after Richard's departure on his Irish expedition, we are suddenly and without warning invited to feel quite differently about the youthful King. The turning point is Act II, scene ii, in which the Queen frets about her husband and learns that the banished Bolingbroke, evidently prepared for rebellion, has returned to be greeted by hundreds of followers. In this scene, the Queen acts as a catalyst for the shift in audience response. Up to this point, we can easily identify with John of Gaunt and sense deeply the injustice of Bolingbroke's banishment (assuming, as most Elizabethans did, that Mowbray was almost certainly Richard's agent in the murder of Woodstock); but here we are abruptly led to sympathize with the King, now highly vulnerable. As the play moves to its closing acts, this identification becomes total involvement with a tragic hero—and all Shakespeare's talents are brought to bear in evoking our sympathy for and understanding of a very sensitive man who is gradually coming to comprehend the full range of his helplessness. So far, the pattern is like that in *Edward II*.

Bolingbroke, however, is not so bluntly handled as Marlowe's Young Mortimer, and in him, finally, is embodied the basic dilemma of this play and of the others we are concerned with. For Bolingbroke is no cutthroat. And although he is ruthlessly ambitious, he is also, as the first Lancastrian king, represented as strong, shrewd, and competent. Whereas in the Marlowe play our sympathies shift violently from Young Mortimer to Edward, in *Richard II* they are deeply and disturbingly divided between Richard and Bolingbroke from the point at which Richard becomes a tragic figure. Following Richard's return from Ireland, we are moved by both the religio-legal aspects of his position and by his capacity to feel

6. *Angel With Horns* (New York, 1961), pp. 23-39.

things deeply. At the same time, we have little doubt of Bolingbroke's qualifications to be king of England—usurper or no. In no other play do the irreconcilable poles of the Tudor myth seem farther apart, and in no other play are the pity and terror at the prospect of this division so successfully evoked. Richard at Pomfret and Henry at court are both tragic figures—Richard the poet, capable of articulating his innermost thoughts and feelings; Henry the strong, silent, clear-headed politician, aware that his reign will include a legacy of continuous rebellion and intrigue. It is impossible to assert that either side is right or wrong, and the play's impact is in the depth and range of our awareness of that impossibility, expressed in part through sudden shifts in appeal to audience sympathy toward its central figures.

So far, we have been concerned only with plays in which the king, though inadequate, is legal possessor of his throne. The problem of the *de facto* king, one whose title is marred in some way, is basically the same. The homily on disobedience precludes rebellion against any monarch, even if his hereditary right is questionable.[7] The idea that divine providence causes the troubles of Henry VI and King John as a result of their illegitimate succession is constantly reiterated in the plays in which they are the central figures, but usually as an excuse for rebellious action or a sign of the King's weakness. The rebels in *3 Henry VI* themselves admit that had Henry married someone "meek" and been more like his renowned father, whose hereditary title was no better than his son's, they would have deferred their claim "until another age" (II. ii. 150–162). The real issue in these plays is still the weak king.

In *The Troublesome Reign* and Shakespeare's *King John,* there is a clear conflict between the king as absolute authority and the king's inadequacies in dealing with the central problems of his reign. John R. Elliot, in his "Shakespeare and the Double Image of King John,"[8] finds that Shakespeare's play, rather than preaching "the cliches of orthodox Tudor political doctrine," dramatized "the most controversial material to be found in his sources," stressing the ambiguities of John's reign. Elliot feels that *The Troublesome Reign* is more sympathetic to John; yet while the emphasis may be somewhat different, John himself acknowledges in the anonymous play that his "sins are far too great" for him "to be the

7. See Alfred Hart, *Shakespeare and the Homilies* (Melbourne, 1934), pp. 29–31.
8. *Shakespeare Studies,* I (1965), 64–84.

man / T'abolish Pope and popery from [the] realm," and abolishing popery in these plays is synonymous with being a successful king. The significant thing is that both plays present scenes inviting sharply varying kinds of audience sympathy. When John acts in the best interests of England by challenging papal authority, we cheer him; but when he surreptitiously plots the death of Prince Arthur, legal successor to the throne, and when he knuckles under to the Church, we condemn him and sympathize again with the rebellious lords. In the final act, innocent despite himself of Arthur's blood, the harassed, fever-ridden, and later poisoned King once more evokes our sympathy. The King's almost criminal weaknesses are emphasized while he is sure of his power; his personal tragedy becomes apparent when he loses his hold on the land. The shifts in appeal to sympathy in these plays are just as sudden as in *Edward II* and *Richard II*. The powerful rhetorical pathos of Shakespeare's play, the real source of its difference from *The Troublesome Reign,* contributes markedly to the atmosphere of uncertainty and terror which accompanies the reign of an unstable monarch.

Shakespeare's *Henry VI,* as a trilogy showing a prolonged decline in national unity, contains a greater number and variety of events than the other plays I have been considering. Shifts in appeal to audience sympathy certainly exist, however, though they are perhaps not so important in the pattern of each individual play. The weak king is the basic issue in all three plays, and a shift in appeal to our sympathies toward Henry definitely seems intended between the final scenes in Part 1 and the end of Part 3. Though his faults are of a different nature from Edward's and Richard's, he is contemptibly weak in allowing Suffolk to arrange the marriage with Margaret and even worse in sitting by while good Duke Humphrey is destroyed. Unlike Edward and Richard, his image remains weak and pusillanimous even when he is at bay—when he is bullied by York into disinheriting his own son. He almost seems to deserve the downfall that has been his inevitable fate from birth. Yet throughout most of Part 3, he alone of all the characters holds our sympathy. The Henry we hear lauding the shepherd's existence while fathers and sons destroy one another in pointless battle evokes feelings comparable to those evoked by Richard at Pomfret.

Henry's enemies can hardly be called sympathetic in the earlier portions of the trilogy—Suffolk if anything resembles the evil Young Mortimer at the end of *Edward II.* But Richard of York is certainly a glamorous figure whose commanding presence and political shrewdness make him comparable to the young Bolingbroke. His claim to legitimacy is moot, but then so is Henry's. Neither side can in fact claim right by descent, so ability has got to be considered a determining factor. And York clearly has the ability. The clue to what the Yorkist rebellion really is, of course, is Cade's rebellion—the signal for the ensuing total chaos to begin. But while Richard of York reveals his piratical schemes along the way, his image of kingly potential remains intact to his death. The fact that sympathies are intended to shift is seen in the character of his venomous son Richard Crookback, who shows the audience all the evil implicit but never fully revealed in his father's ambition.

Henry's Lancastrian supporters are no more appealing than his enemies following the death of Duke Humphrey. Queen Margaret, who can command some sympathy as a result of the disinheriting of her son, with the murder of York appeals to us little more than the crookback. Though opposed in battle, both the supporters of the Yorkist cause and the supporters of the Lancastrian cause assume the position of the King's adversaries in *Edward II* and in the Richard II plays. Set against them all in Part 3 is the pacifistic Henry, whose faults have suddenly become his virtues. The peaceful, holy man, long abused (by us as well as by his associates) for his unmilitant presence and refusal to command, in the perspective of the rapine struggles of the third play, seems to provide the only answer. Our sympathies shift to him when it becomes apparent that neither side is right and that the war, whichever way it goes, can only result in ever-increasing bloodshed. Like the other weak king plays, *Henry VI* presents a dilemma. As Henry's weakness brings his kingdom to ruin, we long for a king with the presence of a Henry V. Yet amid the chaos his own inadequacies have helped to create, this Henry has a vision of the way things ought to be transcending the superficial chivalry which has heretofore governed all political responses. Thus the feelings evoked from us concern not only the conflict of a weak king as God's deputy but all the conventions of medieval warfare as well. Before we are finished, an implicit contradiction between Christian love and chivalric honor has been made. The three parts of *Henry VI* are broader in scope than the other plays we have considered.

Detailed analysis of the artistry of any of these plays has obviously not been my purpose. They are so distinct from one another in quality and

sophistication that such a discussion would have to take a radically
different form from this one. But what they hold in common in their
construction is important. Each demands sudden and seemingly unreasonable shifts in the attitude of its audience toward its protagonist and
antagonists. These shifts form a pattern, when the plays are looked at
together, which suggests their uniform purpose. An inadequate, weak, or
unstable king necessarily evokes our anger and frustration. We would like
to see him replaced. Thus we identify with the rebellious lords who make
such a prospect seem possible. When a rebellion has been successfully
mounted, however, our sense of guilt at disobeying God's deputy is
immediately aroused. We then see not the weak king but the heaven-sent
symbol of order in the land under attack. The rebellious lords no longer
mirror our antagonisms toward the crown but now appear as ambitious
madmen destined to bitter rivalry once their immediate objectives are
achieved. Even Bolingbroke, whose image is better than the one described, nearly destroys his country by his actions. This severe bifurcation
of our sympathies draws from within us (as audience) our inevitable
ambivalence toward the ruler: be it Edward, Richard, Henry, or John—or
perhaps even Elizabeth or the joylessly anticipated James. We are not
responding to individuals, despite all we see and hear them do and say;
we are responding to the situations in which these individuals find
themselves. Images in chronicle and drama of the great kings—Edward
III and Henry V—are wish-fulfillments; images of the devil-King,
Richard III, are warnings of the hell to follow challenges to divine will in
the royal succession. The plays here discussed are neither. They present
monarchs pretty much as we respond to them. While these monarchs
reign secure, we groan at their inadequacies; when they are at bay,
suddenly they are martyrs.

M. C. Bradbrook says the myth and the drama which emerged from it
"provided a reflection of men's hopes and fears." The group of plays
written between 1590 and 1596 that I have considered in this paper—those
dealing with the weak king—by evoking violent shifts in audience response to their central figures, reflect these fears and suggest a close
identity in one aspect of construction and purpose.

The Search for a Hero in
Julius Caesar

MOODY E. PRIOR

B RUTUS IS THE DRAMATIC HERO of *Julius Caesar*."[1] This forthright statement from the Introduction to the New Arden edition of the play
sums up a long and generally accepted critical tradition,[2] but the very fact
of its appearance is a commentary on the play. A similar statement would
not be thought necessary or proper in the introduction to a critical edition
of, for example, *Othello,* or *Hamlet,* or *King Lear.* At best, moreover, it is
not a view which can be maintained without modification. Thus, we also
find in the Arden Introduction the following: "There are four fully
developed figures of absorbing interest in *Julius Caesar:* Caesar himself,
Brutus, Cassius, and Antony. For each of them Shakespeare arouses in us
some admiration and some degree of sympathy; in each he brings out
some conspicuous defects of character. Caesar is the titular hero, Brutus the
dramatic hero."[3] The statement about Brutus as the hero, in spite of its

1. T. S. Dorsch, Introd. to *Julius Caesar,* Arden edition (London, 1955), p. xxxix.
2. The principal critical approaches to the play are briefly reviewed by Mildred
Hartsock, "The Complexity of *Julius Caesar*," *PMLA,* LXXXI (1966), 56–57.
3. Dorsch, Introd. to *Julius Caesar,* pp. xxvi–xxvii. G. Wilson Knight writes: "The
play has, as it were, four protagonists, each with a different view of the action" (*The
Imperial Theme* [London, 1931], pp. 63–64).

forthrightness, does not represent a self-evident fact; rather, it testifies to the existence of a problem.

There are persuasive reasons why the nomination of Brutus as the tragic hero of *Julius Caesar* has appealed to critics of the play. *Julius Caesar* initiates the series of great Shakespearean tragedies, and it is not unnatural to think of it as anticipating them in formal terms and in the idea of tragedy which they embody. Moreover, the understanding of a serious dramatic action is simplified if it can be approached through a central character; for, although it is one of the oldest of principles of dramatic construction that a play does not achieve its unity necessarily by virtue of having a single hero, a play seems easier to get hold of if the interest in the action is concentrated upon a single figure of stature and strong appeal.[4] Caesar, the title figure, is disqualified since he dies at the midpoint of the action, even though his spirit survives to plague and ultimately to defeat the conspirators. Brutus, on the other hand, does seem to qualify. He is prominent throughout, his death terminates the play, and the final eulogy by Antony is about him. But it is chiefly by virtue of what he is and what he foreshadows that he has been chosen for the role of tragic hero. In many ways he suggests kinship with Shakespeare's later heroes—in his initial vacillation, in his distress "between the acting of a dreadful deed and its first motion," in his high sense of honor, and in his participation in an act that tries his moral principles and involves him in disaster. Brutus has, in fact, been regarded as the first dramatic character since antiquity to represent the complexity and irony which we associate with tragic grandeur. This view of the character has been effectively set forth by Willard Farnham:

Shakespeare's Brutus asks admission to the ranks of those creatures of poesy who work out some tragic destiny in the grand manner of profound irony, not as pawns of Fortune or the gods, nor as magnificently defiant sinners, nor as headstrong weaklings, but as men of heroic strength or goodness whose most admirable qualities lead them into suffering. They are often forced to take the wages of what has the appearance of evil action and yet is not to be called evil action in all simplicity because it is dictated by their nobility. This is so with

4. John Holloway observes: "In nearly all of Shakespeare's major tragedies the hero, the protagonist, has a very great and indeed a peculiar prominence. There is no parallel to this in Shakespeare's other plays. . . . Nor is it paralleled in all tragedies by other authors" (*The Story of the Night* [London, 1961], p. 22).

Brutus. Before his appearance we find no protagonist upon the English tragic stage in whom greatness of soul is thus linked with misfortune.[5]

This approach to the play is strengthened by the place of *Julius Caesar* in the canon as the first of the mature tragedies, but the chronological position of the play, coming as it does at the conclusion of the series of history plays, suggests the possibility of viewing it in the perspective of the earlier plays. The histories are the plays through which, concurrently with the comedies, Shakespeare mastered his craft, explored and gave meaning to human behavior, and manifested the originality of his powers. Had Shakespeare written nothing else after *Henry V,* he would command respect as one of the world's chief dramatists. *Julius Caesar* allows us to see how much of Shakespeare's first sustained effort in the composition of serious drama carried over into the later tragedies.

Considered together, the history plays give the impression of a completed grand design. *King John* aside, they dramatize an extensive, coherent period of English history, from the forced break in the medieval succession at the abdication of Richard II, through the ensuing strife in the Wars of the Roses, to the emergence of the Tudor dynasty. This rich panorama of events was not only a source of splendid dramatic materials, but also a kind of natural history of politics and statecraft and a proving ground for ideas about political behavior and for an understanding of the forces which animate and shape great historical events. The interest in this aspect of the material, already evident throughout the three parts of *Henry VI,* formed the basis for the design of the last five plays in the cycle. Beginning with *Richard III,* Shakespeare centered the action of each play on a distinctive aspect of political power and its relation to the condition of a commonwealth. In *Richard III* the protagonist has almost no legal claim to the throne except what he manages to create by force and guile, and he regards the acquisition of power as an end in itself, without regard to legal and human considerations or the good of the state,

5. Willard Farnham, *The Medieval Heritage of Elizabethan Drama* (Berkeley, 1936), pp. 418–419. Cf. also, Virgil Whitaker, *Shakespeare's Use of Learning* (San Marino, 1953), p. 240: "Brutus is the first of Shakespeare's superb tragic figures who fail through false moral choice"; and Ernest Schanzer, *The Problem Plays of Shakespeare* (New York, 1963), p. 68: "Its central character is Brutus, in whom the moral issue is fought out, and whose tragedy . . . is very much of the Shakespearian kind . . . the only person in the play who experiences any inner conflict."

as an amoral exercise of *Realpolitik*. In *Richard II,* the King owes his
power to unquestioned and recognized legal right, but the kingdom
suffers because he lacks the personal and political qualifications for the
exercise of his power. In *Henry IV,* the King is astute and knowledgeable
in the ways of power and possesses the personal and political qualifications to rule in a statesmanlike fashion, but he is hampered and his rule is
marred by a lack of legal right to the kingship and by his destruction of
the mystique of kingly power in forcing the abdication of Richard. In
Henry V, the King's power rests on a strong *de facto* legality, and he has
the personal and political qualifications to exercise his power with success.
Thus in these five plays, the major variations of the basic theme are
represented. This exhaustion of the possibilities of the theme is matched
by the variety in the dramatic means employed. The plays reveal an
extraordinary dramatic inventiveness. No two of them are identical in
dramatic structure and in the method by which the materials are organ-
ized to maximize the effectiveness of the story and its reflection of the
underlying political insight which gives meaning to the events and helps
to illuminate the characters.

Julius Caesar owes a great deal to this creative effort. It reveals the same
interest in the realities of political activity, the same brilliant insight into
the behavior of men in the search for power, and the same artistic
originality in translating political affairs into drama as do the histories.[6]
Moreover, it shows some resemblance to them in the matter of organization. The similarities begin with a detail, the title. King Henry VI gives
his name to three plays in which he is a cause or the victim of the events
which surround him without being in a conventional sense the principal
character. This kind of dramatic design finds its most successful realization in the two parts of *Henry IV.* King Henry IV is not, strictly
speaking, the protagonist of the two plays which bear his name, just as in
the later play Caesar is not the tragic hero although the play is called *The
Tragedy of Julius Caesar.* Henry is, however, the central figure—and the
analogy with the later play continues—in the sense that all the events of
the play find their meaning in relation to his position as king and usurper.

6. J. D. Wilson, who is mindful of the importance of the histories in this
connection, refers to *Julius Caesar* as "perhaps the most brilliant and most penetrat-
ing artistic reflection of political realities in the literature of the world" (Introd. to
Julius Caesar, New Cambridge Shakespeare [Cambridge, Eng., 1949], p. xv).

Henry is a brilliant politician who seized power in a deteriorating political situation, and he hopes to establish a new order in the state; but the uncertainty of his legal position provides the occasion for unrest. A conspiracy to unseat him is formed, and among the conspirators are those who once supported him and helped him to power. In both parts, the movement of the play is precipitated by conspiracies against the King. He never succeeds in bringing about the political order he had hoped to create, and he dies in the middle of the second play which bears his name, upon which occasion his son, once despised as being "given to sports, to wildness, and much company"—to borrow words applied to Mark Antony—takes over and at the conclusion of 2 *Henry IV* is accepted as a capable leader with every expectation of resolving the rebellious disorders and political uncertainties of the past.

The analogies with *Julius Caesar,* though they cannot be pressed too far, are sufficiently cogent to suggest the possibility of approaching the organization of that play on somewhat similar terms. Caesar is the center of all the forces in the play without being its protagonist; the determining principle of order and selection of the events is the political conspiracy against him, and the action comprises the initiation, growth, initial success, and final failure of that conspiracy.[7] The opening scene is, from this point of view, a masterly introduction. None of the principals is present; the effect of the scene is to suggest the state of political unrest and to point to Caesar's rise in power as the cause. It calls attention to the resentment of conservative citizens to Caesar, and it introduces the populace as a key element in the situation—they are the "growing feathers" by means of which Caesar "would soar above the view of men"—and it indicates that in making a bid for power against established traditions of political authority Caesar has courted the favor of the plebeians and encouraged their aspirations. It establishes also the instability of the crowd—"Knew you not Pompey?"—and thus prepares for the emergence of the plebeians

7. A recent study which supports this view primarily through consideration of imagery is that of R. A. Foakes, "An Approach to *Julius Caesar*," *SQ,* V (1954), 259–270. Adrien Bonjour, *The Structure of* Julius Caesar (Liverpool, 1958), p. 24 writes: "Reduced to its simplest terms, *Julius Caesar* is the story of a political murder and a posthumous revenge." Bonjour, however, centers the discussion for the most part on Brutus, and in a chapter entitled "The General Structure of the Play," Cassius is scarcely mentioned.

as the deciding factor in the fortunes of the conspirators and their fluctuation of loyalty first to Brutus and then to Antony. This lively introduction to the general situation is the setting for Caesar's first appearance: Caesar is shown already accepting the ceremonies and privileges usually accorded only to the supreme authority of a state, and we learn by implication of his wish for a male heir. There is also the first hint of a personal weakness, a latent superstitiousness. The scene between Cassius and Brutus acquires its meaning from these preparations. Cassius dominates this episode, with his fierce loyalty to the old republican traditions of Rome, his dislike of Caesar, and his skillful testing of Brutus, pouncing on his prey when the shouts betray Brutus into revealing his fear of Caesar's ambitions for a crown. The scene is interrupted briefly by the return of Caesar and his train from the games, an appearance that provides a hint of Caesar's fear, which like his superstition he does not fully acknowledge but keeps at bay ("I fear him not. / Yet if my name were liable to fear . . ."), and contains Caesar's characterization of Cassius with its contrast of the characters of Antony and Cassius. Later the contrast will be dramatically developed, but at the moment Caesar's speech has the effect of keeping the spotlight on Cassius. Before the scene ends, we are aware that Cassius has the conspiracy well under way and that Brutus will be a part of it.

The next phase of the action consists of the final consolidation of the conspiracy and the successful accomplishment of its purpose in the assassination of Caesar. For this portion of the action Brutus and Caesar become the center of interest. Brutus takes over the leadership from Cassius, almost imperceptibly at first with the objection to an oath, then in the rejection of Cicero, and finally in the fatal decision to spare Antony. Alongside this development, Caesar is dramatically prepared for his doom: he overcomes his physical infirmities, his superstition, and his fear, and in anticipation of the crown triumphs over his limitations to assume the posture of the imperial Caesar who is above other men; in this mood he refuses to look at Artemidorus' schedule and resists the pleas of the conspirators for Publius Cimber, thus giving them the public occasion to strike.

Once Caesar is dead, the interest then moves to the struggle for power—the effort of the conspirators to win over the senators, then Antony, and then the populace, climaxed by their inept loss of this key element to their success through the demagoguery of Antony. The action now moves to the final phase. Antony takes the initiative, demonstrating an unexpected political shrewdness and ruthlessness; the conspirators flee Rome, and the outcome now rests with the test of arms. Shakespeare prepares us for the ultimate catastrophe. To the uncertainties of war Cassius and Brutus add the hazards of quarreling among themselves, failure to agree on a proper plan of battle, and personal dismay—in the case of Brutus the loss of Portia, in the case of Cassius, and more disastrously, the weakening of will through disenchantment and loss of faith in the enterprise which leads him to place the worst construction on Brutus' actions in the battle and to take his own life. The conspirators lose the battle, and Antony assumes power.

Approached in this way the play can be seen to have proportion, closeness of articulation, and a dynamic principle that drives the action steadily from the opening scene to the end. The common criticism that the play divides in the middle with the death of Caesar becomes less relevant. True, nowhere in the portion following the death of Caesar is there anything quite like the tense step-by-step mounting of intrigue and feeling that leads to the assassination, but there is certainly no loss of momentum, nor any lack of firm relationship between episode and episode. If there is a structural flaw, it is possible that our perception of it has been intensified and its importance exaggerated through an inadequate approach to the structure and meaning of the play.[8]

This view of *Julius Caesar* places in relief the affinity which it has with the histories in formal characteristics, specifically in maintaining a strong line of action and achieving unity while dividing the interest among several characters. However, the transitional character of the play is indicated by the way in which it at once resembles yet departs from the histories in the treatment of politics. The action of all the tragedies

8. For example, what happens between the death of Caesar and the appearance of Antony receives scant attention in productions. It becomes clear in this episode that the conspirators have planned for the act of assassination but for nothing else. They seem to be unaware that the death of Caesar will leave an appalling political void, and they seem unprepared for the next step. With the assassination accomplished, they shout slogans, propose announcements to the people, and talk philosophically about death and their readiness for it. And there is the ritual of dipping their hands in Caesar's blood, at the end of which Decius says, presumably with impatience, "What, shall we forth?" Productions usually pass over this significant and dramatically effective scene in huggermugger in order to get to the big entrance of Antony.

involves great affairs of state, and the ways of political power and the conduct of men caught up in public events are as brilliantly dramatized in them as in the earlier plays.[9] But the perspective from which the political aspects are viewed is somewhat different in the tragedies. In the histories, Shakespeare was dealing with English history, and, moreover, history that had a direct bearing on the political situation of his own day. The histories reveal in consequence a nationalistic bias which occasionally comes to the surface—for example in Gaunt's dying encomium to England in *1 Henry IV* and the Bastard's final speech in *King John*—and they imply a preference for a particular conception of the proper organization of the commonwealth and the source of ultimate authority and power in the state, a monarchical idea developed under the Tudors.

Efforts have been made to fit *Julius Caesar* into the Tudor political bias by representing Caesar as the embodiment of kingly power and the play as a commentary on the evils of conspiracy against royal authority even when it is inspired by the most idealistic motives.[10] This view of the play does not hold up very well. Caesar is not a king; the power he exercises has no legal or traditional sanction and has not yet received official approval. He is in fact represented as manipulating circumstances to achieve this goal and in the process undermining an established and traditional form of government and cultivating the power of the masses as a volatile force which he can employ to compel acceptance of his aims. On this last point, his tactics would not have appealed to conservative political opinion in Shakespeare's day, since the deliberate use of the populace as a means to power by ambitious politicians was viewed with considerable fear. But if the play does not present Caesar with the awesome divinity of an anointed king destroyed by rebels, or create any special sympathy for his effort to centralize political authority in himself, neither does it imply condemnation of him as a vile usurper or a rebel against constituted authority. But for that matter, it does not create any greater sympathy for the republicanism of Cassius and Brutus, even though they are trying to

9. Two recent books in which the political aspect of plays other than the histories forms the center of interest are Allan Bloom and Harry Jaffa, *Shakespeare's Politics* (New York, 1964); and Jan Kott, *Shakespeare our Contemporary* (New York, 1964).

10. For a critical study of such views see Irving Ribner, "Political Issues in *Julius Caesar*," *JEGP*, LVI (1957), 10–20.

preserve the established order and the honorable traditions of the past. And certainly the victory of Antony cannot be construed as the triumph of honor, or legality, or right rule as, for instance, is the victory of Richmond in *Richard III*. If there is a political bias in *Julius Caesar,* it is implied so subtly as to render its existence disputable.[11] The play appears to be neutral with reference to the political aims of the different parties to the conflict. Each of the four major figures reveals some defect or weakness or unamiable quality, yet at the same time each is endowed with extraordinary powers and human virtues which make a claim on our sympathies or at least elicit respect and admiration. It is not surprising that comprehensive critical appreciations of the play often end up containing analyses about equal in length of each of the four major figures. The change from English to Roman history thus brought about certain distinct if subtle changes in the approach to the dramatization of political events. The Roman world aroused interest and admiration, but not patriotic sentiments nor a sense of immediate relationship to the kind of political order or theory involved in the situation.[12] In consequence, the merit of

11. Vernon Hall, *"Julius Caesar:* a Play Without a Political Bias," *Studies in the English Renaissance Drama* (New York, 1959), pp. 106–124, discusses critically attempts to demonstrate a political bias.

12. The attitudes toward the civil wars and the principal figures involved in them have been surveyed by Ernest Schanzer, *Problem Plays of Shakespeare,* pp. 11–23; and J. Leeds Barroll, "Shakespeare and Roman History," *MLR,* LIII (1958), 327–343. This material is sometimes appealed to for clues to particular interpretations of the play: for examples see Vernon Hall, *"Julius Caesar,"* pp. 125–126; Virgil Whitaker, *The Mirror up to Nature* (San Marino, 1965), pp. 125–126; J. D. Wilson, Introd. to the New Cambridge edition, pp. xxi–xxiii. No agreement emerges from such studies as to any given way in which these events necessarily impressed themselves on audiences of Shakespeare's day. Ben Jonson, who might be considered an important test case, provides no support for the notion that a Christian audience familiar with medieval and Renaissance writings on Roman history and brought up on Tudor political theory would be unsympathetic with Brutus and Cassius and would regard their destruction as merited. In *Sejanus,* Arruntius, a choral character, lamenting the decline of the Roman virtues, says, " 'Tis true that Cordus says, / Brave Cassius was the last of all that race" (I.i.102–104). The historian Cordus, accused by the Sejanus faction of defaming the present by praising Cassius and Brutus, defends himself by pointing out that Livy names "the same Cassius, and this Brutus too, / As worthiest men—not thieves and parricides" (III.i.420–421; see also ll. 456–460). Schanzer (pp. 25–36) argues effectively that Shakespeare made dramatic use of the

the characters as men is not related directly to the success of their efforts to bring about a healthy political order in the state, and the moral dilemmas in which they find themselves are dealt with sympathetically without reference to their preference for a particular form of political order.[13]

This distinction must, however, be made with reservations. The moral aspects of power enter into the characterizations in the histories also. One source of the complexity and richness of the history plays is the more than implicit awareness of the inherent paradox—or better, the irreconcilable contradiction—at the center of all political involvement. Political power gives a man the opportunity to concern himself with the well-being of society—"power to do good is the true and lawful end of aspiring," as Bacon said—and since it is directly concerned with actions that affect others it lies within the province of ethics; but political action considered as a science or art is as non-moral as engineering, and men deeply committed to a political course, though they may believe that its aims are of the highest merit, cannot always enjoy the luxury of being morally fastidious in the means. Bolingbroke in *Richard II* is perhaps the most conspicuous example of this dilemma among the characters in the histories. His accusations against the King (presented indirectly through his challenge of Mowbray) are just, and he finds support from others who are dismayed by the evils of Richard's rule. His inheritance is unlawfully seized, and he is encouraged by the nobles to use the occasion to help them secure better government, and so, though ostensibly returning from exile to reclaim his lands, he seems willing to be used by them to replace Richard. Yet once started on this course, he finds it necessary to do all manner of things that are morally reprehensible, from political slyness to the murder of the lawful king. He is no Richard III to exult in his political virtuosity and his mastery of the ruthless art of gaining and using

---

conflicting attitudes available in the writings about these men by "playing on his audience's varied and divided views of Caesar" to create an enigmatic character who presents a different image to each of the other principal characters, and in the process creates "his own image of himself."

13. L. C. Knights, "Shakespeare's Politics: With Some Reflection on the Nature of Tradition," *Proceedings of the British Academy*, XLIII (1957), 118: "In *Julius Caesar*, freed from the embarrassments of a patriotic theme, and with the problem projected into a 'Roman' setting, Shakespeare examines more closely the contradictions and illusions involved in political action."

power, and so he cannot repress his awareness of the harsh contradictions in his role. Seeing the dead body of Richard II he exclaims, "Lords, I protest my soul is full of woe / That blood should sprinkle me to make me grow." The contradiction between his political aims and his political means pursues him in the Henry IV plays, and his remorse breaks through in his dying speech of advice to Hal: "God knows, my son, / By what by-paths and indirect crook'd ways / I met this crown."

In *Julius Caesar* all the principal characters confront this dilemma, but it is Brutus and Cassius who are viewed continuously and directly in relation to it. It is as though the contradiction which Bolingbroke is unable to resolve within himself is factored out, and the two parts assigned to Brutus and Cassius respectively. In the opening scenes, Brutus stands out for his explicit concern over the moral issues raised by the conspiracy and his desire to preserve his own high principles while meeting its demands; Cassius, on the other hand, acts as a political realist who attempts to guide the course of the conspiracy by political considerations alone. It is in large part because of this impression of moral earnestness that critics have been attracted to the idea of Brutus as the first of Shakespeare's characters to be conceived in the new tragic mode and hence as the tragic hero of *Julius Caesar;* and once this point of view is adopted Cassius must necessarily suffer at the hands of the critics in consequence. However, the primary distinction between them, so effectively presented at the outset, is only the beginning of a complex development which depicts what happens when an intense political crisis places the ultimate demands upon these two—both equally patriotic but differing in character and political methods—as political agents and as men. In the course of the action, the initial outlines take on subtle shadings, and at the end of the play it is no longer easy to maintain the same simple kinds of sympathy and moral judgment that are generated by the opening scenes.

The original decision which binds Brutus and Cassius in the conspiracy is identical for both of them: the choice as they both see it is between the death of republican Rome and the death of Caesar. Both men, moreover, seem agreed that the patriotic preservation of the old Roman order represents an obligation which makes superior moral claims on them over the principle which forbids murder. It is not, however, the agreement on political principles and moral choice which stands out but rather the disparity between the two men, since our impression of this decision is colored by the differences in temperament which operate in each case. Cassius is more demonstrative emotionally than Brutus, unable to repress his personal feelings in any circumstance, as he acknowledges late in the play when he speaks of Brutus' practice of stoicism with awe upon learning of Portia's death: "I have as much of this in art as you, / But yet my nature could not bear it so." The contrast is established during the initial scene between them. Cassius does not conceal his dislike of Caesar, nor the fact that this dislike colors his decision to thwart Caesar's bid for power. The two feelings merge into one. He is as passionate in the expression of his desire to preserve republican Rome from the power of one man as of his detestation and contempt for the man who has become a dictator and aims to become emperor. Brutus, on the other hand, deliberately separates his personal feelings about Caesar from the grim political decision which he believes he is forced to accept as a matter of principle and honor. Cassius is not, any more than is Brutus, motivated by any ambition for power, nor can it be maintained that he kills Caesar out of envy, though Antony and some critics would have it so. Nevertheless, Brutus' reserve and conspicuous high-mindedness weigh heavily in his favor. Initially, therefore, these temperamental differences serve chiefly to provide an impression of the quality of mind and spirit that is involved in each case in making the same choice.

During the first part of the play, through the scene of the assassination, the contrast in character serves largely to enhance the stature of Brutus, at the expense of Cassius. The skill with which Cassius works on Brutus in their first encounter arouses suspicion of his sincerity and, accordingly, sympathy for Brutus as a possible victim of a political schemer. Caesar's remarks to Antony about Cassius' lean and hungry look have the effect of reinforcing this impression. When Cassius goes out into the storm, baring his "bosom to the thunderstone" and rounding up the conspirators, it is not so much his daring and dedication that stand out as his restless stirring up of trouble. Brutus meanwhile arouses compassion as he broods over the most awful decision of his life. And though Cassius succeeds singlehandedly in creating the conspiracy, no one comes to him, as does Ligarius to Brutus, and begs to devote himself to his cause with no further knowledge than that he heads it. When Brutus imperceptibly takes over the leadership of the conspiracy from Cassius, it is in the manner of a man who assumes that his nobility of mind gives him this right and that it is to be expected that it will be respected by others. But this clear-cut distinction does not survive the enlargement of understanding provided by the course of the play, and the grounds for the reassessment are laid quite early. Brutus agrees to take part in a desperate and violent political enterprise, but its physical and practical aspects offend him. He is shocked at his first view of the faction, heavily muffled to wait upon him clandestinely at night. He regrets the need to shed Caesar's blood, since it is the spirit of Caesar that he opposes, "And in the spirit of men there is no blood." He thus conceives of the act as a sacrifice and is convinced that once this simple act of pious surgery is over he can become morally fastidious again. Cassius knows from the start that what they are planning to do is "Most bloody, fiery, and most terrible" and that the assassination will not absolve them from further ruthless and unpleasant acts. In spite of his passionate emotional involvement, Cassius is able to see things honestly and realistically. Brutus, though impressive in the deliberate separation of his feelings from the demands of principle and duty, is wrapped up in his preoccupation with his honor, and his confidence in his own self-esteem beclouds the realities which confront them and leads him to make one error after another. In two of the great scenes of the play, the consequences of the unique virtues of Brutus as they manifest themselves in these critical political times are brought into dramatic focus. The disaster of the orations brings to a climax his political ineptitude. The quarrel with Cassius exposes openly for the first time the limitations of his sense of moral superiority.

As the scene of the orations marks the turning point in the political fortunes of the conspirators, so the scene of the quarrel marks the turning point in the relations of its leaders. It marks also an alteration of attitude toward them.[14] The failure to appreciate this change as one of the important aspects of the dramatic development is one of the likely casualties of approaching *Julius Caesar* as the tragedy of Brutus. The orations

14. A similar development takes place in *Richard II*. As Richard is debased and humiliated and as he begins to awaken to his failings, sympathy swings to him and diminishes the unpleasant impression left by the ruthless actions and the grandstand monarchizing of the early scenes. Simultaneously, Bolingbroke, the champion of political justice and the unfairly disinherited heir, acquires tarnish as he becomes more and more enmeshed in the unpleasant demands of power politics.

confirm the consistent rightness of Cassius' political judgment; the quarrel provides the first conspicuous opportunity to view him sympathetically as a man. From this point on Cassius appears often in a favorable or at least humanly appealing light. The comparisons between him and Brutus no longer always give the immediate advantage to the latter. Cassius is the first to concede in the quarrel—"I said an elder soldier, not a better. / Did I say 'better'?" He backs down and accepts Brutus' plan for the battle, although as he later confesses to Messala he knows the decision is fatally wrong. Though a disciple of Epicurus, he now broods over omens he once scoffed at. He notes with a touch of sadness that the day of the battle is his birthday, and in the conviction that his "life is run his compass" places the wrong interpretation on the events of the battle and commands his bondman to take his life. The high point in the enhancement of Cassius' human stature in the play is the tribute of Titinius at Cassius' death and the loyalty that prompts Titinius to take his own life:

> But Cassius is no more. O setting sun,
> As in thy red rays thou dost sink to-night,
> So in his red blood Cassius' day is set!
> The sun of Rome is set. Our day is gone;
> Clouds, dews, and dangers come; our deeds are done.
>
> (V.iii.60–64)

This speech will stand comparison with any of the noble benedictions which Shakespeare has provided for his dead heroes. Even more striking is Titinius' speech as he kills himself: "Brutus, come apace, / And see how I regarded Caius Cassius." That Titinius should address himself to the absent Brutus is surely not without significance. The implication of the speech is, in effect, that neither Brutus nor the other characters, nor indeed the auditor, can continue any longer to assume that only Brutus possesses the human qualities that can inspire such total devotion and loyalty. It is as though a claim is being entered for Cassius' right to some share in the sentiments inspired by the representation of the death of men of great spirit in the performance of great actions.

Inevitably, any melioration in our impression of Cassius must affect our view of Brutus and reflect on the initial picture of him. In the quarrel scene, the studied cultivation of nobility of mind and conduct which sets Brutus apart from the other characters and commands their reverence manifests itself in a form that is less than admirable. The illogical contradiction in his attitude toward Cassius in this scene has been often noted. His grievance is that Cassius did not send him money when he requested it—"For I can raise no money by vile means," he explains—yet he threatens Cassius with punishment for trying to raise money by the only means now available to them in the terrible extremity in which they find themselves. Cassius, trying to save a desperate situation, pleads with Brutus, "In such a time as this it is not meet / That every nice offence should bear his comment," and receives the retort, "The name of Cassius honours this corruption, / And chastisement doth therefore hide his head," leaving Cassius helplessly bewildered with no reply save, "Chastisement!" In the concluding episodes, Brutus reveals at times a singular incapacity for awareness. He does not sense the contradictions in his reproaches to Cassius in the quarrel and is insensitive to the cutting harshness and even moral snobbery of his rebukes. He never realizes the extent to which his lack of judgment has doomed the conspiracy, and he can still set aside Cassius' advice on strategy as though to an underling whose experience and wisdom in such matters cannot be seriously entertained. And in the light of everything that has happened, there is an air of unreality and obtuseness of perception about his proud remark to his few remaining followers after the defeat:

> My heart doth joy that yet in all my life
> I found no man but he was true to me.
>
> (V.v.34–35)

This incapacity to confront reality and to see himself is, in fact, one important respect in which Brutus does not measure up to the tragic heroes which follow. He lacks the final full realization of himself and the meaning of his catastrophe, the tragic anagnorisis, which, with the possible exception of Coriolanus, is a distinguishing mark of the Shakespearean tragic hero. This lack of awareness may well be one of the reasons why Brutus does not command throughout the full measure of sympathetic acceptance we grant to the major tragic heroes of Shakespeare.[15]

Through the complex interplay between them and the changing im-

15. For example, Whitaker, *The Mirror up to Nature,* p. 132: "The most serious weakness of the play from the point of view of moral exposition is undoubtedly Brutus' own failure to recognize the enormity of his mistake. . . . we miss the great speeches in which Othello or Lear or Macbeth confess their mistakes and survey the tragic consequences."

pression which they create during the course of the action, the characters
of Brutus and Cassius acquire depth and provide the clues for an understanding in human terms of their downfall. For there are two notable
failures. That of Brutus has chiefly occupied critics, and has been often
dealt with, but the failure of Cassius is also dramatically significant and
developed in considerable detail. It was his energy and passion and skill
that brought the conspirators together in a common enterprise. In every
circumstance his judgment of the proper steps to take and those to avoid
proves to be politically right. Yet he regularly allows Brutus to overrule
him, seemingly overawed like everyone else by Brutus' nobility. But there
is more to Cassius' relations to Brutus than that. Caesar's description to
Antony notes Cassius' inwardness and his lack of an easygoing temper,
which seem to isolate him from ready access to others. But Cassius is not a
cold man. His dedication to his cause, his passionate outbursts of feeling
reveal qualities that render him deficient in the role of political virtuoso in
spite of his political skill and wisdom. Moreover, in his isolation he reveals
a deep need for companionship and unexpected human warmth. "Have
you not love enough," he asks of Brutus at the end of the quarrel,

> to bear with me,
> When that rash humor which my mother gave me
> Makes me forgetful?
>
> (IV.iii.117–119)

And he is all eagerness and gratefulness in his acceptance of the cup of
wine in which Brutus offers to "bury all unkindness":

> My heart is thirsty for that noble pledge.
> Fill, Lucius, till the wine o'erswell the cup;
> I cannot drink too much of Brutus' love.
>
> (IV.iii.158–160)

It is just after this that Cassius once more lets Brutus override him, this
time in the crucial matter of the plan of the battle. No difference in moral
attitudes is involved in this decision, as in the earlier one of sparing
Antony; it is simply a matter of military judgment. Cassius presents his
plan briefly. Brutus begins his more lengthy proposal with, "Good reasons
must, of force, give place to better," and when Cassius in the course of
Brutus' exposition interposes—"Hear me, good brother"—Brutus prevents
him from developing his thought and with "Under your pardon" he

continues. There is nothing explicit offered to explain Cassius' quiet submission: "Then, with your will, go on." But the entire scene of the quarrel and the news of Portia's death lie behind this episode and color it. Can Cassius risk another serious argument over a difference of opinion? In the background hovers the memory of that unfortunate remark about being a better soldier—or was it elder soldier? No matter. Nothing is worth the risk of endangering the pledge of love, more important to Cassius now than the battle which he is confident they must lose.[16]

It is left ambiguous in the opening scene between the two whether Cassius' need for Brutus was entirely political or whether it was also to some extent sincerely personal. How are we to consider his opening gambit?

> Brutus, I do observe you now of late;
> I have not from your eyes that gentleness
> And show of love as I was wont to have.
> You bear too stubborn and too strange a hand
> Over your friend that loves you.
>
> (I.ii.32–36)

Is this anything more than the blandishment of a skillful political manipulator getting to work on his victim? The first scene does not answer the question, but it raises skepticism about the purity of Cassius' motives. There is no question, however, about the genuineness and sincerity of Cassius' sentiments when, "aweary of the world: / Hated by one he loves," he exposes his innermost feelings to Brutus:

> I, that denied thee gold, will give my heart.
> Strike as thou didst at Caesar; for I know,
> When thou didst hate him worst, thou lov'dst him better
> Than ever thou lov'dst Cassius
>
> (IV.iii.103–106)

Now, the political need is clearly unimportant and the personal almost desperate. To have succeeded, Cassius needed the total calculation devoid

16. The importance of love and friendship as they color the political world of *Julius Caesar* has been noticed in recent studies: for example, Adrien Bonjour, *The Structure of* Julius Caesar, p. 132; Schanzer, *Problem Plays of Shakespeare*, pp. 41–42, and especially G. W. Knight, "The Eroticism of *Julius Caesar*," in *The Imperial Theme*, pp. 63–95. In this respect *Julius Caesar* marks a change from the histories, in which the personal and human aspects of an individual's political relations are normally measured by reference to a concept of honor.

of all human considerations which is the mark of the true Machiavellian. His human qualities rendered him unfit for the conspiracy just as surely as Brutus was rendered unfit by his political naïveté, his strong conviction of his own nobility, and his fastidious moral sense. Each man in his own way loses out in the opposition between the remorseless demands of involvement in a political crisis and a capacity for moral rectitude and submission to human feelings and values.

This view of the play appears to be contradicted by the concluding speech of Antony. It has the effect of placing the focus on Brutus and reestablishing his moral preeminence:

> This was the noblest Roman of them all.
> All the conspirators save only he
> Did that they did in envy of great Caesar;
> He only in a general and honest thought
> And common good to all, made one of them.
> His life was gentle; and the elements
> So mix'd in him that Nature might stand up
> And say to all the world "This was a man!"
>
> (V.v.68–75)

The speech asks us, in effect, to reject any complicating and ambivalent impressions made by the latter portions of the play, to pass judgment on Cassius ("in envy of great Caesar"), and to restore to Brutus the idealized image of him which dominates the early episodes ("the noblest Roman of them all . . . 'This was a man!' "). Its rhetorical force is strengthened by its position as the last utterance. Its finality would be endorsed by those critics of Elizabethan and especially Shakespearean drama who accept all such dramatic conventions as soliloquies, asides, and formal concluding statements at their face value, as clues provided by the dramatist to establish lines of characterization, moral value, and the like, and to straighten out the ambiguities of a not always logical or tidy dramatic development. It is open to question, however, whether such critical principles can be applied consistently to Shakespeare without damage to his subtlety. When, for example, Iago states in soliloquy his conviction that Desdemona is in love with Cassio, no one is likely to allow this confidence from the stage to alter the impression of what Desdemona says and does; the more likely result is to wonder what is troubling Iago and to become uncertain about what he says of Othello. And we do not leave *Macbeth* with the impression of having witnessed the story of a "dead butcher, and his fiend-like queen" simply because that is the final sentiment expressed about him in the last speech of the play. It is a proper judgment coming from Malcolm, who expresses the sentiments of a nation rescued from a nightmare, but it is not precisely our verdict. On the other hand, the sentiment expressed by Fortinbras in the concluding speech, that Hamlet, "was likely, had he been put on, / To have prov'd most royal" will receive assent, not only because Fortinbras is a shadowy figure with no previous direct involvement in the action and hence appropriately choral but because—and much more to the point—the qualities which Hamlet has manifested were such as might have proved worthy of kingship under happier circumstances. But even in this instance, though it seems proper for Fortinbras to have four captains bear Hamlet "like a soldier," and this gesture provides a splendid closing theatrical spectacle for the play, we know that Hamlet was also a courtier and scholar and a man troubled by such doubts as have brought upon him the distinction of having become the classic symbol of those who find their world shattered, their familiar values insecure, and themselves in isolation.

The concluding speech of Antony raises its own difficulties. If the eloquent benediction spoken over the dead Cassius, "the sun of Rome," is to be discounted because Titinius speaks as a devoted friend and Antony's eulogy given increased merit because it is spoken by an enemy, does it then become relevant to consider that Antony and Cassius are sharply opposed throughout the play, beginning with Caesar's description of Cassius, and that it is more likely that Antony will find words for Brutus but not for Cassius? Moreover, is the Antony who destroyed Brutus by shattering through innuendo the image of "The noble Brutus" as "an honourable man" ideally suited to assume the choric role and speak the formal lines which restore his claim to those proud titles? And what of Brutus' own eulogy of Cassius?

> The last of all the Romans, fare thee well!
> It is impossible that ever Rome
> Should breed thy fellow.
>
> (V.iii.99–101)

These doubts may be irrelevant; the speech may indeed be choric, and its function to provide a clear and unmistakable perspective on the intent and meaning of the play. In which case Shakespeare wrought more subtly than he knew. The momentary impression of Antony's formal speech should not weigh against the total complex impression made by a sophisticated dramatic art using all the resources of the theater and language. We may be skeptical of the final authority of the shorthand expository devices of the theater, the expected rhetoric of formal dramatic moments, and the dramatic conventions of a particular theater when they reduce the riches of a great play to simpler terms than the art of the play warrants and thus stand in the way of perceiving or appreciating them.

Even for the most admiring of its critics, *Julius Caesar* has not seemed to be as fully realized as the tragedies which follow. Farnham, whose opinion of Brutus as the first distinctively tragic figure in Renaissance drama has been cited, describes *Julius Caesar* as "a play in which [Shakespeare] clearly stands poised between immaturity and maturity in tragic perception." [17] It may be equally appropriate to view it as poised between the great tragedies which follow and the history plays which precede, a play retaining some of the methods and insights which Shakespeare developed in his dramatizations of English history while anticipating those which became the distinctive features of the plays which follow. From this perspective, the play is less likely to appear as an imperfect realization of the qualities and powers of the major tragedies—a conclusion true enough and important in its own way—and more likely to appear as an unusual and original work, unique among the plays of Shakespeare, with its own distinctive artistic merits. The various concepts which we apply to literature offer a means whereby we can come to terms with particular works, appreciate their qualities, understand their art, and comprehend their meaning. The test of the appropriateness of one or another concept as an approach to an individual work is the completeness with which it enables us to bring together all the elements in it into an intelligible and coherent relation with one another, and the effectiveness with which it enables us to examine its distinctive effects exhaustively. *Julius Caesar* is indeed a tragedy, and it is the first of Shakespeare's plays in which the characteristics of the later tragedies are clearly foreshadowed, but to measure the play by applying to it rigorously an idea of tragedy derived from the tragedies which follow it has the effect of obscuring some of its interesting features and of calling attention to its limitations

17. Farnham, *Medieval Heritage*, p. 368.

rather than to its special merits. In particular, the attempt to find the source of its unity and to identify its special powers through the centripetal effect of a dominating protagonist analogous to Othello or Lear or Hamlet tends to distort the structure and in some respects to impoverish the play. It is very doubtful whether the most fruitful way to approach *Julius Caesar* is as the tragedy of Brutus.

Virtue's Holiday: Thomas Dekker and Simon Eyre

JOEL H. KAPLAN

I$_N$ Thomas Dekker's *Shoemakers' Holiday* the fraternal spirit of a generous and exuberant professional guild rapidly takes possession of an entire nation. Trades, Dekker tells us, were first "ordaind to be *Communities*,"[1] and in the course of this play the fervent and jocund sense of community retained by a brotherhood of shoemakers triumphs over the intrigues of a suspicious and "subtle" society. As Simon Eyre, the mad cobbler of Tower Street, rises from master of a single shop to sheriff, to alderman, and finally to Lord Mayor of London, the craft of an older order is swept aside by the honest energy of artisans "not subtile, (But in *Handi-crafts*.)"[2] *The Shoemakers' Holiday* is, all in all, a merry piece of work. And yet on closer examination the play's central episodes seem to

1. *The Seven Deadly Sinnes of London*, in *The Non-Dramatic Works of Thomas Dekker*, ed. Alexander B. Grosart (London, 1884–86), II, 74.
2. *The Double PP.*, in *The Non-Dramatic Works*, II, 190. Eyre makes a similar pun in *The Shoemakers' Holiday*, V. v. 9–10: "I am a handi-crafts man, yet my heart is without craft . . ."

bristle with moral ambiguities that are concealed by the vitality of its surface. Although Simon Eyre clearly wins our approval, he makes his fortune through a rather dubious business venture. Likewise, Rowland Lacy, the comedy's romantic intriguer, gains our sympathy in spite of his defection from the King's army. The license that permits us to gloss over these incidents is to be found in Simon's rhetoric, which has been accused, understandably, of obscuring the more serious issues raised by Dekker's material. Jonas Barish has termed the shoemaker's language "a red herring, designed to secure an illegitimate sympathy for the character," [3] while Harry Levin has denounced Simon as a "Shylock masquerading as Falstaff." [4] In one sense these indictments are surely justifiable, although we might argue about whether or not the sympathy secured in this manner can be called "illegitimate." What is even more surprising is to discover that in a number of instances Dekker does not cover his tracks well enough, and we are made aware of the play's anomalies. This might be ascribed to the playwright's reputed carelessness if a pattern did not emerge in his handling of Simon's rhetoric. Eyre's language is permitted to justify the shoemaker's own behavior in the context of Dekker's play, but when Simon faces moral disparities which are inherent in the actions of others we are allowed a brief glimpse of these ambiguities before they are dissolved in his verbal euphoria. What we are left with is the impression not of a disreputable shoemaker, but of a disreputable society that seems to melt away in his presence. Eyre is presented as an exuberant and overwhelming creature not to cloud moral judgments but to move beyond them, making possible an admittedly illogical leap from the profession of virtue to its energetic celebration. Proscriptive morality is not so much ignored as subsumed in the rush of goods and throng of words by which Simon imposes his vitality and will upon society at large, transforming virtue into festival and creating a new order by an act of sheer verbiage.

3. *Ben Jonson and the Language of Prose Comedy* (Cambridge, Mass., 1960), p. 282. Peter Ure raises a similar objection to Dekker's Orlando Friscobaldo, an invention "in the Simon Eyre vein" in "Patient Madman and Honest Whore: The Middleton-Dekker Oxymoron," *Essays and Studies 1966,* Vol. XIX of the New Series of Essays and Studies Collected for the English Association, pp. 18–40.

4. Cited by Barish "in conversation," *Ben Jonson,* p. 282.

I

In *Old Fortunatus,* an allegorical comedy either written or revised for Henslowe in 1599,[5] Dekker attempted a similar translation of virtue into festival. However, this endeavor to distinguish a holiday form of virtue from its merely passive shadow was frustrated by the morality framework of Dekker's play. In *Old Fortunatus* theatrical effect remains at odds with the didactic nature of a genre that demands strict judgment, and the resulting denouement seems less a metamorphosis than a dramatic trick. The problem arises with Ampedo, one of Fortunatus' two sons. From the very outset of the play Ampedo remains committed to a purely negative type of virtue, believing that his moral obligations extend no further than the repudiation of vice. This is also the view that Dekker's audience is encouraged to take, especially as Ampedo is called "brother vertue" and contrasted with Fortunatus' second son, Andelocia, who is called "brother Vice" and who behaves abominably throughout the piece. When both brothers meet wretched deaths, we naturally assume that we have witnessed the operation of a wanton and indiscriminate Fortune. But in the play's final scene Virtue disowns Ampedo, reproaching him and:

> those that (like him) doe muffle
> *Vertue* in clouds, and care not how shee shine,
> Ile make their glorie like to his decline:
> He made no vse of me, but like a miser,
> Lockt vp his wealth in rustie barres of sloth:
> His face was beautifull, but wore a maske,
> And in the worlds eyes seemd a Blackamore.
> So perish they that so keepe vertue poore.
>
> (V.ii.272–279) [6]

5. Whether Dekker wrote or merely revised the play, he must take responsibility for the form in which the piece has come down to us. Interestingly enough, though, speculations upon Dekker's additions usually credit him with the Fortune, Virtue, Vice scenes, which we are concerned with here. See, among others, M. L. Hunt, *Thomas Dekker, A Study* (New York, 1911), pp. 29–30; and Fredson Bowers' textual introduction to *Old Fortunatus* in *The Dramatic Works of Thomas Dekker* (Cambridge, Eng., 1953–61), I, 107. Una Ellis-Fermor regards the Vice-Virtue allegory as one of the play's original elements, but does not deny Dekker's authorship; see *The Jacobean Drama* (London, 1936), p. 121, n. 2.

6. All citations for the plays of Dekker are to *The Dramatic Works,* ed. Fredson Bowers, 4 vols. (Cambridge, Eng., 1953–61).

Ampedo's good, apparently, is not good enough. His passive virtue does as much harm to Virtue's true cause as does his brother's outright villainy. In retrospect we realize that the play's punishments are not arbitrary but deserts justly meted out to Virtue's foes. What appeared to be a victory for Fortune is suddenly transformed into a celebration of Virtue and confirmed by an appeal to Eliza, the "true" virtue. Fortune's song of praise, sung by her minions in Act I, is now altered to a closing hymn in praise of Virtue's triumph and holiday:

> *Vertue* smiles: crie hollyday,
> Dimples on her cheekes doe dwell,
> *Vertue* frownes, crie wellada,
> Her loue is Heauen, her hate is Hell.
> Since heau'n and hell obey her power,
> Tremble when her eyes doe lowre.
> Since heau'n and hell her power obay,
> When shee smiles, crie hollyday.
>   Hollyday with ioy we crie,
>   And bend, and bend, and merily,
>   Sing hymnes to *Vertues* deitie:
>   Sing hymnes to *Vertues* deitie.
>
> (V.ii.347–358)

Yet this conclusion is not entirely satisfactory. Dekker asks us to make a retrospective judgment, reversing our entire impression of Ampedo on the basis of the play's final scene. The impossibility of doing this may be gauged by the work's critical reception. Very few of Dekker's readers indeed are able to recall Virtue's rejection of Ampedo.[7]

II

In *The Shoemakers' Holiday* Dekker works in a tradition that is saturnalian and festive rather than proscriptively moral, and his celebration is more successful. Simon Eyre is the comedy's presiding genius, and as he climbs from shop master to Lord Mayor he brings the vigorous

7. The play is often cited for its "riotous inconsequence of structure" (Ellis-Fermor, *Jacobean Drama*, p. 121), but J. W. Ashton has even presented Ampedo's "good intentions" as evidence of the lack of "poetic justice" in the work. See "Dekker's Use of Folklore in *Old Fortunatus, If This Be Not a Good Play*, and *The Witch of Edmonton*," *PQ*, XLI (1962), 240–248.

spirit of the shoemakers to larger and larger segments of society. As well, in his role as madcap Simon brandishes an asyndetic rhetoric that prospers where alternative modes of speech and action fail. The varieties of deliberate speech employed by Eyre's antagonists, the subtle blank verse of Lincoln and Otley, or Hammon's stichomythic repartee pale beside the spontaneous and fantastical tropes of this "wild ruffin." There is seldom any rational progression in Simon's outbursts, but rather an incessant pounding of epithets, a constant reshaping of terms by an outrageously energetic presence:

Away you Islington whitepot, hence you happerarse, you barly pudding ful of magots, you broyld carbonado, auaunt, auaunt, auoide Mephostophilus: shall *Sim Eyre* learne to speake of you Ladie *Madgie?* vanish mother Miniuer cap, vanish, goe, trip and goe, meddle with your partlets, and your pishery pasherie, your flewes and your whirligigs, go, rub, out of mine alley: *Sim Eyre* knowes how to speake to a Pope, to Sultan *Soliman,* to *Tamburlaine* and he were here: and shal I melt? shal I droope before my Soueraigne? no, come my Ladie *Madgie,* follow me *Hauns,* about your businesse my frolicke free-booters: *Firke,* friske about, and about, and about, for the honour of mad *Simon Eyre* Lord Maior of *London.*

(V.iv.46–57)

Proclaiming "Prince am I none, yet am I princely borne," [8] Simon swears "by the Lord of Ludgate" and a host of preposterous monarchs both real and mythical. He seems, in fact, almost a Lord of Misrule, swiftly propelled to the pinnacle of his society amid the jangle of the morris dance and the clang of the pancake bell. His rhetoric is wholly Dekker's and markedly different from the speech of Eyre in Deloney's *Gentle Craft.* In Deloney, Simon is a simple and rational businessman and speaks accordingly. His syntax is one of cautious accounting, in which even the prospects of advancement and material accumulation must be viewed with a sense of sobriety and solemn obligation:

to bee Sheriffe of *London* it is no little cost. Consider first . . . what house I ought to haue, and what costly ornaments belong thereto, as hanging of

8. This proverb, attributed to Iphicrates by Thomas Deloney, assumes a thematic importance in *The Gentle Craft, Part I,* the principal source for *The Shoemakers' Holiday.* It even appears on the title page of Deloney's collection. As a metaphor for Eyre's jaunty monarchy Dekker could hardly have chosen a fitter phrase. See *The Gentle Craft, Part I,* in *The Novels of Thomas Deloney,* ed. Merritt E. Lawlis (Bloomington, Ind., 1961).

Tapistrie, cloth of Arras, and other such like, what store of Plate and Goblets of Gold, what costlie attire, and what a chargeable traine, and that which is most of all, how greatlie I shall stand charge beside to our Soueraigne Lord the King, for the answering of such prisoners as shall be committed to my custody, with an hundred matters of such importance, which are to such an Office belonging.[9]

While Deloney's shoemaker steps aside to weigh and consider, Dekker's Eyre plants himself firmly in the midst of things. He stands at the center of a charmed circle, exercising within its boundaries a magical power to animate or rejuvenate through language alone. The story of *The Shoemakers' Holiday* is the expansion of this circle and the enlargement of Simon's influence until an entire country is seized with his genial madness.

The world that is in need of such "redemption" is introduced in the play's opening scene. Sir Roger Otley, the Lord Mayor whom Simon will eventually replace, is engaged in a courteous, formal, and hypocritical conversation with the Earl of Lincoln. Their subject is the rumored attachment of Rowland Lacy, the Earl's nephew, to Sir Roger's daughter, Rose. Neither wishes to see the match prosper, yet to maintain social proprieties each must seem to oppose it through courtesy to the other, and beneath the niceties of their dialogue both courtier and citizen participate in a neat bit of verbal fencing. Lincoln begins the exchange with a perfunctory mention of Otley's "courtesy":

> My Lord Maior, you haue sundrie times
> Feasted my selfe, and many Courtiers more,
> Seldome, or neuer can we be so kind,
> To make requitall of your curtesie:
>
> (I.i.1–4)

We might note that the feast motif that assumes a major importance with Simon's rise to power is first introduced in this scene and that Otley's tables are set not for merry madcaps "of what degree soeuer," but for the Earl of Lincoln and "many Courtiers more." These opening lines are themselves the sort of polite "requitall" that might characterize an Otley feast, cold compliments and easily dispensible. Indeed, when Lincoln means to get down to business he must and does break off, "But leauing this . . ." and our play proper begins:

9. *Ibid.*, pp. 155–156.

> I heare my cosen *Lacie*
> Is much affected to your daughter *Rose*.
>
> (I.i.5-6)

After the matter is broached and Otley censures his daughter's "boldnesse in the chace," the Earl issues what amounts to a challenge, asserting his prerogatives in an aristocratic couplet:

> Why my lord Maior, think you it then a shame,
> To ioyne a *Lacie* with an *Otleys* name?
>
> (I.i.9-10)

Otley can only retreat, humbling himself still further, yet in the process he manages a veiled slur at genteel prodigals:

> Too meane is my poore girle for his high birth,
> Poore Cittizens must not with Courtiers wed,
> Who will in silkes, and gay apparrell spend
> More in one yeare, then I am worth by farre,
> Therefore your honour neede not doubt my girle.
>
> (I.i.11-15)

Lincoln counters by granting Otley's premise and professing an honest concern for the citizen's fortune:

> Suppose your daughter haue a thousand pound,
> He did consume me more in one halfe yeare,
> And make him heyre to all the wealth you haue,
> One twelue moneth's rioting wil waste it all,
> Then seeke (my Lord) some honest Cittizen
> To wed your daughter to.
>
> (I.i.32-37)

But in the course of his argument the Earl is able to express his indignation that Lacy, in his prodigal poverty, once stooped to a citizen's trade and:

> Became a Shoomaker in *Wittenberg,*
> A goodly science for a gentleman
> Of such discent. . . .
>
> (I.i.29-31)

Mutual contempt and hostility are never very far beneath the rhetorical patina of this old order, and both Lincoln and Otley realize it. The latter now replies under his breath: "Wel Foxe, I vnderstand your subtiltie" (l.

38),[10] and returns Lincoln's remark with a twist, implying that such a trade might be a gentleman's only redeeming feature:

> And yet your cosen *Rowland* might do well
> Now he hath learn'd an occupation,

(I.i.42–43)

If Dekker's audience is still uncertain as to how it must interpret these backhanded compliments, Otley completes his speech with an aside: "And yet I scorne to call him sonne in law" (l. 44).

This false "politeness" gives way to Simon's festive license in the course of Dekker's play. Eyre's holiday madness provides him with a compelling vitality that is able to frustrate the intrigues of Lincoln and Otley. Moreover, when the shoemaker succeeds Otley as Lord Mayor of London, his animated rhetoric and behavior become the official mode of a cockney utopia that replaces the more calculating and somber regime of his predecessors. Fittingly, Simon's gradual takeover may be seen in the three feasts that are mentioned or presented in *The Shoemakers' Holiday*. The first of these is the "courteous" feast Lincoln speaks of in Act I. As Lord Mayor, Otley has given "sundrie" banquets for those "many Courtiers" he is obliged to entertain. Yet Otley's generosity goes no further than obligation, and if we may judge the mood of his banquets by the quiet hypocrisy of Act I, scene i, they seem incredibly tense and self-conscious affairs. The play's second feast occurs in Act III, scene iii, midway through Simon's ascent and Dekker's comedy. Otley is still Lord Mayor, now compelled to entertain Eyre, who has just been appointed "shiriffe of the Citie." This banquet is held at Otley's country estate, to which Simon brings his "crue of good fellowes" and his own morris. The shoemaker and his "Mesopotamians" impinge upon the rustic serenity of Old Ford with tabor, pipe, and jig. Otley's reception is at first a mannerly apology for his own "bad cheere," but Simon corrects his gentility as he enlivens his banquet:

Good cheere my Lord Maior, fine cheere, a fine house, fine walles, all fine and neat.

(III.iii.5–6)

and, for the moment, even Otley is won over, speaking more wisely than he knows:

---

10. Lincoln echoes this sentiment: "To approue your loues to me? no, subtiltie . . ." (I.i.71).

> Now by my troth Ile tel thee maister *Eyre,*
> It does me good and al my bretheren,
> That such a madcap fellow as thy selfe
> Is entred into our societie.
>
> 　　　　　　　　　　　　(III.iii.7–10)

In this scene Eyre asserts his superiority over Otley, carrying his own merry world to the Lord Mayor and transforming the feast at Old Ford. Furthermore, Simon's morris becomes the means for another triumph over the Lord Mayor. Lacy, who is now disguised as one of Eyre's apprentices, uses the dance to reveal himself to Rose, furthering his own counter-intrigues against Otley and the Earl of Lincoln. At the play's third and final feast Simon is in complete control. He is now Lord Mayor and spreads his tables for an enormous Shrove Tuesday meal. It is a banquet to end all banquets, with "an hundred tables fiue times couered" for all the prentices in London. Dekker's shoemaker lords it over a wild pre-Lenten fling and is saluted by *"all good Fellowes, Professors of the Gentle Craft; of what degree soeuer"*:

> ALL
> Oh braue shoomaker, oh braue lord of incomprehensible good fellowship, whoo, hearke you, the pancake bell rings.
> 　　　　　　　　　　　*Cast vp caps.*
> 　　　　　　　　　　　　　(V.ii.200–201)

At the height of these festivities, Simon is joined by the King of England, who confirms him in office and partakes in the banquet. When Lincoln and Otley arrive to protest the union of their children under Simon's suzerainty, the previous Lord Mayor appears as a mere shade, already fading from memory:

> KING
> [to Lincoln] Who seeks, besides you, to diuorce these louers?
> 　　　LORD MAYOR [i.e., Otley]
> I do (my gracious Lord) I am her father.
> 　　　　　　　KING
> Sir *Roger Oteley,* our last Maior I thinke?
> 　　　　　　　　　　　　　(V.v.72–74)

The King denies Sir Roger's suit, approving the marriage in terms that ironically echo Lincoln's taunt in Act I, scene i:

KING
Why tell me *Oteley,* shines not *Lacies* name,
As bright in the worldes eye, as the gay beames
Of any citizen?

(V.v.98–100)

and reinforce Simon's position as lord of the feast.

III

The hub of Eyre's world is his workshop; but a workshop is a commercial as well as a fraternal venture, and from the outset Simon is as much merchant as madcap. Dekker reconciles the two strains by using Eyre's "bandog and bedlam" rant to provide a rhythm for impetuous industry. If his journeymen can hammer away to "derie, derie, down," Simon can set his establishment in motion with:

Where be these boyes, these girles, these drabbes, these scoundrels, they wallow in the fat brewisse of my bountie, and licke vp the crums of my table, yet wil not rise to see my walkes cleansed: come out you powder-beefe-queanes, what *Nan,* what *Madge-mumble-crust,* come out you fatte Midriffe-swag-belly whores, and sweepe me these kennels, that noysome stench offende not the nose of my neighbours: what *Firke* I say, what *Hodge?* open my shop windowes, what *Firke* I say.

(I.iv.1–8)

In this manner sharp business practice can be presented (and accepted) as prank or merry jest. For example, when Eyre's workmen threaten to leave, Simon recalls them to the tune of twelve cans of beer but cuts the number to two when their backs are turned. We are hardly offended:

EYRE
. . . auant boy, bid the tapster of the Bores head fil me a doozen Cannes of beere for my iourneymen.
FIRKE
A doozen Cans? O braue, *Hodge* now Ile stay.
EYRE
And the knaue fils any more then two, he payes for them: a doozen Cans of beere for my iourneymen, heare you mad Mesopotamians, wash your liuers with this liquor, where be the odde ten?

(II.iii.66–72)

Eyre's larger ventures are excused in a similar manner. With a like gusto he dresses as an alderman to obtain enough credit to purchase a ship "laden with sugar Candie." In Deloney, this transaction was so secret that Simon's journeyman, who first mentions the prospect, is never told of his master's design.[11] *The Shoemakers' Holiday* presents the enterprise as a jolly project for Eyre's entire shop:

Peace *Firk*, silence tittle tattle: *Hodge*, Ile go through with it, heers a seale ring, and I haue sent for a garded gown, and a damask Casock, see where it comes, looke here *Maggy*, help me *Firk*, apparel me *Hodge*, silke and satten you mad Philistines, silke and satten.

(II.iii.94–98)

Indeed, Eyre's opportunism and madness are most often inseparable,[12] and his accumulation of wealth and offices may be seen as the translation of his "accumulative" rhetoric into the material world. If the objection is raised that "the instant we peer behind the facade of heartiness, we discover 'Shylock masquerading as Falstaff,' "[13] we need only reply that Dekker never lets us peer behind the façade. The moment we do so we are no longer talking about his play.

This dual energy, Simon's sportive madness and his mercantile drive, maintains the state of agitated well-being that pervades his world. The center of this world, as suggested above, is Simon's shop, and we find the

11. *Novels of Thomas Deloney*, pp. 141–146. Another interesting difference in the two versions of this transaction is that, while Deloney's Simon deals in dry goods, Dekker's shoemaker purchases a more festive lading that includes foodstuffs. There is no historical basis for either cargo, so that Dekker differs here from his usual practice of altering Deloney only for the sake of historical accuracy or dramatic compression. See W. K. Chandler, "Sources of Characters in *The Shoemaker's Holiday*," MP, XXVII (1929), 175–182.

12. If this hard core of mercantile opportunism is neglected in production, audiences will be given an Eyre who is merely wishy-washy, and the comedy will not hold together. This was the experience of a number of critics who reviewed Ted Berger's adaptation of the play, produced at the Orpheum Theatre in New York in March, 1967. Dan Sullivan, writing for the *New York Times*, March 3, 1967, laments the reduction of Dekker's "roistering magnifico" to "a harmless father figure . . . whom everyone follows because he's such a Nice Guy," while Edith Oliver, reviewing for *The New Yorker*, March 11, 1967, pp. 127–128, complains that the production's "department-store Santa Claus has little to do with the rough-tongued, big hearted Simon Eyre."

13. Barish, *Ben Jonson*, p. 282.

shoemaker's exuberance reflected in varying degrees and qualities in its inhabitants. Firk possesses his master's madness in a cruder and more physical form.[14] Eyre talks to embrace the world, ranting in terms biblical, historical, and mythological, but his "fine firking iourneyman," as the pun on his name implies,[15] revels primarily in the sexual *double-entendre*. If Simon sees journeyman Rafe as surpassing Hector, Hercules, and the knights of Arthur's table, to Firk he is:

as good a workman at a pricke and an awle, as any is in our trade.

(I.i.139–140)

Likewise, the French wars, viewed by the Earl of Lincoln as an expedient, by Lacy as an obstacle, and by Simon as an opportunity to display his verbal fireworks on behalf of the gentle craft, are seen as a chance to "firke the *Basa mon cues*" for his sake. In one respect Firk appears even as a purer madcap than Simon. The journeyman does not benefit from his exuberance as his master does. Firk's pranks, such as the misdirection of Otley and Lincoln to Rafe's wedding, are for wit's sake alone, as is his gratuitous and continuous corruption of language ("cormorant," "porpentine," "vennentorie," "Oatemeale," etc.). Firk is, in short, as much of a vice figure as an honest craftsman may be, but he *is* an honest craftsman and jealously guards his position in Simon's establishment. He has both of his master's instincts but in a simpler form, and the balance between them has been readjusted.

Mrs. Eyre also possesses both of her husband's drives, but if the balance in Firk is heavily weighted towards madness, Margery embodies Simon's materialism. Like Firk she is proficient in bawdry, but her primary concern is with goods. This preoccupation is most comically apparent as she contemplates her husband's rise to sheriff in terms of the accouterments proper to a sheriff's wife:

14. Firk's propensity for "flesh" has been noted by Harold E. Toliver in *"The Shoemakers' Holiday:* Theme and Image," *Boston University Studies in English,* V (1961), 208–218. This article also contains an excellent discussion of the play's two songs.

15. See entry under "firk" in Eric Partridge's *Shakespeare's Bawdy,* rev. ed. (London, 1955). For Dekker's use of the term with obscene innuendos see "A new Ballad of y⁽ᵉ⁾ dauncing on y⁽ᵉ⁾ ropes to y⁽ᵉ⁾ tune of a rich Merchant man, &c," reprinted as an appendix to F. D. Hoeniger's "Thomas Dekker, the Restoration of St. Paul's, and J. P. Collier, the Forger," *RN,* XVI (1963).

. . . prethee let me haue a paire of shooes made, corke good *Roger,* woodden heele too.

HODGE

You shall.

WIFE

Art thou aquainted with neuer a fardingale-maker, nor a French-hoode maker, I must enlarge my bumme, ha ha, how shall I looke in a hoode I wonder? perdie odly I thinke. . . . I must get me a fan or else a maske. . . . Fie vpon it, how costly this world's calling is, . . .

(III.ii.28–34,44,46)

And, as is the case with Firk, the simplification of Simon's qualities implies a gentle criticism. Once the delicate balance maintained in Eyre himself is shifted, the interdependence of his festive and commercial energies becomes apparent. If industry is used to justify madness, mirth and good fellowship are equally important in justifying materialism; when one or the other predominates, as in Firk or Margery, its shortcomings are revealed.

If anyone in Simon's shop achieves something of Eyre's synthesis, it is Hodge. Sim's foreman can indulge, and participate in, Firk's pranks and obscenities, but he is also able to run his master's shop. Indeed, in Act IV, scene i, after Eyre has become Lord Mayor, we see Hodge in charge of Simon's old establishment, merrily exhorting the prentices to "worke apace":

to it pell mel, that we may liue to be Lord Maiors, or Aldermen at least. . . . they say seuen of the Aldermen be dead, or very sicke.

(IV.i.3–4,34–35)

Together with Firk and Margery, Hodge helps form what we might call a corporate Simon, and when the three are viewed as a group, the excesses of Firk and Madge maintain a balance similar to Eyre's. This accounts in part for the impression that Simon's presence permeates his shop, having an existence beyond the shoemaker himself. His shop is, in fact, Simon's first conquest, completed long before the opening of Dekker's comedy. Within the play Eyre makes further conquests that bring the spirit of his shop to a nation and its ruler.

Simon's ability to transform the incongruity of his own behavior may also be seen in his manner of dealing with the moral anomalies of society. The same type of festive energy succeeds in dissolving the disparities of the non-festive world outside Eyre's shop, but with an important differ-

ence. In presenting Simon as both madcap and merchant Dekker resolves
the contradictions in his material below the threshold of dramatic perception. That is to say, while we can isolate instances of disreputable behavior
in Eyre's conduct, his actions do not invite criticism in context. When
Simon and his followers face the world of Lincoln, Otley, or Lacy,
however, Dekker presents moral ambiguities more directly, as challenges
to be overcome by the shoemaker's exuberance. A brief example will
illustrate the technique. In the play's initial scene Lacy tells us that he
does not intend to accompany his men to France, but will remain at home
to court Rose. No sooner has this decision been reached than we see Lacy
approached by Rafe, one of his recruits, who pleads for a discharge so that
he may remain at home with his wife. All the elements for irony are
massed as Lacy, resolved on desertion, comforts Rafe's bride:

> . . . God (no doubt) wil send
> Thy husband safe againe, but he must go,
> His countries quarrel sayes, it shall be so.
>
> (I. i. 178–180)

Yet before we are able to condemn Lacy as a hypocrite, Simon arrives to
argue for Rafe's release, loosing a torrent of fantastical vitality that is
overwhelming in effect:

> gentlemen, captaines, colonels, commanders: braue men, braue leaders, may it
> please you to giue me audience, I am *Simon Eyre,* the mad Shoomaker of
> Towerstreete, this wench with the mealy mouth that wil neuer tire, is my wife
> I can tel you, heres *Hodge* my man, and my foreman, heres *Firke* my fine
> firking iourneyman, and this is blubbered *Iane,* al we come to be suters for this
> honest *Rafe,* keepe him at home, . . .
>
> (I. i. 125–131)

When, however, Simon sees that his request will be denied, he promptly
shifts his position "rau[ing] in commendation of *Rafe*" and the honors to
be won in war. He appeals, as Lacy had, to Rafe's patriotism and even
reworks Lincoln's earlier *sententiae* on honor (ll. 92–97) into a corporate
rather than a personal ideal. This second explosion sends logic reeling as it
changes the direction of the scene, creating a situation that seems positive
and vital from one that was initially ironic:

> take him braue men, *Hector* of *Troy* was an hackney to him, *Hercules* and
> *Termagant* scoundrelles, Prince *Arthurs* Round table, by the Lord of Ludgate,
> nere fed such a tall, such a dapper swordman, by the life of *Pharo,* a braue
> resolute swordman: . . . *Raph,* heres fiue sixpences for thee, fight for the

honour of the *Gentle Craft,* for the gentlemen Shoomakers, the couragious Cordwainers, the flower of saint *Martins,* the mad knaues of Bedlem, Fleetstreete, Towerstreete, and white Chappell, cracke me the crownes of the French knaues, a poxe on them, cracke them, fight, by the lord of Ludgate, fight my fine boy.

(I. i. 164–168, 211–216)

As the hypocrisy of Lacy's position disappears in Simon's sweet smoke of rhetoric, we might be tempted to accuse Eyre, like Falstaff, of wrenching "the true cause the false way" with his "throng of words." We should not, however, lose sight of an important distinction between the two. Falstaff throws the moral anomalies of his society into high relief, drawing attention towards injustices but leaving them unresolved, while Simon renders such anomalies irrelevant by his very presence. The logic-chopping of Falstaff's mock encomiums produces a satiric effect as it exposes the pretensions of his society. Simon's non-logical or associative prose can stir up a tempest of boisterous conviviality that makes the world of Lincoln and Otley appear shabby indeed, but it is criticism by inference only. The shoemaker is able to animate concepts that have otherwise gone stale as he reinforces the romantic and heroic ideals of his society by exuberant restatement. In *The Shoemakers' Holiday* faith is encouraged in the energy of a madcap lord of mirth who can wonderfully and magically revitalize a commonweal.

IV

On a larger scale Simon's success can be gauged by his relationship to the play's two love triangles. To remain in Eyre's merry world ensures good fortune, and if Lacy wins Rose by becoming a member of the gentle craft, Rafe's problems first begin with his "exile" from Simon's demesne. As courtier, Lacy cannot gain Simon's approval:

Be rulde sweete *Rose,* th'art ripe for a man: marrie not with a boy, that has no more haire on his face then thou hast on thy cheekes: a courtier, wash, go by, stand not vppon pisherie pasherie: those silken fellowes are but painted Images, outsides, outsides *Rose,* their inner linings are torne. . . .

(III. iii. 38–42)

But as shoemaker he can. When Lacy disguises himself as Hans and accepts a place in Eyre's shop, he vindicates himself by becoming, like his

master, both madcap and merchant-craftsman. He can jest with Firk and
the rest, but he also possesses the business acumen to arrange the purchase
that makes Eyre wealthy. Lacy becomes, in brief, part of Simon's circle
and is thus entitled to the cobbler's protection. Eyre, as we might expect,
simply sweeps away Lacy's doubts about the opposition his marriage will
arouse. In an outburst of rhythmic prose Simon obliterates the reservations implicit in Lacy's hesitant couplet:

LACY
This is the morning that must make vs two
Happy, or miserable, therefore if you—
EYRE
Away with these iffes and ands *Hauns,* and these *et caeteraes,* by mine honor
Rowland Lacie none but the king shall wrong thee: come, feare nothing, am
not I *Sim Eyre?* Is not *Sim Eyre* Lord mayor of *London?* feare nothing *Rose,*
let them al say what they can, . . .

(V. i. 3–9)

Merely proclaiming his identity is enough. Moreover, Eyre proves to be
even better than his promise; at the play's concluding feast, amid the
general revelry Simon has so fantastically prepared, the King himself
pardons Lacy's "vile treason," knights him, and heartily blesses the
match.

The story of Lacy and Rose is tied to the play's second love interest, that
of Rafe and Jane, by a common third party. "Proper" Hammon, the
antagonist in both romances, stumbles into Dekker's comedy from the
vernal world of Greene or the Shakespeare of *Love's Labor's Lost.*[16] He is
totally out of tune with the rhythms of Simon's London, and is, significantly, the only major character in the piece who never meets the shoemaker.[17] If Lacy succeeds because he is absorbed into Eyre's society, and

16. R. A. Law has suggested that *Romeo and Juliet* might have supplied Dekker
with a model for Hammon in the character of Paris. Although the differences seem
to me to be far greater than the similarities, both characters do embody the
courteous formalities of a more romantic and lyrical mode of drama that is
elsewhere absent in Dekker's play. See *"The Shoemaker's Holiday* and *Romeo and
Juliet,"* SP, XXI (1924), 356–361.
17. Robert Langbaum makes a similar point about Falstaff's sphere of influence,
from which both Hotspur and Henry IV are excluded. Yet while this exclusion
works to Falstaff's disadvantage in Shakespeare's histories it works to Hammon's
disadvantage in *The Shoemakers' Holiday.* Dekker's comedy, in fact, would seem to

Rafe resumes his merry life only after he is reincorporated into his master's band of amity, Hammon is utterly excluded from the shoemaker's world and fares accordingly. His is a form of speech and behavior that is anachronistic in its opposition rather than villainous, and his stichomythia seems strangely out of place, either in London or at Old Ford:

> ROSE
> Why doe you stay, and not pursue your game?
> SIBIL
> Ile hold my life their hunting nags be lame.
> HAMMON
> A deere, more deere is found within this place.
> ROSE
> But not the deere (sir) which you had in chace.
> HAMMON
> I chac'd the deere, but this deere chaceth me.
> ROSE
> The strangest hunting that euer I see,
> But wheres your parke?
> HAMMON
> Tis here: O stay.
> ROSE
> Impale me, and then I will not stray.
>
> (II. ii. 28–35)

In Hammon, Dekker seems to vindicate Simon's manner by showing us the impotence of a way that is more deliberate than Eyre's, even if it is unmalicious.

V

Rafe's return from the wars in Act III is one of Dekker's most striking scenes, in the theater [18] as well as in the study. As Margery and Hodge

---

challenge Langbaum's statement that "Falstaff's genius for creating his own environment is dangerous, since the single vision of life cannot be identical with reality and must eventually collide with it." Surely, it *may*, but this is determined by the individual work in question. In *The Shoemakers' Holiday* Eyre's single vision, his "created" environment, becomes the play's reality, plain and simple. See *The Poetry of Experience* (New York, 1957), p. 176.

18. For Walter Kerr, reviewing the Minneapolis Theater Company's 1967 production, it was just at this moment that "the whole performance takes shape . . . in the urgency that gathers about one distressed figure" (*New York Times*, June 6, 1967).

await Firk's return from the guildhall with news of Simon's election to sheriff, Rafe enters *"lame,"* a fugitive from a world that threatens beyond the perimeter of Eyre's conjuring circle. He has lost a leg in France and now finds that his wife has disappeared from Simon's shop. Margery, however, is so taken with her own vision of future possessions that she finds little time for Rafe. His lameness is dismissed with a bawdy joke:

the left leg is not wel: t'was a faire gift of God the infirmitie tooke not hold a litle higher, considering thou camest from *France:*

(III. ii. 64–66)

and his concern for Jane almost callously received:

O *Rafe* your wife, perdie we knowe not whats become of her: she was here a while, and because she was married grewe more stately then became her, I checkt her, and so forth, away she flung, neuer returned, nor saide bih nor bah: and *Rafe* you knowe ka me, ka thee. And so as I tell ye. *Roger* is not *Firke* come yet?

(III. ii. 79–83)

Here, if anywhere, Simon's method is brought to the test. In the juxtaposition of Margery and Rafe, Dekker sets the less admirable qualities of Eyre's world alongside a challenge to that world. For just a moment a careful balance is maintained between Rafe's pathos and Margery's comic pretensions, but before we are permitted to draw any logical conclusions, Firk comes scurrying back with the news of Simon's election:

Enter Hans, *and* Firke *running.*

FIRKE

Runne good *Hans,* O *Hodge,* O mistres, *Hodge* heaue vp thine eares, mistresse smugge vp your lookes, on with your best apparell, my maister is chosen, my master is called, nay condemn'd by the crie of the countrie to be shiriffe of the Citie, for this famous yeare nowe to come, and time now being: . . .

(III. ii. 103–107)

And as we are once more caught up in the excitement and utter madness of Eyre's world, the French wars are made to seem not so much a challenge to the shoemaker's exuberance as the grim alternative to such a whirligig. Here, by implication, is also the answer to Rafe's dilemma: for the moment, the French wars might still be painfully outside of Simon's protection, but they are now juxtaposed with the energetic expansion of his world. Rafe, who can ply the gentle craft in spite of his lameness, is able to become a part of it all, and we next see him as one of Eyre's cheery "Mesopotamians" enjoying Otley's banquet with his brother cobblers. If

Rafe's wounds keep him from actually participating in the shoemakers' morris, they do not prevent his "spiritual" reunification with his fellow journeymen and do not stop Firk and the prentices from helping him reclaim his bride. Nor is Rafe hindered from partaking in the play's concluding feast.

We have already looked at this final banquet as the culmination of Simon's rise to power and his ultimate victory. At the feast the shoemaker's mad language and behavior are sanctioned by Dekker's King, who is presented as the play's official source of value,[19] to be set "cheeke by iowle by Saint Hugh," the patron saint of cobblers. The King's function is largely ceremonial (if the word is not too pretentious for the play), confirming Simon's achievements in three central areas—love, mirth, and commerce. Lacy and Rose, who have eloped with Simon's help, are symbolically remarried, Eyre himself royally dubbed "my mad Lord Maior (that shall be thy name)," and his new market in Cornhill readily approved:

> One honour more Ile doe thee, that new building,
> Which at thy cost in Cornehill is erected,
> Shall take a name from vs, weele haue it cald,
> The Leaden hall, . . .
>
> (V. v. 127–130)

Simon's business and madcap aspects are further confirmed when the King grants the shoemaker's two boons: the patent for market days that Eyre requests is conferred, and the King agrees to join Simon's feast before he himself embarks for France.

Simon's effect on the King, however, is as important as the King's on Simon. Eyre is also able to confer identity by naming, and with a single pun (Hugh=you) makes his monarch patron of shoemakers:

EYRE

All Shooemakers, my Liege, all gentlemen of the Gentle Craft, true Troians, couragious Cordwainers, . . . all kneele to the shrine of holy saint *Hugh.*

ALL

God saue your maiesty.

> (V. v. 145–148)

19. The situation resembles the denouement of *Old Fortunatus,* in which Virtue enlists the aid of Queen Elizabeth in consolidating her victory over both Vice and Fortune. In *The Shoemakers' Holiday,* however, this consolidation takes place within the boundaries of Dekker's play world.

As the King affirms Simon's worth, Simon assimilates the King, making him titular head of his spirited world of craftsmen. By extension all of England becomes a shoemaker's shop, and all the people in it members of the gentle craft, of what degree soever. Simon's vitality cannot put an end to the wars that the King and his subjects must fight, but it can at least unite them in their struggle, and it is this sense of expanded fraternity, and not the war itself, that is stressed at the end of Dekker's play. *The Shoemakers' Holiday* closes with a movement outward and away from Simon's shop but presents a vision in which his cockney paradise is translated into a glittering patriotic future, the success of which is as assured as the abundance of pancakes on Shrove Tuesday, and as free from pain.[20] If, as it has been suggested,[21] the play's anonymous monarch is intended to be Henry V, perhaps we are meant to complete this vision ourselves. Dekker's contemporaries certainly knew that the miraculous and painless victory at Agincourt was won on the shoemakers' feast of Crispin-Crispian.

20. Jonas Barish, in correspondence.
21. L. M. Manheim, "The King in Dekker's *The Shoemakers' Holiday*," *N&Q*, IV (1957), 432–433.

The Theme of Forgiveness in the Plot and Subplot of A Woman Killed with Kindness

JOHN CANUTESON

I̲N̲ H̲I̲S̲ R̲E̲C̲E̲N̲T̲ S̲T̲U̲D̲Y̲ O̲F̲ *A Woman Killed with Kindness* David Cook suggests that if the play were performed more frequently, many of the objections raised by critics would prove untenable. Such a revival would show that the play "is not just a pleasing pastiche by a pocket Shakespeare, but a major work in its own right which must be very favorably compared to any other work of the same kind in English."[1] Even a reading of the play will reveal its stage-worthiness;[2] but while production might void the unfavorable criticisms, I suspect that in the after-theater parties we would hear again the interpretive rancor to which Heywood alludes in the epilogue:

1. David Cook, "*A Woman Killed with Kindness:* An Unshakesperian Tragedy," *ES,* XLV (1964), 372 (hereafter cited as "Cook").

2. A particular excellence of the play is the use of "unifying symbols" such as those pointed out by Ray Heffner in Ben Jonson's comedy (*English Institute Essays,* New York, 1955). The domesticity of the main plot is summarized by the table which appears again and again onstage; in both the main plot and the subplot relationships of the characters are frequently indicated by what they do with, or say about, their hands; and music, with the chief symbol being Anne's lute, is used to dramatize the decay of happiness in both plots.

"Taste it," quoth one. He did so. "Fie!" quoth he,
"This wine was good; now't runs too near the lee."

Another sipp'd, to give the wine his due,
And said unto the rest it drunk too flat.
The third said it was old, the fourth too new.
"Nay," quoth the fifth, "the sharpness likes me not." [3]

Such disagreement would no doubt arise between the historically oriented critic and the uninformed theatergoer. A modern spectator lacking historical insight would not accept the interpretation that Heywood's intentions were to show "the relationship between the loving husband and the erring wife" or to show "his audience that the more gentle course, the Christian course, brings satisfactions impossible to vindictive punishment of any kind." [4] Likewise a spectator today would deny that Sir Charles exhibited "a very high type of honour." [5] In the simplest terms he would say that Frankford is a beast and Sir Charles is a fool, and I would cheer him, because I think the instinctive reaction to the play is sound.

In this paper I would first like to discuss some standard objections to letting our modern conscience be our guide in interpreting this drama and then go into detail to show how the subplot functions as a testing ground for the moral principle established in the main plot by Frankford's unusual judgment.

Hardin Craig tried to explain and correct the discomfort which he experienced in reading the play thus:

We rarely admire the heroics of bygone ages, nor do we put such a value upon matrimony; but the discovery of such disparities is inevitable in reading the literature of other times. We can at least understand, and in understanding sympathize. [6]

The difficulty with Craig's corrective is that in other plays the disparity is not so disruptive. Who for example would call Othello "a most dreadful cad" [7] because he stabs Desdemona for her apparent infidelity? Something in *A Woman* leads us to question Frankford's action toward his wife,

3. Thomas Heywood, *A Woman Killed with Kindness,* ed. R. W. Van Fossen (The Revels Plays; London, 1961). I will be using this edition throughout the paper, and it will be cited hereafter as "Van Fossen."
4. *Ibid.,* pp. xxx–xxxi.
5. Hardin Craig, *The Enchanted Glass* (Oxford, 1952), p. 135.
6. *Ibid.,* p. 136.
7. Walter Prichard Eaton, *The Drama in English* (New York, 1930), p. 129.

whereas in *Othello* we both "admire the heroics" and "put such a value upon matrimony."

Freda Townsend, who argues that Heywood "could not have failed to intend the dramatic contrast between the chaste Susan and the unchaste Anne, between the honorable Sir Charles and the dishonorable Wendoll, between the rewards of virtue and the wages of sin," [8] uses as evidence to support her reading a statement by Heywood in *An Apology for Actors:* "Women . . . that are chaste, are by vs extolled, and encouraged in their vertues. . . . The vnchaste are by vs shewed their errors." [9] That Heywood could have intended Anne as a lesson can be further supported by Anne's direct address to the audience after her discovery:

> O women, women, you that have yet kept
> Your holy matrimonial vow unstain'd,
> Make me your instance: when you tread awry,
> Your sins like mine will on your conscience lie.
>
> (xiii.141–144)

Further there is the matter of the expensive "blacke velluett" gown which Anne would have worn from scene xvi to the end of the play in contrast with Susan's white wedding dress—probably the same white dress that Anne wore in the first scene. The divergence in virtue should be just as obvious.

But audiences rarely interpret plays the way they are told. On the contrary they can see dramatic meaning that can refute such blatant moralizing and symbolism. Furthermore, the quotation from *An Apology* comes from Heywood's exploration of the social function of drama. He is justifying the medium where

Thou mayest see many of their fates and ruines, who haue beene dishonorable, uniust, false, gluttenous, sacrilegious, bloudy-minded, and brochers of dissention. . . . It followes that we proue these exercises to haue beene the discourers of many notorious murders. . . .

> (G 2ᵛ)

Heywood presents three examples, two of which involve women who, struck with remorse by the plays they were watching, confessed the murder of their husbands—the first by poisoning and the second by

8. "The Artistry of Thomas Heywood's Double Plots," *PQ,* XXV (1946), 102.

9. Thomas Heywood, *An Apology for Actors,* ed. Richard H. Perkinson, Scholars' Facsimiles & Reprints #27 (New York, 1941), Gᵛ.

driving a nail through her husband's skull. Either Heywood has created a much subtler character than he intended in Anne Frankford, or, in *An Apology,* he was writing not as a practicing dramatist but as a generalizing apologist in the face of detractors and was not considering Anne specifically.

The third and greatest barrier to following our instinct in reading the play lies in the Elizabethan treatment of adulteresses, both onstage and off. In the theater the unfaithful wife was usually dealt with summarily, though as Waldo McNeir has shown, Heywood had precedents for a forgiving husband in Gascoigne and Greene, as well as in "the condemnation of wrathful vengeance by classical, medieval, and Renaissance authorities." [10] Outside the theater, if the promiscuous wife was not killed by her husband, she was required by the church to do public penance. But, as Van Fossen has pointed out, the real ordeal for the woman came after the public penance, when, "as a social outcast and a woman, she would have had a most difficult time." [11] Van Fossen then quotes Thorp to conclude, "Frankford's real kindness to Anne consists not 'in sparing her life but rather in his continuing to shelter her from an unfeeling world after she has forfeited all right to such protection.'" [12] However, under these circumstances, Frankford's kindness is qualified, limited— hardly as lethal as the title of the play indicates.

Just as the nature of Frankford's judgment of Anne may trouble us, the relation of the subplot to the main plot has been a stumbling block to critics who look for classical unities and do not find a close connection between the action of Sir Charles, Susan, and Acton; and Frankford, Anne, and Wendoll. Madeleine Doran, though not dispraising the work, says that "the rivalry of Acton and Mountford, without essential connection to the Frankford story, follows even a quite different time scheme from the main plot." [13] In *A Woman,* however, a thematic unity can be

10. "Heywood's Sources for the Main Plot of *A Woman Killed with Kindness,*" in *Studies in the English Renaissance Drama,* ed. Josephine W. Bennett *et al* (New York, 1959), p. 207.

11. Van Fossen, p. xxx.

12. *Ibid.,* p. xxxi. Cf. W. Thorp, *The Triumph of Realism in Elizabethan Drama 1558–1612* (London, 1928), p. 113.

13. *Endeavors of Art* (Madison, Wis., 1954), p. 290.

found, and the most fruitful reading of the play, as Cook has suggested, would involve charity rather than chastity.[14]

As a practicing dramatist Heywood could depend on the popularity of adultery and revenge on the stage; and as a sensitive man, or a Christian, he would also see the barbarity of the traditional handling of those problems, both in the theater and in the world around him. He could not write anything approaching a homily on the subject of forgiveness and hope to have his play live to see its second performance. What he seems to have done, on the other hand, is to set up a drama to consider the proper method of dealing with a sin of passion, show the protagonist following a course of action, and use a subplot as a referent by which we can judge the merits or failings of the action of the protagonist. To some he has probably created a quintessential adultery-revenge tragedy: A woman sins against a man with every good quality, and he kills her without even touching her, nay, ironically, with "kindness." But to others, he has presented the possibility of dealing with a moral crisis by the use of the Christian code, and in particular, by forgiveness. The treatment of the play always depends on the personality of the director, but he has a wealth of material to use to investigate Christian charity.

In the first scene of the play we see the marriage celebration of a man of considerable means and the daughter of a nobleman, attended by two men of the nobility. Frankford, Anne, Acton, and Mountford are not the only celebrants, however, as Master Wendoll, "a gentleman of a good house, somewhat press'd by want" (iv.32–33) and Masters Malby and Cranwell are also present. We have been told by the Prologue to "Look for no glorious state" (l. 3), and the festivities here have all the marks of the middle class. The knights joke lustily about "The Shaking of the Sheets"; there is dancing offstage—Sir Francis observes that the floor will be "peck'd and dinted like a millstone" (l. 89)—and at one point Sir Francis turns pleasantly to the audience to give proverbial advice to the young blades:

> Mark this against you marry, this one phrase:
> "In a good time that man both wins and woos
> That takes his wife down in her wedding shoes."

                                                              (i.46–48)

14. Cook, p. 363.

So relaxed are the proceedings that we are virtually unaware of the significance of Acton's and Mountford's knighthood or of Anne's noble birth. For all practical purposes, the major distinction between Acton and Mountford, and Wendoll, and even the spectators in the pit, who would have seen numerous weddings of this sort (if only from the position of the servants in scene ii) would be the distinction of wealth. Money of course will be quite important in the play, and here it is the possession of £200 and not the gentility which decides who can gamble on hawks and dogs with class.[15]

After the celebration of the servants in scene ii, "a burlesque parallel of the action in scene i,"[16] Acton and Mountford meet for their wager, accompanied by Malby, Cranwell, Wendoll, two falconers, and two huntsmen. The familiarity of everyone with the terminology of hawking makes the scene vividly exciting, but in the midst of our excitement, we are stunned to hear the two gentlemen fall to quibbling, then to quarreling. We are more surprised to see them convert their squabble to a courtly insult:

> SIR FRANCIS
> How, knight?
> SIR CHARLES
> So, knight? You will not swagger, sir?
> SIR FRANCIS
> Why, say I did?
>
> (iii.31–33)

The argument heats up swiftly, but without grace, the knights neither knowing nor caring about the progression of giving the lie and completely forgetting the lie direct. Where fisticuffs should have done, swords are drawn and the hawking party divides to fight. However, social distinctions are ignored as Sir Charles and Sir Francis fight not each other, but anyone of the opposition. What began as a jovial wager between two wealthy men has proceeded through the assumption of a knightly code archaic in terms of the play to a fatal donnybrook, as Mountford unheroically kills Acton's falconer and huntsman.

15. We can assume that Master Frankford could have gone hunting if he were not already committed to a "sport" (l. 92).

16. Lloyd E. Berry, "A Note on Heywood's *A Woman Killed with Kindness*," *MLR*, LVIII (1963), 64–65.

Mountford immediately realizes that his rage has led him to commit murder and that he must pay for it:

> It was not I, but rage, did this vile murder;
> Yet I, and not my rage, must answer it.
>
> (iii.51–52)

Since he was a sympathetic character up to the time of his anger, our question now is, What must he do to pay for his error?, or abstracted, What is the proper penance for a sin of passion? Mountford's error is a crime subject to civil law in addition to being a sin. For the sin alone, we know that Mountford is repentant (l. 49); moreover the laws and Acton's use of them will be superfluous to Mountford's inner atonement since

> My conscience is become my enemy,
> And will pursue me more than Acton can.
>
> (iii.72–73)

We soon learn what constitutes social retribution as the sheriff arrives and leads Sir Charles off to prison, "To answer for the lives of these dead men" (l. 105).

Meanwhile, the happiness of the first scene has not been diminished for Frankford by scene iv. His wife was praised at length before, summed up as "beauty and perfection's eldest daughter" (i.23), and now Frankford, after reviewing his other comfortable possessions concludes,

> But the chief
> Of all the sweet felicities on earth,
> I have a fair, a chaste, and loving wife,
> Perfection all, all truth, all ornament.
>
> (iv.9–12)

The audience should catch the clues: "A woman repeatedly summed up with reference to the idea of perfection: this is the woman who falls, without visible struggle, to the first temptation offered." [17] The audience now would wonder who her partner will be, and at this moment Wendoll rides up. He is suggested as the seducer by such word play as "Prithee, Nan, Use him with all thy loving'st courtesy," and Anne's reply to Frankford, "As far as modesty may well extend" (ll. 79–81); and by

---

17. Patricia Meyer Spacks, "Honor and Perception in *A Woman Killed with Kindness,*" *MLQ*, XX (1959), 323.

Nicholas' unfounded hostility to Wendoll: "Zounds! I could fight with him, yet know not why" (l. 87).

Wendoll brings word of Sir Charles's crime which Frankford hears and then says,

> Sir Charles will find hard friends; his case is heinous,
> And will be most severely censur'd on.
> I am sorry for him. Sir, a word with you:
>
> (iv.60–62)

with which he suddenly offers Wendoll his "table and purse." We recognize the circumstances being arranged for Anne's fall, but more importantly, by the sudden enjambment of the two plots, we can compare Charles's sin and crime with Anne's imminent sin and consider the attitudes of others to these sins.

We soon learn that Sir Charles has been released in spite of Acton's demands for his death, but at the price of "All the revenues that his father left him." His former position of wealth is demolished,

> And he is now turn'd a plain countryman
> Reform'd in all things.
>
> (v.7–9)

In addition to his sincere repentance for his sin, he has now done social penance for his crime by forfeiting the wealth that placed him in a position to wager £200 on hawks and dogs. The fatal courtly badinage of scene iii is reviewed as Mountford becomes "The poorest knight in England" (l. 17).

With Mountford having only a summerhouse and £500 left to support himself and his sister Susan, Shafton comes onstage as a possible means of relief to Sir Charles's penury. He is liberal with Mountford, and we hope momentarily that Mountford's former happiness will be somehow restored; but we soon learn that Shafton is concerned only with his own "gain and pleasure," and we can forecast more vexing problems for Sir Charles.

Anne's sudden fall in the next scene should give us few problems. Hallett Smith places Anne in the Jane Shore tradition and notes that the women lamented not the "seduction itself or the struggles they had gone through before they finally fell, but . . . [in the case of Higgins and

Daniel] their guilt and punishment." [18] Otelia Cromwell reminds us that the most important issue in the plot is "the nature of Frankford's revenge," and not the fall itself, [19] and Cook stresses Anne's moral insensibility: "This patently is her first encounter with passion—of which she knows nothing after her secluded youth and calmly affectionate marriage." [20] I can only add that in this scene the relationship of Wendoll and Frankford, with the betrayal of a friend, is the moral issue, debated even after Anne comes in. For the new but similar moral problem of a woman's infidelity to her husband to be considered in detail would be somewhat cumbersome. The result is that the decision to sin is Wendoll's, and though we cannot excuse Anne, we can at least temper our attitude toward her guilt by blaming Wendoll as Nicholas does:

> It is that Satan hath corrupted her,
> For she was fair and chaste.
>
> (vi.179–180)

Anne is just beginning her sin of passion when we see Mountford and Susan reduced to ordinary farmers as the price for Sir Charles's crime. Shafton enters and demands the £300 which he had lent Mountford earlier, plus the accrued interest. Mountford cannot raise that amount because of his poverty and because he will not sell his few remaining acres. His reasoning betrays again his pride in his nobility:

> If this were sold, our names should then be quite
> Raz'd from the bead-roll of gentility.
>
> (vii.36–37)

But at the same time, it is clear that he is being victimized because of his crime; that is, he suffers beyond what is just. Not only does Shafton have Sir Charles arrested for the debt, but also Shafton says,

> . . . I'll sue thee by a late appeal
> And call thy former life in question.
>
> (vii.59–60)

Sir Francis of course loves every minute of Mountford's torment—it is literally music to his ears (ll. 76–77). His motive is revenge, and he wants

18. *"A Woman Killed with Kindness," PMLA,* LIII (1938), 14.

19. *Thomas Heywood: A Study in the Elizabethan Drama of Everyday Life, YSE,* LXXVIII (1928), 55.

20. Cook, p. 357.

to pursue it to the limit, even to the bribing of Susan to dishonor herself by lust (ll. 79ff.). Malby, his companion, realizes the exaggerated revenge:

> Methinks, Sir Francis, you are full reveng'd
> For greater wrongs than he can proffer you.
>
> (vii.85–86)

Nevertheless, Acton sees Susan and decides to flout her poverty, and is only stopped by a glance from her eye. He then acts as if he has fallen in love at first sight with the sister of his adversary. His state of mind is not exclusively love, but a "violent humour of passion and of love" (ll. 108–109). That his attitude is not pure love is shown later when he tries to tempt Susan with gold (ix.41 ff.), and when finally he acknowledges his base behavior:

> Stern heart, relent;
> Thy former cruelty at length repent.
>
> (xiv.118–119)

In scene viii Frankford first hears of his wife's infidelity from Nicholas and from this point Van Fossen's claim that Frankford is "the Christian gentleman"[21] seems to me to be unfounded. Frankford's response to Nicholas is simple:

> What didst thou say? If any word that touch'd
> His credit or her reputation,
> It is as hard to enter my belief
> As Dives into Heaven.
>
> (viii.61–64)

The reference to Dives, though biblical, is proverbial. Frankford could have used "camel through the eye of a needle," except that the Dives metaphor allows him to associate his own mind with Heaven. He further denies the possibility of her faithlessness with such assurance that he is willing to "Hazard the dear salvation of my soul." Aside from his certain loss at this wager if he were in earnest, it is interesting that he bandies about what a Christian gentleman would be loath to lose. Christian terms are to Frankford little more than bywords with which to measure his faith in his wife, as when he says,

> For should an angel from the heavens drop down
> And preach this to me that thyself hast told,

21. Van Fossen, p. xlii.

> He should have much ado to win belief,
> In both their loves I am so confident.
>
> (viii.83–86)

Less faith in heaven is shown here than in *A Challenge for Beauty,* scene
iv: "*Unless* an Angell . . . [etc.] It wins with me no credence" (italics
mine).

The most galling use to which Frankford puts religious terms is when
he repeatedly compares himself with the divine, as in the Dives metaphor
above and, at line 102,

> But he, that Judas that hath borne my purse,
> And sold me for a sin. . . .

This presumption, as we shall see, reaches its climax in scene xiii.

All this time we realize that Anne is engaged in sin. While Frankford
slowly discovers it, we wonder what he will do about it when he has
conclusive proof or when he catches them in *flagrante delicto.* We have an
idea what Nicholas, forever reaching for his dagger, would do—the same
thing that almost any husband would do. Perhaps Frankford, like Hamlet, has too deliberative a bent. Whatever his course of action will be, the
subplot is still exploring the treatment afforded sins of passion, as in scene
ix, when Susan approaches kindred and friends for financial help.

Old Mountford's response to Susan is to deny kinship to Sir Charles,
charging him with moral irresponsibility:

> You say my nephew is in great distress—
> Who brought it to him but his own lewd life?
> I cannot spare a cross. I must confess
> He was my brother's son; why, niece, what then?
> This is no world in which to pity men.
>
> (ix.1–5)

Susan counters his callousness by kneeling [22] and beseeching him first as a
Mountford to have pity, but then "for Christianity, Nay, for God's sake"
(ll. 9–11). He replies with more stuffy, uncharitable moralizing:

> Money I cannot spare; men should take heed.
> He lost my kindred when he fell to need.
>
> (ix.16–17)

22. Susan has to kneel in this scene on the evidence of x. 66: "I begg'd, I su'd, I
kneel'd." One effective place to insert the stage direction is in the middle of line 9.

Susan turns to her cousin Sandy, who likewise disowns her and denies
her suit: "I knew you ere your brother sold his land" (l. 22). Similarly,
the man whom Sir Charles allowed to live rent-free on his farm has a
cocky answer to her plea, and another cousin charges Sir Charles again
with moral irresponsibility. Susan sums up the whole encounter,

> O Charity, why art thou fled to Heaven,
> And left all things on this earth uneven?
>
> (ix.37–38)

The complete lack of charity in Susan's kinsmen and friends is followed
by the false charity of Acton, who, through Malby, attempts to prostitute
Susan with gold. She recoils, protesting that her "honour never shall for
gain be sold" (l. 54); and Acton, with his intent somewhere between love
and lust, decides on another approach to woo her:

> Well, I will fasten such a kindness on her
> As shall o'ercome her hate and conquer it.
>
> (ix.66–67)

An unmistakable verbal link with the main plot is presented here, and it
is significant that Acton plans in effect to buy Susan's love by paying for
Sir Charles's freedom—his "kindness" is little more than another attempt
at prostitution.

Sir Charles feels his ultimate forgiveness has come when his debts are
paid, as he thinks, by his kinsmen. His too-long torment actually stemmed
from the perversity of men rather than from his sin, however; and his
release is effected by a man with, at best, questionable motives, not by his
kinsmen. Of the latter Susan reports,

> O brother, they are men all of flint,
> Pictures of marble, and as void of pity
> As chased bears. I begg'd, I su'd, I kneel'd,
> Laid open all your griefs and miseries,
> Which they derided—more than that, deny'd us
> A part in their alliance, but in pride
> Said that our kindred with our plenty died.
>
> (x.64–70)

In the subplot, "plenty," or financial security, was the state of happiness of
the first scene before Sir Charles's sin of passion. In the main plot
happiness was the condition of wedded bliss, also in the first scene and
before Anne's sin. Frankford who counted his chaste wife as his chief

possession likewise will claim "in pride . . . that our kindred with our plenty died."

When Sir Charles finds that Acton has bought his financial forgiveness, he is overwhelmed. He considers how he should "requite that grace," had it come from, in order, father, friends, a stranger, an enemy (ll. 105–118), and ends in perplexity. He might understand forgiveness by a kinsman, but by a stranger it is inconceivable. What Sir Charles thinks he is experiencing is a forgiveness akin to Christian charity—the nonunderstandable love of one's enemy, remarkable here because it has surpassed by so far the love of kinsmen who are "by the law of nature . . . most bound in offices of love."

Having seen the action of what Sir Charles would consider Christian charity we return to the main plot for the scenes preceding the exposure. At supper, Cranwell remarks that Frankford might have tried to persuade Acton to be more lenient toward Sir Charles. Frankford replies,

> Did not more weighty business of my own
> Hold me away, I would have labour'd peace
> Betwixt them, with all care; indeed I would, sir.
>
> (xi.28–30)

This is nothing short of a selfish refusal to be a peacemaker: the contrast with Anne's behavior follows when Anne says that she will write to her brother, Acton, and is commended by Wendoll for her gesture:

> A charitable deed,
> And will beget the good opinion
> Of all your friends that love you.
>
> (xi.32–35)

Later, in order to have Wendoll stay with Anne, Frankford assumes the guise of good-natured charity when he declines to have Wendoll accompany him:

> Fie, fie, that for my private business
> I should disease my friend and be a trouble
> To the whole house.
>
> (xi.78–80)

The plot necessitates Wendoll's staying in the house with Anne, and Heywood has effected it via a bit of false charity on the part of Frankford.

When Frankford leaves we see Anne and Wendoll in the foreplay of
sin, with Anne's theologically nearsighted rationalization that (1) she did
not know what she was getting into before, and (2) she must now
continue through fear (ll. 110–114). Frankford returns with Nicholas
clandestinely, uses false keys to enter the house, eventually sees his wife
asleep with Wendoll and, after a soliloquy, returns to wake them. When
Wendoll runs across the stage pursued by Frankford, his patron charges
him with ingratitude and again analogizes his own situation to Christ's:
"Go, to thy friend / A Judas . . ." (xiii.75–76). By placing himself in the
role of the betrayed Christ, he keynotes his handling of Anne's sin. From
first to last he is concerned not with the sin against God but the sin
against him.

Anne enters with such an awareness of her sin that she thinks herself
beyond forgiveness:

> O by what word, what title, or what name
> Shall I entreat your pardon? Pardon! O
> I am as far from hoping such sweet grace
> As Lucifer from Heaven. To call you husband—
> O me most wretched, I have lost that name;
> I am no more your wife.
>
>   (xiii.78–83)

She understands first of all that by tradition her sin has destroyed her
marriage. Secondly, because she acquiesces to her husband's placing himself in the position of the divine, or simply because of her extreme guilt,
she thinks her sin is primordial and unforgivable. We have to agree that
according to custom her marriage is doomed, but we also have to correct
her theology. No relationship among men can be compared to God's
treatment of Lucifer, because no mortal has the right to withhold forgiveness—only God can judge. In no Elizabethan or Jacobean tragedy does a
character blamelessly decline forgiveness to a penitent. That Frankford
does not forgive Anne immediately removes him from consideration as a
Christian gentleman, since the one thing that we can be certain of in this
scene is Anne's repentance:

> I deserve a thousand thousand fold
> More than you can inflict . . .
>
> . . . womanhood—to which I am a shame

> I am not worthy that [i.e., the phrase of the re-
> turned prodigal son] I should prevail
> In the least suit . . .
>
>   (xiii.94 ff.)

Anne is here concerned with her mortal condition rather than her immortal soul; and Frankford is interested not in her eternal forgiveness but in his own besmirched honor: "Now, I protest, I think 'tis I am tainted" (l. 86). She anticipates the usual physical abuse, but Frankford denies her this. He internalizes his abuse, gives her a psychological grilling, and then brings out their two children to shame her; but his aims are those of a man of clouded honor, not of a Christian gentleman. He dwells on "regard of honour," "The blemish of my house," and asserts that "her spotted body / Hath stain'd their [i.e. the children's] names with stripe of bastardy" (ll. 117 ff.).

Frankford retires to consider a judgment; Anne laments her mistake at length; the servants enter to intone piously, "O mistress, mistress, what have you done, mistress?" (l. 145); but Nicholas saves the scene from its grotesqueries by shushing everybody, " 'Sblood, what a caterwauling keep you here!" (l. 146). Frankford returns and announces his sentence which, presumably via a vow, is "regist'red in Heaven already" as he stands before Anne, who, like the suppliant Susan before her kinsmen, is on her knees.

> I'll not martyr thee
> Nor mark thee for a strumpet, but with usage
> Of more humility torment thy soul
> And kill thee even with kindness.
>
>   (xiii.153–156)

Frankford, like old Mountford before the kneeling Susan, does not consider forgiveness: he assumes that when one sins he deserves the consequences of his act. The only question for Frankford, then, is just what kind of punishment should be used. The torment he chooses, with the name and superficial appearance of kindness, is in fact death. He banishes her from her children and from himself. He charges her not to try to contact him,

> . . . as thou hop'st for Heaven, as thou believ'st
> Thy name's recorded in the Book of Life.
>
>   (xiii.172 ff.)

Frankford most hypocritically thinks that his decree and God's are one. When Anne replies to Frankford, "A mild sentence," Cook asks, "Cannot this show him what a harsh sentence in fact it is?" [23]

To understand what went wrong with the judgment, apart from Frankford's simple refusal to forgive Anne as Sir Charles's kinsmen refused to "forgive" him, we turn in the next scene to the subplot, with Sir Charles bringing his sister "trick'd . . . like a bride," to Acton, whose £500 have set Mountford free. Rather than remain dishonorably indebted to his enemy, Sir Charles plans to offer Acton his sister. The problem emerges that Susan holds her honor as dear as her redemption (xiv. 54–55); likewise, Sir Charles holds her honor as dear as his own soul (l. 61). His own honor he has "kept as spotless as the moon" (l. 27)—he seems to have forgotten the murders. Yet he is willing to sacrifice the one honor for the other, hers for his: he

> . . . rather would engage [her] unstain'd honour
> Than to be held ingrate.
>
> (xiv.80–81)

Not only does Sir Charles's reasoning exhibit the code of honor extended to absurdity, but his actions also dishonor him. He becomes a pander bringing his sister to be deflowered by his enemy.

Sir Francis, who dealt to the extreme with Sir Charles before, can appreciate the forced code of honor. When addressed as a knight of honor, he responds again as a man of chivalry:

> Stern heart, relent;
> Thy former cruelty at length repent.
> Was ever known in any former age
> Such honourable wrested courtesy?
>
> (xiv.118–121)

Acton and Mountford are living in an age when chivalric behavior should be dead. They are landed gentlemen who revert to antiquated codes to deal with moral problems. But even in a former age Mountford's action would be "wrested," or distorted. By placing this scene directly after the judgment scene, Heywood forces us to consider the two solutions of moral dilemmas. In the first, Frankford, concerned with his honor, disregards simple forgiveness to comply with the demands of the time for punishment of unfaithful wives, while Mountford, to save his honor, does the

23. Cook, p. 365.

ultra-honorable thing in offering his dear sister to (as he sees him) an honorable enemy to whom he is indebted. Both actions appear to be virtuous moves: Frankford's decision seems kind because it is not violent, Mountford's noble because it is daring. But in reality Mountford is dishonoring himself by maintaining an archaic code with such vigor, and Frankford is exposing himself as a refined revenger of his tainted honor while he protests to be acting out of kindness. Both Frankford and Sir Charles fail to adopt genuinely new solutions—in both characters there is an essential lack of imagination despite the unusualness of their actions.

Frankford shares with Sir Francis an extremism. After Anne has gone to Frankford's manor house, Sir Francis hears of Anne's sin and opens scene xvii with this statement to Charles and Susan:

> Brother, and now my wife, I think these troubles
> Fall on my head by justice of the Heavens,
> For being so strict to you in your extremities.
>
> (xvii.1–3)

Acton would be the last to charge Frankford with unusually harsh treatment. On the contrary he says that Frankford "show'd too mild a spirit" (l. 16). But his former statement ironically expresses the truth of the matter, that in a way it *is* just that a man who avenges with such spirit should have his sister submitted to the same strict measures. Acton actually praises Frankford's actions (ll. 19–20), leaving us to consider any judgment praised by a man of this sort.

At the sight of his sister preparing for death, even Acton softens:

> I came to chide you, but my words of hate
> Are turn'd to pity and compassionate grief;
> I came to rate you, but my brawls, you see,
> Melt into tears, and I must weep by thee.
>
> (xvii.63–66)

Frankford who has agreed to come, having examined "the general circumstance," (l. 47), enters and offers a pious disclaimer of responsibility:

> Good morrow, brother; good morrow, gentlemen.
> God, that hath laid this cross upon our heads,
> Might had he pleas'd have made our cause of meeting
> On a more fair and a more contented ground;
> But He that made us, made us to this woe.
>
> (xvii.68–72)

Anne again abjectly asks for Frankford's pardon and adds,

> My fault so heinous is
> That if you in this world forgive it not,
> Heaven will not clear it in the world to come.

(xvii.86–88)

Anne is again theologically naïve, not knowing that one need not be forgiven on earth to receive God's forgiveness. She cannot kneel as she did before, because of her weakness, but she is on her "heart's knees" (l. 90). To her pleas for forgiveness Frankford responds for the last time as a substitute for Christ:

> As freely from the low depth of my soul
> As my Redeemer hath forgiven His death,
> I pardon thee.

(xvii.93–95)

The curious thing is that Anne has added nothing—indeed she could not—to her former request for Frankford's forgiveness. She has repented to God, but this was not Frankford's aim in banishing her. The very fact that he forgives her now, following the same pleas that he heard before, shows conclusively the useless extremity of his revenge. Perhaps Frankford abandons his sacrilegious presumption when he admits that he too has a redeemer, and when he says:

> Even as I hope for pardon at that day
> When the Great Judge of Heaven in scarlet sits,
> So be thou pardoned.

(xvii.105–107)

But to assume that Frankford has received a tragic insight is to miss his single-mindedness.

Cook maintains that "It is Frankford's realization of his own wrongness which makes the final packed climax of the play,"[24] and "Frankford's inadequacy is transfigured in self-realization." However, I can see nothing in the last scene which indicates that Frankford realizes his mistake. He is simply pleased with Anne's repentance, and is willing to forgive her.

> Though thy rash offence
> Divorc'd our bodies, thy repentant tears
> Unite our souls.

(xvii.107–109)

---

24. *Ibid.*, p. 362.

He rewards her penance for her sin against him with a kiss, symbolic of their remarriage, and acknowledges that her purification is complete:

> Though thou art wounded in thy honour'd name,
> And with that grief upon thy deathbed liest,
> Honest in heart, upon my soul, thou diest.
>
> (xvii.118–120)

Sir Francis points out that a conventional treatment of Anne would not have effected "such true sorrow," and Frankford agrees: "I see it had not" (l. 136). In other words, he thinks his method of dealing with Anne's sin was both carefully considered and successful. He carries out his plan to kill Anne with kindness right up to the last line of the play, when he composes her epitaph.

To summarize, Frankford's novel judgment has pretentions to charity. But because it is unusual, we must evaluate it in terms of the charity offered in the play as a possible method of dealing with sins of passion. We learn from Sir Charles and Sir Francis that punishment for a sin can be too severe and that one can carry the notion of honor too far, and the parallels with the main plot confirm our suspicion that Frankford is not a tragic figure but a despicable one. Heywood has come as close as he could to extolling the virtues of Christian forgiveness before the current practices of his society and the conventions of the theaters. To assume that Frankford has acted either wisely or well, or even kindly, would be to misread the lesson of the subplot.[25]

25. I would like to thank Mr. Mark Stavig and Mr. R. W. Van Fossen for their valuable comments on earlier drafts of this paper.

Religion in Massinger's
The Maid of Honour

PETER F. MULLANY

PHILIP MASSINGER's *The Maid of Honour* (c. 1625), based on a story from Painter's *Palace of Pleasure,* combines a romantic plot concerning the hero's love for a virtuous heroine with a humours subplot parodying the main action. The romantic complication, or "blocking agent,"[1] is provided chiefly by the hero's vow of celibacy as a member of the Knights of Malta,[2] while in the subplot a Signior Sylli vows that he shall not marry a woman unless she can resist his beauty for a month. *The Maid of Honour,* together with *The Virgin Martyr* and *The Renegado,* has often been taken to illustrate Massinger's interest in religion, particularly Roman Catholicism, because in each of these plays there is a main plot

---

1. Northrop Frye, *Anatomy of Criticism* (Princeton, 1957), p. 165.

2. The founding of the Knights of Malta in 1099 in Jerusalem, their dedication to the service of the poor and of pilgrims, and their adoption of the Augustinian rule with a habit consisting of a black robe with an eight pointed cross is summarized in E. J. King's, *The Grand Priory of the Order of the Hospital of St. John of Jerusalem in England: A Short History* (London, 1924), pp. 1–11. See also Elizabeth Wheeler Schermerhorn, *On the Trail of the Eight Pointed Cross: A Study of the Knights Hospitallers in Feudal Europe* (New York, 1940), pp. 1–13.

based on religious experience and because they are suffused throughout with numerous religious references.[3] Critics have also taken these plays to represent Massinger's serious moral concerns and his didactic bent. Professor T. A. Dunn in his study of Massinger speaks of the playwright's orthodoxy and conservatism: "His standpoint in all his plays is that of a morality unquestioned and venerable, and behind all his morality lie the generally unstated but undeniable sanctions of Christianity."[4] Such judgments have their basis in the explicit moralizing that pervades Massinger's plays. Paris in *The Roman Actor,* for instance, is believed to profess what essentially was Massinger's view of the purpose of drama when he argues along well-established lines defending the drama against Puritan attacks:

> But, 'tis urged
> That we corrupt youth, and traduce superiors.
> When do we bring a vice upon the stage,
> That goes off unpunish'd? Do we teach,
> By the success of wicked undertakings,
> Others to tread in their forbidden steps?
> We show no arts of Lydian panderism,
> Corinthian poisons, Persian flatteries,
> But mulcted so in the conclusion, that
> Even those spectators that were so inclined,
> Go home changed men.
>
> (I.iii) [5]

Throughout his plays Massinger does homage to such sentiments as those expressed by Paris by safely moralizing his conclusions in a rich

3. W. Gifford first stated that Massinger was a Catholic in the introduction to his edition of *The Plays of Philip Massinger,* 4 vols. (London, 1805), I, ix.

4. *Philip Massinger: The Man and the Playwright* (London, 1957), p. 177. Dunn concludes as follows: "What does seem to emerge quite clearly from the plays is that, Anglican or Roman Catholic, Massinger had a respectful tolerance in matters of faith rare in his century. He was never polemical or satirical or flippant where religion was concerned. He respected piety, devotion, and sincerity; he abhorred impiety, blasphemy, and sham" (p. 191). Cf. also A. H. Cruickshank, *Philip Massinger* (London, 1920), p. 3; and Maurice Chelli, *Le Drame de Massinger* (Lyon, 1923), pp. 328 ff.

5. *The Plays of Philip Massinger,* ed. W. Gifford, 3rd ed. (London, 1850). All citations are to this edition in which line numbers are not indicated.

dispensation of poetic justice.[6] In *The Maid of Honour* the religious conflicts, the moral stances, and the concluding apotheosis of the heroine reveal Massinger's kinship with his frequent collaborator John Fletcher. The moral dilemmas in *The Maid of Honour* are exploited for the same theatrical ends that characterize Fletcherian tragicomedy; they are not really indicative of Massinger's moral earnestness. To assert that "In *The Maid of Honour* religion is presented as the most important matter in life"[7] indicates a serious response to dramatic material which I believe was intended to move audiences, but hardly to persuade them of religion's significance.

Set in fourteenth-century Sicily, *The Maid of Honour* presents the common tragicomic clash between love and honor, here particularized in the opposition between passion and a religious vow of celibacy and by the inequality in rank of the central figures. Bertoldo, a Knight of Malta, is rejected by Camiola at first because of his vow and their different ranks. However, later in the play Camiola professes affection for Bertoldo. In a surprising theatrical coup she then reverses this position and renounces the world to enter a convent. Meanwhile Bertoldo returns to his order, presumably with a renewed dedication to celibacy. The intricacies of this romantic plot are set against a pseudo-historical background of contending factions and political alliances in Sicily which gives a semblance of actuality to the highly improbable events of the Bertoldo-Camiola affair. Roberto, Bertoldo's brother and the king of Sicily, is pictured at first as a stern ruler whose political schemes extend so far as to refuse to ransom Bertoldo from captivity and suffering, but ultimately they too are reconciled.

The love plot of *The Maid of Honour* is further thickened by three

6. The general critical response to Massinger's "moral earnestness" is indicated in the following works: Thomas M. Parrott and Robert H. Ball, *A Short View of Elizabethan Drama* (New York, 1958), pp. 256 ff.; Benjamin Townley Spencer, "Philip Massinger," in *Seventeenth Century Studies,* ed. Robert Shafer (Princeton, 1933), pp. 3–119; Philip Edwards, "Massinger the Censor," in *Essays on Shakespeare and Elizabethan Drama in Honor of Hardin Craig,* ed. Richard Hosley (Columbia, Mo., 1962), pp. 341–350. A. L. Bennett, "The Moral Tone of Massinger's Dramas," *Papers on Language and Literature,* II (1966), 207–216, surveys nineteenth-century attitudes and concludes that while Massinger revealed a sound moral vision in his satires, his turning to romantic tragi-comedy caused this vision to become unclear.

7. Spencer, "Philip Massinger," p. 75.

contrasting suits for Camiola's hand waged by humour figures. Roberto's minion, Fulgentio, is the conventional court sycophant whose shining exterior cloaks his inner corruption. After his true nature has been revealed and after Camiola has rejected him, it is her mercy that saves him from ruin and reconciles him to Roberto. Adorni, on the other hand, is the traditional faithful follower who loves Camiola nobly at a distance and who must serve against himself in his embassy to Bertoldo from Camiola. Camiola's third suitor is Signior Sylli, who is foolishly possessed by the humour that his beauty is an irresistible temptation to females. A reverse parody of the conventional romantic heroine, Signior Sylli imposes the conditions and trials prior to the winning of his hand. His vow that none shall marry him until they resist his charms for a month is a ridiculous parallel to Bertoldo's sacred vow. The comic humor and the occasional bawdiness of this plot may be seen not only as a contrast in situation but also as a contrast in tone to the major romantic emphasis of the play.

Massinger structures *The Maid of Honour* in the Beaumont and Fletcher manner; surprise, reversal, and emotional climaxes are his dramatic goals. A hypothetical situation serves here, as in the Beaumont and Fletcher tragicomedies, to provide a seemingly real dramatic conflict which is so manipulated that we are led through a series of theatrical highpoints to the surprising denouement which dispels the initial hypothesis. Bertoldo's vow of celibacy as a member of the Knights of Malta, references to the divine right of kings, the appearance of Paulo, Camiola's confessor, and the numerous verbal allusions to religion provide the audience a counter by which they may juxtapose their world with the dramatic world. Massinger deliberately makes it appear that the emotional crises of his characters involve problems testing religious commitments because he seeks to engage his audience in an emotional response to situations which are unreal. In *The Maid of Honour* this stock dramatic counter of religion is used to move audiences emotionally in situations which are basically analogous to the continued moments of theatrical and rhetorical excitement in *A King and No King,* wherein Fletcher leads us to believe that incest is at the heart of the play's conflict and then dissolves this hypothesis by means of a fortuitous conclusion. In an analogous manner, with the ostensible religious concerns of *The Maid of Honour* Massinger asks for serious responses to materials which he has not taken very seriously, for they are no more than the means to sensationalist ends.

The Maid of Honour begins with a series of contrasts revealing Bertoldo's honor, King Roberto's desire for peace, and Fulgentio's unsavory favor with Roberto. These contrasts are heightened throughout Act I by the rhetorical arguments urging the rival claims of justice and mercy, military honor, and peaceful content as Bertoldo tries to convince his brother to help Ferdinand, Duke of Urbin, who, having conquered Siena in a desperate attempt to win the Duchess Aurelia, now stands in peril of attack by Gonzaga, a Knight of Malta and leader of Aurelia's forces. The intensity of tone characterizing the clear-cut opposition of Bertoldo and Roberto is revealed by a lengthy speech in which Bertoldo castigates court vices and reminds his brother that Sicily, like England, must go beyond her borders to achieve true greatness. Roberto, displeased by Bertoldo, grants that volunteers may join his brother in an expedition to Siena, but he refuses to give them any aid. Bertoldo, a Hotspur-like man of action, thus succeeds to some extent in his first rhetorical encounter.

Scene ii turns from political wars to the personal war of passion and reason, love and honor. Again Massinger structures the scene by presenting a clash between antithetical positions. Bertoldo maintains his love for Camiola, but she argues on grounds of honor against his suit. The symmetry with scene i where Bertoldo argued honor's cause is apparent except that now he reverses positions to press his passion. Prior to his entrance Camiola delivers a soliloquy which reveals the conflicts that are to be worked out later in their confrontation:

> Camiola, if ever, now be constant:
> This is, indeed, a suitor, whose sweet presence,
> Courtship, and loving language would have stagger'd
> The chaste Penelope; and to increase
> The wonder, did not modesty forbid it,
> I should ask that from him he sues to me for:
> And yet my reason, like a tyrant, tells me
> I must nor give nor take it.
>
> (I.ii)

Her speech conceals for the moment the particular reasons why she must resist Bertoldo's suit because Massinger wishes to exploit them for surprise and climactic ends. He builds the scene to points of maximum intensity as

Camiola first tells Bertoldo that disparity in rank, a conventional "block-ing agent" of romance stories, prevents their union although she acknowl-edges Bertoldo's preeminent virtues. She then reveals the greatest obstacle to their love:

> . . . the stronger bar,
> Religion, stops our entrance: you are, sir,
> A Knight of Malta, by your order bound
> To a single life; you cannot marry me;
> And, I assure myself, you are too noble
> To seek me, though my frailty should consent,
> In a base path.
>
> (I.ii)

This revelation comes as a surprise, for until now Bertoldo's vow has not even been mentioned. He immediately proposes a dispensation from his vow, but Camiola shuts the door on this possibility by remaining constant to reason and honor:

> When what is vowed to heaven is dispensed with,
> To serve our ends on earth, a curse must follow,
> And not a blessing.
>
> (I.ii)

Bowing beneath Camiola's "irrevocable" decision, Bertoldo parts from his "fairest cruel" to serve the cause of honor in military action. Throughout this scene, then, Massinger uses religion to impose an air of seriousness on the theatrical legerdemain, since ostensibly Camiola and Bertoldo are faced with choices involving religious commitments. But, as we shall see, this religious hypothesis is the foundation upon which a series of startling reversals in character and action are constructed.

The religious character of membership in the Knights of Malta is particularly evident in Act II when Gonzaga, after defeating Bertoldo's forces at Siena, recognizes Bertoldo as a fellow member of the sacred order. Gonzaga quickly reverses his earlier praise of Bertoldo's military prowess to denounce him for breaking faith with the sacred rule. Gonza-ga's impassioned rhetoric builds to the scene's high point when he tears the cross from Bertoldo's robe and has him put in prison.[8] Sworn to guard

---

8. Historically the rule of the Order called for this serious penalty whenever a Knight turned from fighting an enemy in a just war. On this point see E. J. King, *The Grand Priory* . . . , p. 11. In *The Knight of Malta* (1618) by Fletcher,

ladies from oppression, Bertoldo's violation of his vow makes his sufferings doubly great. In Act I his vow separated him from Camiola, while in Act II his pursuit of military honor leads him into further violation of his vow. Either horn of Bertoldo's dilemma impales him because both involve a parallel offense against the rule of the Knights of Malta. Massinger develops things then so that Bertoldo at the end of both Acts I and II suffers a defeat. His vow with its special obligations is the chief cause for Bertoldo's plight, and Massinger withholds this vital information until the end of each act in order to build to a surprising and exciting climax.[9]

Camiola in Act II appears in a situation parallel to her scene with Bertoldo in Act I. Fulgentio, Roberto's minion, supposing that Bertoldo's absence removes all obstacles, comes to woo Camiola. The gift of a ring from Roberto, Fulgentio believes, will command Camiola's affection. The situation provides an antithetical contrast to the noble suit of Bertoldo since Camiola abhors Fulgentio as a canker in the state, a view confirmed by his bawdiness and ultimate resort to invoking the King's authority to force Camiola to yield. Camiola, however, firmly states that the King cannot command her mind in a base path, and she rejects Fulgentio. Signior Sylli, meanwhile, takes comfort in Fulgentio's rejection and believes it to be sure proof of Camiola's affection for him; this parallels exactly his reaction to Bertoldo's rejection in Act I. In addition Adorni, a silent admirer of Camiola, overhears her claim that Bertoldo, if he were at home, would revenge the insults of Fulgentio, and so Adorni decides to take the task upon himself. In terms of dramatic structure Acts I and II are strikingly similar; both contrast the main plot and subplot by use of antithetical actions sharply contrasting love, nobility, and honor with the court virtue of Fulgentio and the foolish pretensions of Sylli. Both acts are also schematically arranged, dividing attention between the pseudo-historical military events and the conflicting suits for Camiola's favor.

Inconsistency of character is a staple ingredient of *The Maid of Honour,* since Massinger, seizing at every opportunity for rhetorical pyrotechnics, is concerned with contriving exciting situations. In Act III Camiola

---

Massinger, and Field, the villain Mountferrat harbors so great a lust that the sacred cross of the Order falls off his robe in horror, and at the end of the play he is formally expelled from membership.

9. On this as a standard feature of Massinger's dramaturgy see Dunn, *Philip Massinger,* p. 57.

charges Adorni with ambition after he defeats Fulgentio in a duel and hopes thereby to win Camiola's favor. Immediately thereafter, though, Camiola ignores considerations of rank to assist Bertoldo, who has been imprisoned and denied ransom by the King. The moving rhetoric of her speech elicits sympathy for an action which she now judges honorable:

> O more than impious times! when not alone
> Subordinate ministers of justice are
> Corrupted and seduced, but kings themselves,
> The greater wheels by which the lesser move,
> Are broken, or disjointed! could it be, else,
> A king, to soothe his politic ends, should so far
> Forsake his honour, as at once to break
> The adamant chains of nature and religion,
> To bind up atheism, as a defense
> To his dark counsels? . . .
>
>   O, my Bertoldo,
> Thou only sun in honour's sphere, how soon
> Art thou eclipsed and darken'd! not the nearness
> Of blood prevailing on the king; nor all
> The benefits to the general good dispens'd,
> Gaining a retribution! But that
> To owe a courtesy to a simple virgin
> Would take from the deserving, I find in me
> Some sparks of fire, which, fann'd with honour's breath,
> Might rise into a flame, and in men darken
> Their usurp'd splendor. Ha! my aim is high,
> And, for the honour of my sex, to fall so,
> Can never prove inglorious.

(III.iii)

Camiola's problem in Act III parallels Bertoldo's in Act I; she places herself against Roberto's will in an attempt to rescue Bertoldo from captivity, much as he tried earlier to rescue Ferdinand. Her sudden shift from the constant maintenance of her decision to reject Bertoldo because of his rank and his vow of celibacy to a course of action prompted by love indicates Massinger's desire to avoid exploring the serious implications of such a decision so that he can exploit the theatrical potential of Camiola's passion.

Throughout Act IV Massinger develops a series of complications conse-quent to Bertoldo's ransom by Camiola which further delay their anticipated union. In Adornis' presence Bertoldo willingly swears to the solemn contract binding him to marry Camiola and says that such was ever the aim of his ambition:

> Swear it! Collect all oaths and imprecations,
> Whose least breach is damnation, and those
> Minister'd to me in a form more dreadful;
> Set heaven and hell before me, I will take them;
> False to Camiola! never.
>
> (IV.iii)

Rhetorically Bertoldo intensifies his commitment to Camiola by pledging her a religious devotion: "I'll build to thee / An altar in my soul, on which I'll offer / A still-increasing sacrifice of duty." In a rhetoric charged with hyperboles of passion, Massinger once again carefully dwells on the extreme commitment of love in order that he may later exploit by contrast the reverse of what is stated here. The variety of emotional tones sounded here is a deliberate part of the recurring balance and contrast in situation, character, and statement in *The Maid of Honour;* the reversals of Act IV, as we shall see, make this singularly apparent.

The return of Aurelia, the Duchess, to Siena introduces new complications to the Bertoldo-Camiola affair. After pardoning Ferdinand, Aurelia asks to see Bertoldo who, as Gonzaga reminds her, injured her in violation of his vow to defend ladies. Aurelia, though, is suddenly smitten with Bertoldo and makes him her prisoner of love, despite comments on her wantonness. She justifies her sudden change from a long-standing reserve toward men by asserting that her majesty places her above censure and therefore allows the "violence of her passions." Bertoldo too undergoes a sudden reversal:

> No, no; it cannot be:—yet, but Camiola
> There is no step between me and a crown.
> Then all my ingratitude! a sin in which
> All sins are comprehended! Aid me, Virtue,
> Or I am lost.
>
> (IV.iv)

In this tragicomic world of slippery ethics, it is to be expected that Bertoldo should violate his sacred promise to Camiola in an ambitious quest for a crown. Massinger has already provided thematic exposition on the subject of ambition in Camiola's upbraiding of Adorni for aspiring to her love. Thereby he has prepared audiences to respond appropriately here to Bertoldo's action. Bertoldo's reversal is mirrored further in Adorni, who now hopes that Bertoldo's fall will elevate him in Camiola's favor. For the third time in the play then, Bertoldo has violated a sacred obligation. In the first instance, his love of Camiola violated the vow to his order; in the second instance, his aid of Ferdinand violated his obligation as a Knight of Malta to defend ladies from oppression. Now Bertoldo, joined to Camiola by the terms of the marriage contract, rushes from her in an ungrateful and ambitious alliance with Aurelia.

Meanwhile, in Act IV, scene v, Camiola confronts King Roberto and rejects his attempt to force Fulgentio upon her, insisting that she owes his sacred person no allegiance. She maintains that it is not the prerogative of kings to compel affections, because such action is tyranny. Her argument has been taken as an indication of Massinger's political thinking and of his attitude toward the person of the King. Benjamin Townley Spencer summarizes Massinger's general political thought in the following words:

The Prince is to be educated in a generally liberal way as well as in the specific points of statesmanship. Though not directly appointed by God, his majesty is sacred, and no individual may justifiably assassinate him. Yet he must conform to moral and Divine laws. Rather than giving the prince unlimited freedom in his actions, the office of Kingship indeed restricts him; for, obligated to his people, he must restrain personal desire for the good of the state. He must beware of the favourite, and must not depend to a great extent on the counsellor. Although war is often nationally beneficial in counterbalancing the decay of luxury, a policy of peace is generally advisable.[10]

Massinger in *The Maid of Honour,* as well as in other plays such as *The Emperor of the East, The Bondman, The Great Duke of Florence,* and *The Roman Actor,* makes special use of the commonplace of divine right.[11] Here he has Camiola impose a common limitation upon royal power in a scene that presents an argument between King and subject. Roberto, who has come to punish Camiola's disobedience, reverses himself when Camiola argues:

10. "Philip Massinger," p. 119. Cf. also pp. 91-119.
11. Dunn, *Philip Massinger,* pp. 163-176. Allen Gross, "Contemporary Politics in Massinger," *SEL,* VI (1966), 279-290, has maintained that Massinger's plays do not include specific political allusions.

> Say, you should love wine,
> You being the king, and, 'cause I am your subject,
> Must I be ever drunk? Tyrants, not kings,
> By violence, from humble vassals force
> The liberty of their souls. I could not love him;
> And to compel affection, as I take it,
> Is not found in your prerogative.
>
> (IV.v)

This argument convinces Roberto to reform, and thereupon he sentences Fulgentio to death for spreading malicious lies against Camiola with the condition that only Camiola's plea for mercy can possibly save him.

Massinger's use of divine right with its religious implications and the religious references throughout Camiola's speeches provide the necessary stimulus for the stirring scene. Divine right is called upon as the means to another theatrical highlight—Roberto's reversal. Camiola's concluding sententious couplet provides a specious moral for the events:

> Happy are subjects, when the prince is still
> Guided by justice, not his passionate will.
>
> (IV.v)

Although this scene illustrates such transformation, Massinger's dramatic intention is not to explore the human significance of divine right, but to exploit a political and religious commonplace so as to give an appearance of seriousness to a scene constructed exactly like those which have gone before. Here, as elsewhere, Massinger's dramatic end is the use of a sudden reversal of character in order to structure rhetorically exciting confrontations.

Signior Sylli in the final act is quickly rid of his humour because he breaks his oath and attempts to kiss Camiola. With this ridiculous suitor disposed of, Camiola then hears Adorni's report of Bertoldo's return with the Duchess of Siena. Adorni accuses Bertoldo of ingratitude and perjury, and Camiola, repeating her earlier accusation of Adorni, now charges him with malice for taking joy in Bertoldo's inconstancy. Her speech, laden with religious references, sustains the religious atmosphere of the play and the appearance that religious issues and problems are the dramatic concern:

> In this you confess
> The devilish malice of your disposition.

As you were a man, you stood bound to lament it;
And not, in flattery of your false hopes,
To glory in it. When good men pursue
The path mark'd out by virtue, the blessed saints
With joy look on it, and seraphic angels
Clap their celestial wings in heavenly plaudits,
To see a scene of grace so well presented,
The fiends, and men made up of envy, mourning.
Whereas now, on the contrary, as far
As their divinity can partake of passion,
With me they weep, beholding a fair temple,
Built in Bertoldo's loyalty, turn'd to ashes
By the flames of his inconstancy, the damn'd
Rejoicing in the object.—'Tis not well
In you Adorni.

(V.v)

Camiola decides to pursue the justice of her contract with Bertoldo and to force him to marry her.[12] Thus after having argued so vigorously against Roberto's attempt to constrain her affections, she is placed in a new situation and resorts to her own form of constraint. Massinger, omitting any interest in Bertoldo's violation of his religious vow by entering into the contract, instead concentrates on the dramatic possibilities inherent in Camiola's quest for justice. She pleads her case before Roberto, whom she reminds of his obligation to dispense justice impartially. Her history of Bertoldo's abject fortunes and her payment of his ransom refute all arguments against her claim. Charging Bertoldo with "barbarous ingratitude" and "ambitious hopes" to win Aurelia, Camiola's passionate denunciation wins the admiration of the court and elicits sympathy for her fortunes.

After all obstacles to marriage have been removed, the anticipated ending is averted in a surprising close. Bertoldo, admitting his guilt, wins Camiola's forgiveness, but she says to him:

You have been false once. I have done: and if,
When I am married, as this day I will be,

12. Bertoldo's promise would be tantamount to marriage, requiring only the religious ceremony to make final the intent expressed before Adorni. Cf. Ernest Schanzer, "The Marriage Contracts in *Measure for Measure*," *ShS*, XIII (1960), 81–88.

> As a perfect sign of your atonement with me,
> You wish me joy, I will receive it for
> Full satisfaction of all obligations
> In which you stand bound to me.

(V.ii)

With Bertoldo's rejection, Camiola's announcement of her impending marriage introduces a new note of suspense. Hope is even stirred anew in Signior Sylli's breast by Camiola's words. Aurelia states her own and the audience's bewilderment: "For my part / I cannot guess the issue." Then in a culminating surprise Father Paulo, Camiola's confessor, enters and seizes her for religion. Camiola "marries" into a life of prayers as she says "I am dead to the world. . . ." She bestows a portion of her estate on the faithful Adorni, wins pardon for Fulgentio, and finally restores Bertoldo to his order. Gonzaga returns the white cross to Bertoldo, and Bertoldo promises to live forever a member of the Knights of Malta.

The symmetry of acts and scenes, the recurrent use of surprise and reversal, the impassioned rhetoric of protean characters, and the conflicting opposites make *The Maid of Honour* a play clearly in the manner of the characteristic Beaumont and Fletcher tragicomedy.[13] Massinger's dramatic intention, like that of Beaumont and Fletcher in *A King and No King,* is to create theatrical excitement in an improbable and escapist drama whose aim is not to explore human motives and action. The seeming reality of *The Maid of Honour* provided by the religious atmosphere and the conflicting loyalties dissolves upon examination of the play's structure. Massinger writes to create the exciting moment and the stirring scene, not the well-developed plot of a purposeful narrative. Religion lends an aura of seriousness and suggests the capacity for choice by characters facing dilemmas. However, as we have seen, this is no more than the means to theatrical excitement and moving rhetoric. Indeed the conclusion with all of its overtly religious fireworks clearly indicates Massinger's constant use of surprise and the way in which he builds up to the big moments in each act. Camiola's "marriage" comes as a surprise, an effect won by having her enter the convent. To speak of Camiola's

13. Eugene Waith, *The Pattern of Tragicomedy in Beaumont and Fletcher* (New Haven, 1952), pp. 36–42. The Fletcherian element in Massinger and his anticipation of Restoration drama are treated by James G. McManaway, "Philip Massinger and the Restoration Drama," *ELH,* I (1934), 276–304.

renunciation of the world in terms of human motivation for such action, or to discover in it serious moral and religious significance [14] reveals a failure to recognize the artificial nature of the play and the artifice of religion in it. Characters in *The Maid of Honour* are types; they possess whatever motives lead to theatrical and emotional excitement. Shifting from one extreme to the other, but never developing, these characters are mouthpieces for the moral and religious issues that suggest serious concern but in reality serve only to excite, to move, and to thrill. Eliot's remarks on romantic drama are especially applicable to *The Maid of Honour:*

The debility of romantic drama does not depend upon extravagant setting, or preposterous events, or inconceivable coincidences; all these might be found in a serious tragedy or comedy. It consists in an internal incoherence of feelings, a concatenation of emotions which signifies nothing.[15]

Religion, then, is Massinger's dramatic means to a brilliant display of heightened and conflicting emotions in *The Maid of Honour;* it has no other real significance.

14. Such a reading may be found in Philip Edwards, "Massinger the Censor," p. 346. Mr. Edwards finds Camiola's conception of honor "austere and stern," but "consistent." For another view of Camiola's decision as an example of religious exaltation, see Chelli, *Le Drame de Massinger,* pp. 332–338.

15. "Philip Massinger," in *Essays on Elizabethan Drama* (New York, 1956). p. 154.

Love, Lust, and Sham: Structural Pattern in the Plays of John Ford

JULIET McMASTER

C RITICISM OF THE PLAYS of John Ford has nearly always been restricted to his main plots. In their attitude toward his subplots and comic sequences, his critics seldom go beyond a tacit wish that he had not written them,[1] or at most an acknowledgment that his baser characters sometimes act as foils to the noble ones.[2] I do not intend to defend Ford's frequently maladroit attempts at comedy nor the distorted melodrama of such plots as those concerned with Ferentes in *Love's Sacrifice* or Hippolita in *'Tis Pity She's a Whore;* nevertheless, his plays are worth considering as whole units, because it is evident that he was consciously using a structural pattern which he intended to have thematic significance. Not just once, but repeatedly, Ford bases the structure of his plays on a pattern of

---

1. See, e.g., H. J. Oliver, *The Problem of John Ford* (Melbourne, 1955): "One can only wish that [Ford] had had the courage of his convictions and had omitted the comic relief altogether" (p. 57).

2. E.g., Clifford Leech, *John Ford and the Drama of His Time* (London, 1957), p. 15. G. F. Sensabaugh, however, has pointed out Ford's use of subplots about lust as a contrast to his main plots about love. "John Ford and Elizabethan Tragedy," *PQ,* XX (1941), 442–453.

contrasts between kinds of sexual relationships, each kind being handled separately in the main plot or one of the subplots.

Nearly all his plays have a triple plot. The main one is always seriously if not tragically conducted; the secondary one may be wholly serious or partly comic as well, and it is frequently somewhat melodramatic; the tertiary plot, often concerned with the treatment and cure of a humour character, is always comic. Sometimes, as in *Love's Sacrifice,* these three elements of the story are so distinct that the play seems in danger of falling apart. The typical way in which these plots are related to each other is by contrasts between love, lust, and sham love.

The relationship of the main plot is love proper, between the hero and the heroine. Ford conceives such love as the greatest and most irresistible of the passions: but it is irresistible only up to a point. The hero and the heroine cannot help feeling desire for each other, or declaring it; but they can and must control themselves in its physical fulfilment. The formula, True Love equals Desire plus Control, determines the mood of many of Ford's dramatic situations and makes him distinctively the dramatist of frustration.[3] It is also worth noticing that the love relationship of the main plot is always serious, regardless of whether the play is nominally a tragedy or a comedy. Shakespeare's lovers—Biron, Orlando, even Romeo —are figures we can laugh at, at least occasionally. But though *The Lover's Melancholy* is supposedly a comedy, we are scarcely permitted to smile at Palador, let alone at Orgilus or Fernando.

Lust, in a more or less acute form, is the typical relationship of the secondary plot. Desire is again the main element, though usually there is less than in true love, but of course control lapses, and there is a corresponding lapse in dramatic intensity: Ford is not particularly good at conveying the sort of sexual appetite we see in Falstaff or Marston's insatiate countess Isabella. None of the characters of Ford's main plots would be capable of a second love; but the characters moved by lust typically have three different liaisons in the course of the play. This emphasis on quantity can be amusing, and the secondary plots sometimes include some sour humor. They also contain what is characteristically lacking in the main plots—action and denouement. Ford is chiefly concerned with situation rather than process, and in his main plots he usually

3. For a treatment of the theme of frustration in Ford's plays, see Alan Brissenden, "Impediments to Love: a Theme in John Ford," *RD,* VII (1964), 95–102.

presents a situation that has already developed before the play begins and proceeds by a series of agonized tableaux in which his characters are seen in passion rather than action.[4] But the secondary plot is the level for action —often, indeed, for melodrama. Here the conflict of desire and continence gives way to motives of outraged vanity and revenge as well as sexual passion. Ferentes is ritually murdered by the three women he has dishonored; Levidolche employs her own husband to revenge her lover's rejection; Hippolita tries to poison her faithless lover at his wedding but is tricked into taking the fatal cup herself and dies cursing and in agony.

The tertiary plot is not really concerned with desire at all; but its basis is nearly always a satire on the love convention. The lover's appearance and behavior had become so formalized—what with the "folded arms and melancholy hat,"[5] the green and yellow complexion, the "bonnet un-banded" and "sleeve unbuttoned" that Rosalind talks of, the sighing, the gazing on pictures, the compulsive versifying and so forth—that Marston, for instance, could give the stage direction *"Isabella falls in love"* and expect the actor to be able to convey this to the audience's satisfaction.[6] And the emotion that an actor can convey by a standard set of gestures is suspect: hence Ford's satiric tertiary plots, which are designed to set off the reality of the love in the main plot by presenting a love that is merely appearance. The personnel of this level of the story—Cuculus in *The Lover's Melancholy,* Bergetto in *'Tis Pity,* Mauruccio in *Love's Sacrifice,* and Guzman and Fulgoso in *The Lady's Trial*—are the votaries of Dan Cupid, "Regent of love-rhymes, lord of folded arms"; they wear the uniform and adopt the pose of the lover, without being dignified by love or even lust. Their "love," of which they constantly prate, is all sham, because in fact the only person each loves is himself. They are caricatures of the love convention, extremes either of conformity, like Cuculus, or nonconformity, like Bergetto and Fulgoso. Indeed, one reason for the failure of Ford's comic attempts is that he evidently feels more contempt

4. See Una Ellis-Fermor, "John Ford," *The Jacobean Drama* (London, 1936).

5. The tag that described Ford in William Hemminge's *Elegy on Randolph's Finger* (London, 1659); but the pose and garb are traditional, as testified by Burton's illustration of the lover in the frontispiece of *The Anatomy of Melancholy.*

6. *The Insatiate Countess,* Act II, scene i. See Lawrence Babb, "The Lover's Malady in Elizabethan Literature," *The Elizabethan Malady* (East Lansing, Mich., 1951).

than sympathy for his comic characters. Just as he cannot smile at his main characters, so he cannot see any potential for pathos in his buffoons. Bergetto is the only one of them who really does fall in love, and he is perhaps the one who comes nearest to being funny.[7]

Love's Sacrifice is the play that exemplifies this typical structural pattern most clearly. The main plot is concerned with the tragic love of Fernando and Bianca; the secondary with the tragicomic lust of Ferentes; and the tertiary with the comic humor of Mauruccio, who turns courtier and lover in his old age.

The central love of Fernando and Bianca is the one for which our sympathy is enlisted; and though it is adulterous, since Bianca is married to the Duke Caraffa, Fernando's friend, Ford intends it to be taken as a deep and admirable kind of love. Fernando's passion may be violent, it may override all the reasons he himself can urge against it, yet he can claim when he pleads his cause that his love is chaste:

> And do not think that I have cull'd this time
> From motion's swiftest measure to unclasp
> The book of lust: if purity of love
> Have residence in virtue's breast, lo here,
> Bent lower in my heart than on my knee,
> I beg compassion to a love as chaste
> As softness of desire can intimate.
>
> (II. iii, p. 47) [8]

This is an avowal that I believe Ford means us to accept; and it is true not only of Fernando but of all the lovers in the main plots of his plays (with the notable exception of Giovanni and Annabella in *'Tis Pity She's a Whore*). Their passion, we are to understand, is great, but is matched by their ability to control it. Even when Bianca comes to Fernando's bed in her nightdress and offers herself to him, he can prove the purity of his love by not taking the body which she swears she will kill after the act.

> Heaven forbid that I
> Should by a wanton appetite profane

7. T. S. Eliot singles out the subplot concerned with Bergetto as the least bad of Ford's comic sequences. "John Ford," *Selected Essays* (London, 1932). The depiction of Guzman in *The Lady's Trial* sometimes achieves humor.

8. *The Works of John Ford,* ed. W. Gifford, with additions by A. Dyce, 3 vols. (London, 1895). All quotations are from this edition.

> This sacred temple! 'tis enough for me
> You'll please to call me servant.
> . . . I'll master passion, and triumph
> In being conquer'd.

(II. iv, pp. 53–54)

Fernando cannot help his love for his friend's wife, and being in love, he cannot help speaking. Ford makes it clear that he is acting under compulsion up to this point—he "must speak or burst" (II. i, p. 34). But when it comes to the physical consummation of the passion, Fernando can and does control himself, and this constitutes his virtue, and Bianca's.

Juxtaposed with this story of undeniable but controlled love is the story of the plain lust of Ferentes. He takes pride in being a professional seducer, at one point congratulating himself, after a successful attempt on a maid, " 'Slife! I have got the feat on't, and am every day more active in my trade" (I. ii, p. 19). During the course of the play he seduces three women, Julia, Colona, and Morona. In the main plot Fernando is silenced by Bianca's serious "Fernando, / Jest not at my calamity" (II. iv, p. 53), but in this secondary one, though lives and honors are still at stake, there is some humorous treatment. Ferentes is in the same comic category as Spenser's Squire of Dames, for his opportunities exceed his capabilities. We are evidently meant to be amused at his sexual fatigue when he is pursued by Julia with her *"nunquam satis"* (I. ii, p. 20). And there is a grim humor in the symmetry of the revenge enacted by the three women in the dance, with their three illegitimate children brought forth as witnesses to their father's guilt.

The central figure of the tertiary plot is the senile Mauruccio. If the seat of Fernando's love is his heart, and of Ferentes' his genitals, the seat of Mauruccio's love is his tongue. He is a student of "courtship," an inventor of phrases and love conceits, a spewer-forth of rhyme, and the chief admirer of his own technique in wooing. Ingenuity is perhaps his greatest virtue as a lover. The conceit of which he is proudest is the elaborate one of having his own portrait painted with a heart-shaped mirror showing in the doublet—this to be given to his beloved, so that every time she has occasion to "cleanse her teeth, or conform the hairs of her eyebrows" (II. i, p. 32), she will see her image enthroned in his heart. But all the actual wooing he ever does is to his own looking glass, and when he is confronted with the lady of his choice he is tongue-tied. Appropriately desiccated, he can only assume the trappings of a lover, but he cannot be one. And he is entirely ridiculous.

In *The Lady's Trial* the central story is of the virtuous love of husband and wife, Auria and Spinella. He sets out to make his fortune fighting Turkish pirates abroad while, as one courtier puts it, she is left "to buffet / Land-pirates here at home" (I. i, p. 10). She is indeed attacked by the accomplished seducer, Adurni; and, as a wife who has been bereft of the marriage bed, she finds the temptation real. In the face of Adurni's importunate suit, she apostrophizes her absent husband,

> Auria, Auria,
> Fight not for name abroad; but come, my husband,
> Fight for thy wife at home!
>
> (II. iv, p. 42)

Nevertheless, she is still able to resist Adurni, and reproach him for his lack of self-control:

> How poorly some, tame to their wild desires,
> Fawn on abuse of virtue!
>
> (II. iv, p. 42)

In spite of this, however, a man who has seen her in what he considers to be a compromising situation accuses her to her husband when he returns. But Auria's steadfast faith in her matches her resolute fidelity to him.

A foil to this story is that of Levidolche, who is characterized as "a wanton" in the dramatis personae. Here, with more subtlety and delicacy than in *Love's Sacrifice,* Ford shows the alternate remorse and backsliding of a passionate but essentially weak-willed woman. Levidolche, having divorced a low-born husband to become the mistress of the lord Adurni, has finally come to prostitution and humiliation, when she encounters her husband again and remarries him with the resolution, this time believable, that this is a contract "which death only must divorce" (III. iv, p. 63).

Thirdly, there is the story of the lisping maid, Amoretta, who will not marry the deserving Trelcatio because she has exalted ideas of one day marrying a "printh" (IV. ii); and she is cured of her snobbish humor by the exasperating antics of two incongruous suitors, Guzman and Fulgoso, who have unintentionally, "like wise physicians, / Prescrib'd a healthful diet" (IV. ii, p. 77).

In fact the same pattern based on kinds of love emerges as was evident in *Love's Sacrifice*. Levidolche is not so extreme a case of lust as Ferentes, but she again is associated with three different men: Benatzi, Adurni, and Malfato. Nor is Amoretta a full parallel with Mauruccio, but her part in the play is as much concerned with satire of the love convention because of her two suitors: Fulgoso, with his elaborate expositions on courtship, and Guzman, the soldier with the tattered clothes and the breath which overcomes his beloved as it has overcome armies, respectively represent the opposite extremes of convention and boorishness in wooing.

Even *The Lover's Melancholy,* which seems more tightly constructed because of the interweaving of the love and blood relationships, exhibits much the same pattern. The primary and secondary plots are closely linked by the fact that Eroclea is a central figure in both of them; nevertheless, we can recognize that the story of how Eroclea is restored to her lover and her father is a different one from that of how Thamasta, after a deluded love for a boy who turns out to be a girl in disguise, comes to love the long-disdained Menaphon at last.

Ford is so concerned to make a statement about the chastity of the central love of Palador for Eroclea that he gives Palador a speech to conclude the fourth act, just after Eroclea has been restored to him, that is apparently unrelated to what has gone before:

> Blush, sensual follies,
> Which are not guarded with thoughts chastely pure:
> There is no faith in lust, but baits of arts;
> 'Tis virtuous love keeps clear contracted hearts.
>
> (IV. iii, p. 87)

Thamasta's passion for the boy Parthenophil, on the other hand, is something she feels she ought to resist, though she finds she has not the power; it is a passion that makes her "sensible of being traitor/ To honour and to shame" (I. iii, p. 27). Thamasta is too noble to personify lust as Ferentes personified it; but her rivalry with her own earthy serving maid and her importunate proposals to a boy far below her rank make her story that of the unbridled passion that is contrasted with the controlled love of Palador. There is not much that is humorous in Thamasta's story, but it does not have the solemnity of the main plot. She herself, still shaken by passion that moved her declaration and forced Parthenophil's revelation, can wryly comment,

> O, the powers
> Who do direct our hearts laugh at our follies!
>
> (III. ii, p. 61)

Finally, there is Cuculus, whose kinship with Mauruccio in *Love's Sacrifice* is obvious. He too is "as rare an old youth as ever walked cross-gartered" (III. i, p. 48), and he too does his wooing in rehearsal rather than in actuality. His main comic scene consists in his practicing various techniques of courtship on his servant. And his name (*cucullus non facit monarchum* is a maxim of Feste's) signifies that he wears the trappings of a lover without being one.

'Tis Pity She's a Whore at first sight seems to be a notable exception to this structural rule of setting off virtuous love with the merely conventional or the merely appetitive; for the central love in this play is not only incestuous, but it is consummated as well. However, our judgment of Giovanni and Annabella is mitigated, partly by the fatalism of the play, but also by the contrast with the figures in the subplot. I do not suggest, as some critics have done,[9] that Ford is in any sense advocating incest or condemning the mores of society that forbid it, any more than Shakespeare was advocating regicide in Macbeth. Central figures in any work of imagination, if their motivation is fully and adequately evoked, will always capture our sympathy, whether or not they have our moral approval. But here Ford is still contrasting a central love which has all the force of being an only and lasting passion (even if in this play it proves irresistible), with the merely sequential liaisons of the secondary plot. And he has made sure that Soranzo, the cuckolded husband, does not detract our attention from Giovanni and Annabella; for having debauched someone else's wife, he can hardly move us to moral indignation by his fulminations on finding his own is unchaste. So Giovanni and Annabella monopolize our sympathy, while it is Hippolita who emerges as the lustful woman: Richardetto, Soranzo, and Vasques are the trio of men in her story. In the tertiary plot, Bergetto provides comedy, not as a ridiculously conventional lover but as a ridiculously unconventional one, like Guzman in *The Lady's Trial*.

In Ford's other plays concerned with love, the same threefold plot structure emerges, but the relation between the plots is slightly different.

9. See, e.g., Sensabaugh's article, "John Ford and Elizabethan Tragedy," cited above.

The main and secondary plots of *The Broken Heart, The Fancies, Chaste and Noble,* and *The Queen* are thematic parallels to each other rather than contrasts.

As *'Tis Pity* resolves Ford's central deadlock between passion and control on the side of passion, *The Broken Heart* is the play in which control and self-denial are triumphant. Penthea, who was married forcibly to the sterile old Bassanes after being betrothed in a love match to Orgilus, steadily asserts to her desperate lover that, even should Bassanes die, she would not marry him, because

> The virgin-dowry which my birth bestow'd
> Is ravish'd by another; my true love
> Abhors to think that Orgilus deserv'd
> No better favours than a second bed.
>
> (II. iii, p. 252)

And Penthea, as her life has been a history of emotional and sexual deprivation, dies by starvation. Like her, Calantha, the central figure of the secondary plot, is unable to consummate her love, in this case because her lover is murdered just before the wedding ceremony. With stoical self-control she refrains from any emotional display when she hears the news but marries the lifeless body of Ithocles, before herself dying of the broken heart that gives the play its name.

The stories of Castamela and Flavia in *The Fancies, Chaste and Noble* are similarly parallel,[10] since each is a virtuous young woman who is arbitrarily disposed of by the man she most trusted. Again, in *The Queen,* Velasco and the Queen in their separate plots both receive first scorn and finally repentance and love from their respective partners. And in all three plays the tertiary plot is concerned with satire of some aspect of the love convention.[11]

Ford's plays are no doubt dramatically the worse for his melodramatic depictions of lust and his clumsy efforts at comedy, and it is not surprising that attempts have been made to excise these elements from editions and

---

10. See my article "Platonic Love in Ford's *The Fancies, Chaste and Noble,*" *SEL,* VII (1967), 299–309.

11. The tertiary plot is only rudimentary in *The Broken Heart.* But it certainly looks as though Ford had once intended to develop the exchange between Hemophil, Groneas, and the court ladies in Act I, scene ii, along the lines of the battle of the sexes in *Love's Labor's Lost.*

productions of the plays.[12] But an analysis of his plot structure at least reveals that he was consciously working according to a thematic pattern. This pattern has more than an aesthetic function. By his use of contrast Ford often successfully controls our response to his characters: Spinella, in *The Lady's Trial,* seems the more virtuous for resisting a man who has seduced Levidolche without difficulty, Annabella and Fernando the more excusable in their juxtaposition with Hippolita and Ferentes. In addition, Ford is at least attempting something like a complete exposition, in each play, of the various aspects of love. From the extreme of continence to the extreme of licentiousness, and from high seriousness to absurdity: this was the range that he found in sexual relationships and which he was concerned to demonstrate in the structure of his plays.

12. E.g., the Bowdlerized version of Gifford's edition, *The Dramatic Works of John Ford* (London, 1831), and Maeterlinck's translation and adaptation of *'Tis Pity,* published as *Annabella* (Paris, 1895).

Commedia dell'Arte Portraits in the McGill Feather Book

BEATRICE CORRIGAN

I

ICONOGRAPHERS of the commedia dell'arte have for some years been aware of the pictures of actors in the so-called Feather Book owned by the Wood Library of Ornithology at McGill University in Montreal.[1]

1. The following articles and books deal with or mention the Feather Book: Gerhard R. Lomer, "Feather Pictures of the *Commedia dell'Arte*," *Theatre Arts Monthly*, XIV (Sept., 1930), 807–810; John H. McDowell, "Some Pictorial Aspects of Early *Commedia dell'Arte* Acting," *Studies in Philology*, XXXIX (Jan., 1942), 47–64; George Speaight, *The History of the English Puppet Theatre* (London, 1955), pp. 16–17, 274, n. 6; "Painting with Feathers," a letter to *Country Life,* CXXIX (March 2, 1961), 457; Casey A. Wood, "Two Hitherto Unpublished Pictures of the Mauritius Dodo," *Ibis,* Ser. XII, Vol. 3 (1927), 724–732, and *An Introduction to the Literature of Vertebrate Zoology* (London, 1931), p. 446.

Allardyce Nicoll in *The World of Harlequin* (Cambridge, Eng., 1963), reproduces the pictures of actors but does not describe the book.

The only Italian scholar as far as I know who has mentioned the Feather Book is Vito Pandolfi in *La Commedia dell'Arte* (Florence, 1957–61); hereafter cited as "Pandolfi." He reproduces the pictures of Policianelo (Vol. III, to face p. 64), Baltram (Vol. III, to face p. 65), and Schapin (Vol. IV, to face p. 49), and suggests that they may be identified respectively as Silvio Fiorillo, Niccolò Barbieri, and Francesco Gabrieli. He describes the book briefly in a caption to the first picture but does not mention its location or acknowledge a source for the reproductions.

167

This volume was purchased in London in 1923 by Dr. G. R. Lomer, then the University Librarian, from the booksellers P. J. and A. E. Dobell, for the sum of £ 175. There is an unverified tradition that it had been owned previously by the dealer Tregaskis, but any earlier provenance is unknown.[2]

The Feather Book no longer exists as a volume, the leaves having been removed from the heavy oak boards covered with leather in which they were originally bound. They are now mounted separately under glass. The book contained 156 pictures, approximately 13 x 19 inches in size. Of these, 112 represent birds, depicted with their own feathers and sometimes skins, with the original beaks and claws often forming part of the composition. According to Dr. Casey A. Wood, these are probably the oldest preserved bird skins in existence.[3]

It was because of its ornithological interest that the volume was purchased by McGill, but few ornithologists seem aware of its existence, and the continuing attention of scholars has been attracted by a quite different series of pictures. Leaf 100 of the book depicts an elegantly dressed young man standing under a tree, which like himself is composed of feathers. Projecting from the tree and pointing at the young man is a sign reading LEANDER, and in the upper right hand corner of the picture is the inscription LICHOMEZI.[4] The latter word has perplexed some students of the book, but there should be no difficulty in interpreting it as LI COMICI, for very appropriately it introduces a series of fourteen pictures of characters from the commedia dell'arte, only two of which are not identified by the artist. As five of the pictures show two characters, the total number of personages portrayed in the Feather Book amounts to nineteen. Many of them bear such time-honored names as Policianelo, Schapin, and Chapitan Mata-moros, and so far scholars who have mentioned or reproduced the pictures have dealt with them only as illustrations of mask characters. Vito Pandolfi alone has attached identifications to three,[5] but I should like

2. I owe this information to the kindness of the Rare Book Librarian, Mrs. C. M. Lewis, who allowed me to examine the Library's file on the Feather Book.

3. See "Two Hitherto Unpublished Pictures of the Mauritius Dodo," and *An Introduction to the Literature of Vertebrate Zoology*.

4. This inscription is printed with ink on a lozenge-shaped strip of paper which is glued to the page.

5. See *La Commedia dell'Arte*.

LEAF 100, the McGill Feather Book. Leander

PASER·SALVTARI

DIONISIO·MINAGGIO
GIARDINERO·DE·S·E·SV
OBERNATOR·DEL·STAT
DI·MILANO·INVENTOR
ET·FECCIT·L·ANO·DEL·☩
1618

LEAF 1, the McGill Feather Book. Title page

LEAF 111, the McGill Feather Book. Actors acknowledging applause

LEAF 114, the McGill Feather Book. Chocholi

LEAF 101, the McGill Feather Book. Baltram and Trapolino

LEAF 110, the McGill Feather Book. Schapin and Speneta

LEAF 102, the McGill Feather Book. Policianelo

LEAF 84, the McGill Feather Book. Bucolic courtship

to suggest that they are all portraits of actual actors, who in nearly every case can be identified, some of them as among the leading performers of their day.

The feather title page of the book shows a tree with a life-size bird labeled *paser salutari* [*sic*] perched on a limb. Underneath the tree sits a much smaller shepherd, tending three sheep and pointing to the middle of the page where, surrounded by a tasseled border, there appears the following inscription: *Dionisio Minaggio Giardiniero di S^a. E^a. Guobernator Del Stat^o di Milano Inventor Et Feccit Lano Del 1.6.1.8.*

Dionisio Minaggio's identity remains a mystery. He was probably not an ordinary gardener but a landscape architect with a distinct talent for work in an unusual medium which I shall discuss later. He evidently was at least an amateur ornithologist and had some education. That he was not used to writing is shown, however, by the frequency of reversed *N*'s in his inscriptions and his irregularities of spelling both in Latin and Italian.

It is strange that such a record of the stage should have been executed in Milan, where ever since the days of Cardinal Carlo Borromeo the Church had opposed theatrical performances.[6] However, the comedians themselves, who found Milan a convenient stopping place on their journeys to and from France, and who were always sure of a good audience if they could secure permission to perform, were sometimes ingenious in mollifying the authorities. In this, particularly as the rigor of the Counter-Reformation diminished, they could generally rely on the support of the Spanish governors. Indeed it was a small porticoed courtyard in the Palazzo Ducale itself that was first used for open-air performances. In 1598 a roof was built over the courtyard, thus supplying the city with its first real theater.[7]

6. For the fortunes of the theater in Milan during this period, see Antonio Paglicci Brozzi, *Contributo alla storia del teatro: Il teatro a Milano nel secolo XVII* (Milano, 1891); hereafter cited as "Paglicci Brozzi."

7. *Ibid.,* p. 15, n. 1; Giorgio Riva, "Teatri paleotecnici nella Milano neotecnica," *Sipario*, No. 242 (June, 1966), p. 6. Guido Canella in *Il sistema teatrale a Milano* (Bari, 1966), pp. 25–35, says that the first Teatro di Palazzo Ducale provvisorio was built in 1594 for performances in honor of the wedding of the Contessa De Haro to the son of the Governor, Don Juan de Velasco. Four years later, when Margherita d'Austria passed through Milan on her way to wed the heir to the throne of Spain, a new theater was built, the Stabile Salone Margherita, which was used until 1698. It

In 1578 an institution for educating female orphans, the Collegio delle Vergine Spagnuole, had been founded, and in 1582 it moved to larger quarters and began to build an expensive church. By 1601 it was in such financial difficulties that it appealed to the Governor, Don Pedro Enríquez de Acevedo, Conde de Fuentes, and he granted it a percentage of the receipts from performances given in the Palazzo Ducale or elsewhere in Milan. Though this met with opposition from the City Treasurer, the Collegio secured in 1611 a monopoly of the chair and refreshment rights in all halls rented for public performances.[8] Thus the players could maintain that they made an important contribution to a charitable institution operated by a religious order, and though they still had to reckon with the prejudices and whims of changing administrations, both civil and ecclesiastic, several companies managed to establish fairly regular seasons in Milan.

Though the Feather Book is dated 1618, it must have taken at least two or three years to complete, and I should like to try to trace the affiliations and movements between approximately 1615 and 1618 of the actors whom I believe it portrays. Unfortunately few archives dealing with the theater of the period survive in Milan, but the theatrical companies concerned are so famous that they have left other records behind them.

II

The characters named in the Feather Book in alphabetical order and in the original spelling are:

BAGATINO (leaf 113)
BALTRAM (101)
Dotor CAMPANAZ (103)
CHOCHOLI (114)
CHOLA Napolitano (109)
CIETRULO (113)

---

was in the Teatrino that formed part of this Salone that the Comici performed. In 1622 the Jesuits, always ready to turn the unavoidable to profit, built the second theater in Milan in the Piazza S. Fedele.

8. Paglicci Brozzi, chap. IV; K. M. Lea, *Italian Popular Comedy* (Oxford, 1934), I, 309 (hereafter cited as "Lea").

FLAVIA (105)

FLORINDA (106)

LEANDER (100)

MARIO (105)

Chapitan MATA-MOR (108)

POLICIANELO (102)

POMBINO (107)

RICOLINA (104)

SCHAPIN (110)

SPENETA (110)

TRAPPOLINO (101)

TRASTULO (104)

The unnamed actor and actress appear on leaf 111, which indicates that they are part of the series.

FLORINDA, who stands handsome and imperious in the elaborate costume of a court lady, her hand upraised as she addresses an unseen listener on her left, was a member by marriage of one of the great theatrical families of the age and so may fittingly take precedence here over her fellow players. Born Virginia Ramponi in 1583, she married Giovan Battista Andreini in Milan in 1601 and so became the daughter-in-law of a famous acting couple who had also won acclaim as authors, Francesco and Isabella Andreini.[9] Their company, the Comici Uniti, had visited Milan that year with the special permission of the Governor,[10] and it was on this occasion that he granted to the Vergine Spagnuole the privilege I have mentioned. In 1603 Giovan Battista, who inherited the literary as well as the dramatic talent of his parents, wrote the tragedy *Florinda* which gave Virginia Ramponi her future name *nell'arte* and which launched the young couple on a career as distinguished as that of their elders. The play was published in Milan in 1606, and the author dedicated it to Don Pedro Enríquez,[11] who in the meantime had become the godfather of

9. For a full account of the Andreini family, see the *Enciclopedia dello spettacolo* and the *Dizionario biografico degli italiani*.

10. Paglicci Brozzi, p. 11.

11. Don Pedro was governor of Milan from 1600 until his death in that city in 1610, and it is evident from the repeated visits of the players during those years that he was partial to the theater. In *Florinda* the author played the part not of the heroine's husband but of her brother, Filandro. G. B. Andreini's own stage name

his child, in words which though flowery still have the ring of sincerity.

Besides her talent for acting, Virginia had a beautiful voice and a certain gift for composing verse.[12] Giovan Battista was a talented play-wright,[13] and his *Florinda,* turgid though much of its poetry is, intro-duced some interesting dramatic innovations and elicited complimentary poems not only from his wife but from Florentine poets and dramatists such as Vincenzo Panciatichi and Francesco Vinta.[14] The Feather Book unmistakably portrays Florinda in a tragic role, perhaps indeed as the eponymous heroine of her most famous play. The resemblance of the portrait of Florinda to that of the unnamed actress on leaf III encourages the supposition that the actor with her may be Lelio, the stage name of G. B. Andreini. Andreini was almost the only important *capocomico* of his day who played romantic and tragic rather than comic dialect roles, and the unlabeled feather picture may well represent Lelio and Florinda, elegantly dressed, acknowledging the applause of an audience with ges-tures of heartfelt gratitude. It would be particularly fitting that they should close the series of Li Comici, for Andreini, like his parents before him, was a great favorite in Milan, and most of his plays were performed in the theater of the Palazzo Ducale.

In 1613 Andreini visited Milan with his own company, the Fedeli and

---

was Lelio, taken from the scenario which he later turned into a comedy, *Lo Schiavetto,* first published in 1612 in Milan. In this play, Lelio is a wandering actor in search of his sister, Florinda.

12. She sang the title role in the Rinuccini-Monteverde *Arianna* when it was performed in Mantua in 1608. Mrs. Louise George Clubb has discovered in the Folger Shakespeare Library a composition by Virginia Ramponi and her husband which has until now been unmentioned by bibliographers. It is: *Il Congedo. O ver L'Addio di Florinda Comica, & humilissima serva della Sereniss. & Augustiss. Casa Gonzaga in partendo dalla Cesarea, Real servitù di Ferdinando d'Austria, e di Eleonora Gonzaga. Alla stessa sovrana Imperatrice de Florinda dedicato* (Viennae Austriae, Typis Casparis ab Rath, Bibliopolae. Anno M.DC.XXIX). Only the first composition (in prose) is by Florinda; the rest of the volume is a collection of brief *Composizioni Poetiche,* some in dramatic form, by Lelio. Florinda's beauty was famous. Complimentary verses were addressed to her by G. B. Marino, and her portrait was painted by Alessandro Allori.

13. For an estimate of his dramatic work, see the *Enciclopedia dello spettacolo,* and Lea, I, 320–327.

14. Fellow members of the Accademia Spensierata to which he had been elected, a great honor for an actor.

there performed his celebrated *Adamo,* with which Milton was familiar. Two other plays, *La Veneziana* and *La Campanaccia,* must have been composed in scenario form before 1618, since the characters for whom Andreini wrote them appear in the Feather Book. *La Veneziana,* however, in which CHOCHOLI figures, was not published until 1619, and *La Campanaccia,* the principal character in which is Dotor CAMPANAZ, not until 1627. Vito Pandolfi considers *La Veneziana* of particular historical importance because it marks the transition from the dialect Venetian comedy of the sixteenth century to the dialect comedy of Goldoni. The character of Sier Cocalin de i Cocalini da Torzelo, Academico Vizilante dito el Dormioto, was almost certainly performed by Federico Ricci, the celebrated Pantalone of the troupe, who had joined the Fedeli in 1609.[15] After spending some years in Naples he played again in Milan with Pier Maria Cecchini's Confidenti in 1616, which is probably the date of this portrait.[16] He is shown as bent, white-haired, dressed in black with the traditional Venetian black velvet cap trimmed with fur, in heel-less slippers, and carrying a pair of spectacles.

Federico Ricci's son, Benedetto,[17] is the handsome LEANDER who introduces the series of LI COMICI in the Feather Book. He shared his father's associations with various companies[18] and died in 1620 at the age of twenty-eight at Chambéry in France on his way to Paris. As his youth, good looks, and elegant costume indicate, he played the role of the *innamorato,* and his stage name appears among the characters of Andreini's *Le due commedie in commedia,* published in 1623.

Dotor CAMPANAZ was the Bolognese hero of *La Campanaccia,* the scenario of which had probably been written for Bortolomio Bongiovanni

15. Pandolfi, III, 135. In 1620 Andreini played Cocalin himself—ruefully, for he considered comic roles unworthy of him (Lea, I, 287). Cf. Gino Damerino, "La Veneziana," *Il Dramma,* fasc. 330–331 (March-April, 1964), 31–39. The play was successfully revived in Venice and Milan in 1965 (*Il Dramma,* fasc. 349 [Dec., 1965], 69–70, 75).

16. Ulisse Prota-Giurleo, *I teatri di Napoli nel '600* (Napoli, 1962), pp. 29, 34 (hereafter cited as "Prota-Giurleo"); Lea, I, 285. Luigi Rasi says in *I comici italiani* (Florence, 1897), I, 965, that Federico Ricci was known as Il Pantalone della Podagra, which would account for his almost deformed bearing. By 1627 he was so crippled by gout that he could barely move on the stage (Lea, I, 302).

17. Son, not nephew as Lea says (II, 498). Cf. Prota-Giurleo, p. 37.

18. Lea, I, 297–298.

of Piacenza. He also had been an original member of the Fedeli company
and had remained when the troupe amalgamated with the Accesi, led by
Tristano Martinelli in 1612–14, and by Cecchini in 1617.[19] He played the
part which bore the generic mask-name of Gratiano and appears in the
Feather Book as the typical Doctor of Laws, his dress rich but conservative, with the Bolognese broad bonnet, a long fur-lined coat, a fluted ruff,
and a pair of gloves which he holds in his right hand as he emphasizes
some telling legal *conclusione.*

A second actor-author is represented in the Feather Book in the role of
BALTRAM. Beltrame was the stage name assumed by Niccolò Barbieri, born
in Vercelli in 1570 and the writer of *La Supplica,* one of the most
important contemporary documents on the commedia dell'arte.[20] In 1600
he had become a member of the Gelosi company; later he joined first the
Fedeli, playing in Milan in 1606 and 1612, and after that the Confidenti,
so that he (like the Ricci father and son) would have been in Milan in
1616.[21] Barbieri's life in the theater was a long one, for he did not die until
1641. He was devoted to his profession and jealous for its prestige, and in
1628 he composed a brief defense of actors from the criticisms based on
moral or religious grounds. This proved so popular that he enlarged it,
and it was republished at least twice.[22] It is he who describes Carlo
Borromeo's opposition to the theater and points out that when the company of the Uniti had been bidden in 1582 to leave Milan its leader,
Adriano Valerini, appealed to the Cardinal, who issued a decree in their
favor and himself altered some of the scenari which they submitted to
him, so that there might be no further difficulties with the authorities.

19. *Ibid.,* II, 483. This is a period of constant reorganization of companies and
regrouping of actors.

20. For the best account of Barbieri's career, see the *Enciclopedia dello spettacolo,*
and also the *Dizionario biografico degli italiani.*

21. Lea, I, 285.

22. *Discorso famigliare di Nicolao Barbieri detto Beltrame intorno alle Comedie
moderne, Dov'egli dice la sua opinione, come fanno quei virtuosi, che scrivono, o
ragionano in publico, & in privato di tal professione* (Ferrara, 1628). Revised as *La
Supplica, discorso famigliare . . . diretta a quelli che scrivendo o parlando trattano
de comici trascurando i meriti delle azzioni virtuose* (Venice, 1634). Third edition:
*La Supplica, ricorretta et ampliata. Discorso famigliare . . . virtuose. Lettura per
que' galanthuomini che non sono in tutto critici, nè affatto balordi* (Bologna, 1636).
Quotations in the text are from the third edition.

According to Barbieri, the Pantalone of the company preserved for many years the manuscript which the future saint had corrected with his own hand.[23]

Barbieri describes the Comici as devout, studious, and charitable, helping as they do to maintain convents and orphans, both male and female ("Conventi, Orfani, Orfanelle");[24] the latter possibly a reference to the Vergine Spagnuole which, as we have seen, profited from the players' visits.

He pays special tribute to Francesco and Giovan Battista Andreini, with both of whom he had acted, and mentions that the latter had been shown marks of favor by princes on many occasions and at Mantua had even been given the title of Master of the Hunt for several places in that state.[25]

He praises too the leader of the Accesi, Pier Maria Cecchini, and speaks with particular affection of his close friend Francesco Gabrieli, the famous Scappino, calling him "the best Zanni of our times and the inventor of fantastic instruments as well as the writer of delightful songs and airs. He taught the Spanish guitar," Barbieri continues, "to his Most Christian Majesty and to Her Royal Highness of Savoy, to the Empress while she was at Mantua, and to many other Princes and Princesses of France, and he has always been received by the great as a talented musician, not as a buffoon."[26]

SCHAPIN is portrayed in the Feather Book with his famous Spanish guitar, serenading SPENETA, in real life his wife, Spinetta Gabrieli, like himself a member of the Confidenti. Her role was that of a maid servant. From the tree beside which Scappino stands hang eight of his musical instruments.[27]

23. *Ibid.*, pp. 164–165.

24. *Ibid.*, p. 186.

25. *Ibid.*, p. 40. "È stato favorito da' Principi in molte occasioni, & in Mantoa hebbe fino titolo di Capitano di Caccia di certi luoghi in quello Stato."

26. *Ibid.*, p. 41. "Scappino il miglior Zanni de' nostri tempi, inventor de' fantastici instrumenti, & di canzonette e arie gustevoli, è stato maestro di Chitarra alla Spagnuola del Re Cristianissimo [Louis XIII, to whom Barbieri dedicated the third edition of *La Supplica*], della Reina Regnante [Anne of Austria], di Madama R[eale] di Savoia [Marie Christine, sister of Louis XIII, wife of Vittorio Amadeo I of Savoy], dell'Imperatrice mentr'era a Mantoa [Eleonora Gonzaga, cf. note 12], e di tanti altri Principi, e Principesse della Francia, ed è stato sempre accettato tra Grandi come virtuoso, e non come buffone."

27. Spinetta's real name is uncertain, but Rasi (*I comici italiani,* I, 295) suggests

It was Niccolò Barbieri who wrote for Gabrieli the comedy of *L'Inavvertito ovvero Scappino disturbato e Mezzattino travagliato,* published in 1629 but probably based on an earlier scenario. It is this play which was the source for Molière's *L'Étourdi.* It also contains a part for Barbieri's own character, Beltrame, as the father of the heroine.

Rejecting indignantly the accusation that the theater is a school of vice, Barbieri points out in *La Supplica* that while men are in the theater they can neither gamble, dance with other men's wives, drink, quarrel, nor risk their lives on the water or in hunting or in watching fireworks, but are innocently recreating their spirits and receiving lessons in virtuous behavior. He is proud that his own comedy role of Beltrame represents "a father and head of a household from the valleys of Bergamo, who gives many people great delight (when they understand his dialect) by his rustic speech; and I often have occasion to rebuke my disorderly household and uphold moral rectitude." [28] It is thus that the artist in feathers has portrayed him, black-visaged but in the sober dress of a respectable citizen,[29] pointing out to the reprobation of the audience the startled young rogue, TRAPPOLINO.

Trappola was originally a knavish servant in Ariosto's *Cassaria,* and later

---

that she was Luisa Gabrieli-Locatelli. The instruments hanging by Scappino have been identified by Professor Harvey Olnick of the Faculty of Music in the University of Toronto as: one curved and two straight cornets, small lute, folk violin (peg board is of guitar type) and curved bow, coloscione, another lute, single bagpipe, two folk zithers, and xylophone with hammer. Professor Olnick points out that some of the instruments are unusual in construction, which is in keeping with Barbieri's reference to Gabrieli as an inventor of instruments.

Another series of pictures in the Feather Book, leaves 77 to 84, depicts musicians playing instruments, also sometimes unconventional. These figures are unidentified but may well be players associated with the actors, as many plays of the period had incidental music. The man playing a bagpipe for a seated woman with a distaff and spindle on leaf 84 may well have been taken from one of the bucolic comedies then so popular. The young man playing a coloscione on leaf 80 is identical in appearance (though not in costume) to Leandro.

28. *Ibid.,* p. 121. "Lodo Iddio di rappresentare un padre di famiglia delle vallate di Bergamo, che porge (ove la lingua è intesa) a molti gusto per lo grossolano parlare; ed ho sovente occasione di riprender la viziosa famiglia, e portar moralità."

29. This costume is also depicted with some later fantastic exaggerations on the title page of the 1634 edition of *La Supplica,* reproduced by Pandolfi, Vol. III, to face p. 392.

in G. B. Della Porta's *Trappolaria*. He was also the Captain's servant in the elder Andreini's *Bravure del Capitan Spavento*. The diminutive of the name for a variation of the mask was first used in the sixteenth century by an actor called Giovan Paolo (Zan Polo). Later the role was performed by a youthful actor, Giovan Battista Fiorillo, who had come to Milan in the troupe of his famous father, Silvio.[30] As the wooden sword held by the boy indicates, the mask of Trappolino was a variant of Arlecchino, and Beltrame is possibly rebuffing the impudence of the young servant who abets his son's dissolute behavior. In *L'Inavvertito* there is such a scene between Beltrame and a presumptuous servant whom he treats with dignified disdain.

Silvio Fiorillo himself, the third of our actor-authors, appears in the Feather Book in two of his most famous roles. The stage name he assumed was that of Captain MATTAMOROS, and the artist has portrayed him in the part, handsome and fierce, in a plumed hat, slashed doublet, knee breeches, and a fur-edged short cloak, his gloved left hand on the hilt of a large sword. It is interesting to compare this picture with one first published in 1611 which adorns the title page of several plays written by Fiorillo, *La Ghirlanda,* for instance, and *La Lucilla costante*. It is evident that though in general the costume remains the same, the feather portrait shows a change of fashion. The earlier hat is bell-crowned, the later a broad-brimmed felt turned up at one side. The cloak, still trimmed or lined with fur, has become shorter and less voluminous. The Spanish ruff has been replaced by the French flat collar fringed with fur.

In 1609 Silvio Fiorillo had invented the mask of POLICIANELO, which satirized a certain Neapolitan contractor, Mariotto Policenello, who had blocked the entrance to the theater where the actors were performing with piles of wood, the overflow from his stock.[31] The portrait in the Feather Book is the earliest example known of what was to become the typical Neapolitan mask. The character wears baggy trousers and a thigh-length smock with long sleeves and a leather belt below the hips, through which he thrusts his thumbs, standing in that attitude of disciplined oafishness ("disciplinata goffagine") which Pier Maria Cecchini called typical of the part as played by its inventor. This is the only picture, as far as is still

30. Lea (II, 491) has found no trace of G. B. Fiorillo in the role of Trappolino before 1630, but by that time he had made the name his own.
31. Prota-Giurleo, chap. X.

known, of Fiorillo in the role.[32] It is evident that the personage was originally conceived without the hooked nose or the hump and paunch that later became Pulcinello's trademark.

The role of CIETRULO is generally supposed to be a variation of Pulcinella and so may also have been played by Fiorillo.[33] But the Feather Book shows him as a much less fantastic character, dressed conservatively in black with a short cloak, a small ruff, a close-fitting cap and a short sword, clapping his hand on the shoulder of the frightened BAGATINO. The earliest Bagatino of whom there is a record was a member of Gabrieli's Confidenti in 1627,[34] and this portrait would connect him with the troupe at least eleven years earlier. His motley costume and flat sword bear out Gabrieli's reference to him as a second Arlecchino, and it is possible that Cetrullo is playing the part of a *sbirro*. The sword which he wears supports this theory, and he is certainly making the traditional gesture of arrest. Officers of the Bargello were often represented in the comedy of the period, and nearly always as figures of fun. The cast of Andreini's *Schiavetto,* for instance, contains a Bargello and *diversi sbirri,* who suffer a pelting before they are able to make their arrest. Two *Caporali di sbirri* also figure in Fiorillo's *Tre capitani vanagloriosi.*

Another Neapolitan actor with the Accesi and Fedeli troupes was Aniello di Mauro, who is portrayed in the Feather Book as CHOLA. His playing was so highly admired that in 1608 he had been sent by the Duke of Mantua to Paris as a replacement for the great Arlecchino, Tristano Martinelli. As the substitution was considered satisfactory it is probable that Chola was a Neapolitan version of the Bergamask Arlecchino, equally knavish and grotesque and equally acrobatic. We know that Aniello's dancing was highly admired and imitated and that he made a great impression on the little Dauphin.[35] He is shown in the Feather Book capering in a strange distorted attitude, making with his right hand the

32. Though these portraits must have been made during Fiorillo's visits to Milan in 1616 and 1617, his earliest Milanese appearance after creating the Pulcinella role was in 1611.

33. A Citrullo—possibly Fiorillo himself—was a member of Flaminio Scala's company in 1626 (Lea, I, 302).

34. *Ibid.,* p. 301.

35. *Ibid.,* p. 281.

vulgar Neapolitan gesture against the evil eye. Spectacles and an outthrust tongue add to the oddity of his appearance.

POMBINO, another member of the Accesi, was Girolamo Salimbeni, who had first joined the Gelosi company as early as 1590.[36] He too, like Aniello di Mauro, had gone to France in 1608. His mask represented the Florentine rustic, rather an unusual character, for most of the dialect roles were non-Tuscan. It may, however, have originated with the *commedie rusticali* which became popular in Siena in the sixteenth century. From his portrait, Salimbeni seems to have been short in stature and thick-set. His costume is certainly not that of a peasant: indeed it has a decidedly oriental character. The picture may easily represent him as he appeared in some play with a magical or Eastern background, or in which he had to wear a disguise. Ill-at-ease, despite his incongruously fine clothes, he stands with his gnarled peasant hands hanging awkwardly before him at the ends of abnormally long arms, his face almost animal in its stolid blankness.

Four minor members of the Accesi company remain to be mentioned, only two of whom can be identified by name. RICOLINA, generally known as Rizzolina, was Angela Lucchesi, who in 1602 was a member of the company of Carlo Fredi, and so must have been Neapolitan by origin.[37] She is portrayed as a maid servant, dangling a brace of dead pheasants in one hand, and with the other presenting a nosegay to TRASTULO, who in black tights, a flat cap, a sword and spectacles, is strumming a guitar. According to Pier Maria Cecchini, Trastullo was a Sicilian character, and the name appeared as early as 1585 when a Trastullo accompanied Ganassa to Spain.[38] The youthful appearance of the figure in the portrait makes it possible that the part was played by Giovan Battista Fiorillo and that his part was that of the *ragazzo* in attendance on a Captain, possibly on Capitan Mattamoros himself.

36. His original stage name was apparently Zenobio di Piombino, according to F. Andreini's *Bravure del Capitano Spavento,* quoted by Pandolfi, I, 375. He appears as a character in two of Flaminio Scala's scenari (Lea, I, 293; Pandolfi, V, 220), and in one in the Museo Correr collection (Pandolfi, V, 354).

37. Prota-Giurleo, p. 14. By 1605 she had joined the Accesi (Lea, II, 505). Pandolfi deplores that her identity and that of Flavia are unknown (IV, 450).

38. Benedetto Croce, *I teatri di Napoli* (Bari, 1916), p. 31.

MARIO and FLAVIA, who share a picture, played the roles of *secondi innamorati*. Flavia was Margherita Luciani,[39] wife of Girolamo Garavini, the famous Capitan Rinoceronte, and they were in Milan in 1617 as part of the Accesi-Fedeli company. Both she and the still-unidentified Mario are small, rather meager in appearance, and dressed respectably but without the elegance of Florinda and Leander. This probably explains in part why Flavia was such a bitter enemy of Florinda,[40] whom she could not hope to rival in either looks or costume.

III

That these are indeed portraits and not imaginary conceptions is supported by evidence of two kinds. In the first place, several of the masks, such as those of Beltrame and Capitan Mattamoros, were still in their original state and had not yet been played except by their creators. Scappino, for instance, is shown with the musical instruments that appear in well-authenticated later portraits of Francesco Gabrieli.[41] Moreover, he is portrayed with the actress who was actually his wife and stage partner. In every case the ages of the actors who are not wearing masks correspond to what is known to have been their ages in about 1618.

The second argument is that nearly all these players are known to have performed in Milan during the years 1615 to 1618, and the artist was hardly likely to invent pictures of players whom he had before him in the flesh as models. It is instructive to compare these authentic portraits of actors with the fanciful versions of some of the same masks etched by Jacques Callot. His *Balli di Sfessania*, published in Nancy in 1621, had been inspired by the performances of the Italian players in Florence between 1614 and 1621 while he was working with Giulio Parigi, engineer and stage designer at the court of Cosimo II de' Medici. The Confidenti company was under the protection of Don Giovanni de' Medici, and some of the masks portrayed by Callot bear the names of members of that troupe. Among the masks depicted by Callot as well as Dionisio Menag-

39. Lea, II, 502.
40. *Ibid.*, I, 283.
41. As for example the engraved portrait by Carlo Biffi, drawn in Milan in 1633 and reproduced in the *Enciclopedia dello spettacolo*.

gio are (to use Callot's spelling) Pulliciniello, Scapino, Trastullo, and Riciulina. But whereas the Italian artist is interested in the actor as well as in his costume, Callot, with his training in stage design, sees the costume alone, and the phantasmagoric whirl of the figures capers past his eyes so rapidly that he can seize no human semblance, only the exaggerated gestures, the tossing plumes, the jagged garments that flare out around their wearers like flames. Indeed Prota-Giurleo maintains that Callot was sketching dance attitudes rather than actual masks,[42] and this theory is supported when we notice that though Callot's Pulcinella has some likeness to the same character in the Feather Book, his Scapino has no musical instruments, wears a wooden sword, and is almost indistinguishable from Gian Fritello.

If it is to be accepted, then, that we have in the Feather Book a series of actual portraits of actors, it is evidently one of the most important iconographical documents of the early seventeenth century. Many of the portraits are the only ones in existence of the actors they portray: for example, those of Francesco and Benedetto Ricci, G. B. Fiorillo, Aniello di Mauro, Spinetta Gabrieli, Angela Lucchese, and Margherita Luciani Garavini. Others, such as that of Niccolò Barbieri, are earlier than those portraits which had previously been known. If the supposition about leaf 111 is correct, it is the only portrait of Lelio and Florinda together as they appeared on the stage. The picture of Policianelo is the unique record of Silvio Fiorillo in that part and is particularly interesting in showing the original costume of the character. Indeed all the costumes have an unusual authenticity from having been sketched on the actual wearers.

IV

The medium in which the pictures are executed is so unusual as to deserve special mention.[43] The technique of feather design was new in Europe at that date and as far as I know was adopted by no other

42. Prota-Giurleo, pp. 64–65.

43. I should like to express my gratitude for this information on the history of featherwork to Miss Sybille Pantazzi, Librarian of the Art Gallery of Ontario, Toronto, and to Professor Edgardo Moltoni of the Museum of Natural History, Milan.

craftsman-artist on so ambitious a scale. The Spanish explorers of the
New World had been much impressed by the feather decorations worn by
the inhabitants of Brazil and by the pictures made by Peruvians out of
hummingbird feathers. It was during the reign of Pope Paul III
(1534–49) that Mexican feather work was first brought to Europe by
missionaries and explorers.[44] The Mexicans were particularly skillful in
executing not only abstract designs but also actual pictures in feathers,
always of religious subjects. Some of these, probably made in convent
schools, were brought as presents to Paul III and later to Sixtus V, who is
said to have admired particularly a head of St. Francis.[45]

A miter embroidered with feathers, supposed to have been worn by St.
Carlo Borromeo on his visits to the plague-stricken during the pestilence
of 1576–77, is still one of the chief treasures of the Duomo of Milan.[46]
According to tradition, it was offered by "Indian" Catholics to the Milanese Pope, Pius IV, and presented by him to St. Carlo. A similar miter is
in the Museo degli Argenti of the Pitti Palace in Florence. A further
example of ecclesiastical embroidery in feathers survives in the Kunsthis-
torisches Hofmuseum in Vienna. The only secular example of the period
seems to be the shield of Philip II of Spain, representing four Spanish
military victories, the latest of which is the battle of Lepanto, which dates
the work as later than 1571. This is in the Royal Armory in Madrid.[47] In

44. Edmond Lefèvre, *Le Commerce et l'industrie de la plume pour la parure*
(Paris, 1914), p. 25. A manuscript of the sixteenth-century Spanish Fray Bernardino
di Sahaguña on the *General History of the Things of New Spain,* trans. from the
Aztec by Charles E. Dibble and Arthur J. O. Anderson (Santa Fe, 1959), is in the
Biblioteca Laurenziana in Florence. Chapters 20 and 21 of Part X describe with
illustrations methods of making feather pictures.

45. Fernand Denis, *Arte plumaria: les plumes et leur emploi dans les arts au
Mexique, au Pérou, au Brésil, dans les Indes, et dans l'Océanie* (Paris, 1875), pp.
22–23. Denis also mentions (p. 26) the miter of St. Carlo.

46. U. Nebbia, *Il Tesoro del Duomo di Milano* (Milan, 1962), p. 50. The miter is
illustrated in color on p. 52 of *Il Duomo di Milano,* ed. Mia Cinotti (Milan, 1966).

47. Gardner Teall, "Early Ecclesiastical Featherwork Embroidery," *Christian Art,*
III (1908), 38–41. Teall states that the miter in the Pitti collection belonged to
Alessandro de' Medici, later Pope Leo XI, who died in 1605. Nebbia says that it was
given by the Emperor Charles V to Pope Clement VII (1523–1534), which would
make it the earliest example known of featherwork in Europe. This miter is
illustrated both in Teall's article and in Detlef Heikamp's "Les Médicis et le nouveau
monde," *L'Oeil,* CXLIV (Dec., 1966), 16–23 (Fig. 10).

all these works tiny feathers are used to imitate very fine embroidery, whereas Dionisio Minaggio uses feathers of different sizes, cut in appropriate shapes and glued to a paper foundation.

South American birds and objects made from their feathers formed some of the most valued rarities of Manfredo Settala's famous Museum in Milan. They were described by Paolo Terzaghi in his catalogue of the collection, and the magnificent feather cloak, as well as two of the three birds of paradise which the museum boasted, can plainly be distinguished in the engraving which illustrated Terzaghi's book.[48] Still unpublished are the drawings made as further illustrations for the catalogue.[49] These original sketches are in the Biblioteca Estense at Modena and include a water-color drawing of one feather picture, the head of a Carmelite nun, who is depicted in a blue mantle and hood and a white wimple, holding a gold cross; the solid background is green. Above and below the picture are sketches of the birds from whose plumage the picture was made. They resemble hummingbirds, and it is evident from the relative sizes that the picture of a nun was very small. According to Terzaghi's catalogue, Settala's collection contained another feather picture, of the Virgin with the infant Christ and St. John, which Terzaghi calls "opus plane undique admirandum." These are the earliest known examples of feather pictures in Milan. The feather objects in Settala's collection had come from Chile (a *scoppetta,* or little whisk, of ostrich feathers), Borneo (the birds of Paradise), and Peru (the picture of the nun). The feather cloak was from Brazil.

It is natural that pictures made of feathers should appeal to admirers of the "ghiribizzi" of the Milanese Giuseppe Arcimboldi, who of course had only painted the fruit, flowers, fish, and vegetables with which in an earlier generation he had composed his fantastic creatures. It is perhaps not irrelevant that he had painted a "Ritratto d'uomo formato di uccelli," which is now in the Bossi collection at Genoa. Only Dionisio Minaggio,

---

48. *Museaeum Septalium Manfredi Septalae Patritii Mediolanensis industrioso labore constructum* (Dentonae, Typis Filiorum qd. Elisei Violae, 1664).

49. *Disegni originali che sono descritti nell'opera scritta in latino dal Dott. Fis. Collegiale Paolo Maria Terzago tradotta in italiano con aumenti dal Dottor Fis. Pietro Francesco Scarabelli, Stampata in Voghera nel 1661 in un volume in 4° da Eliseo Viola. (MS, Cassetto A3. Ves. 8° A).*

however, seems to have used the technique exclusively for secular pictures, and he employs it with breadth, originality, and freedom. On the left side of each picture in the Feather Book (with one exception) stands a tree with a large branch or branches arching over the top of the page, forming a demi-frame for the scene enclosed. No two trees are alike: most bear strange blossoms, some have leaves only, in which case they are unmistakably laurels. Variegated too are the flowery meadows in which the characters stand.

The artist's skill in depicting dramatic gesture, expression, and costume is remarkable. He can reproduce every variety of texture and material; particularly skillful is his rendering of Campanaz' fur-lined and bordered coat and the differentiation between the white fur on Chocholi's cap and his fluffy white hair, reminiscent of the "oneste piume" of Dante's Cato. Dionisio Minaggio can represent all kinds of musical instruments, as well as all varieties of weapons and spectacles, and can depict convincingly the brick wall of the house from whose window Speneta leans. The feather medium lends a gaiety and charm to every scene, and the soft but unfaded brilliance of the colors can only be appreciated in the original. The detail of the costumes is minute: every ribbon, stripe, and buckle is faithfully rendered, and as the non-dialect actors and actresses are wearing the latest fashions of their day the pictures are invaluable to the historian of style, both in clothes and in hairdressing. Noticeable is the difference between the costumes of the tragic heroine (Florinda), the heroine of comedy (Flavia), and the maid servant (Ricolina).

The contemporary fashion of wearing feathers for ornaments is evident in the pictures.[50] Only Baltram, Cietrulo, Chocholi, Policianelo and Pombino (all sedate or rustic characters) are without feathers in their hats. Both Flavia and Florinda wear aigrettes, and the latter also carries a feather fan in her hand. Her magnificent dress and the handsome suits of some of the male actors were probably presents from noble patrons, for Barbieri says that without such gifts the actors could never have afforded to make a good appearance on the stage.

---

50. Many of the characters in Callot's *Balli* wear long feathers in their hats. The use of feathers in stage costume becomes increasingly popular during the seventeenth century, particularly in fantastic or exotic plays.

V

Though the Feather Book was executed in Milan, its original owner was probably Spanish. The Governor of Milan by whom Dionisio Minaggio was employed was almost certainly Don Pedro de Toledo Osorio, Marquès de Villafranca, who represented the Spanish crown in Milan from January, 1616 to August, 1618, and was a grandson of the more famous Don Pedro de Toledo who had been Viceroy of Naples from 1532 to 1554. In 1552 the Viceroy's son, Don García, married Vittoria Colonna, niece of the famous poetess. Don García had served in the navy as one of Andrea Doria's captains, and in 1535 was made Admiral of the Neapolitan galleys, helping to defend the Italian coast from attacks by Turks and Barbary corsairs. In 1542 he became colonel of the Spanish infantry in Naples, took part in the attack on Tunis in 1550, and aided his kinsman the Duke of Alba in his campaign against Pope Paul IV in 1555.[51] For a time he was in charge of the household of Philip II's unhappy son, Don Carlos, and after the latter's death in 1565 was appointed Viceroy of Sicily.

The second Don Pedro, then, was half-Italian by birth and spent part of his youth in Naples, becoming Admiral of the Neapolitan fleet after his father's death in 1578. It was a period when Naples rivaled all Italian cities in its love for the theater.[52] Unlike Milan, which had to depend on traveling companies, it had produced its own school of actors, who were welcome, as we have seen, abroad as well as in the cities of Northern Italy. In July, 1608 Don Pedro was sent by Philip III to France to negotiate with Henry IV for the three Franco-Spanish marriages which the Spanish

51. Both the Colonna and the Toledo families held feudal estates in the Kingdom of Naples and were allied not only by marriage but by their determination to defend their properties against papal attempts to diminish Spanish and feudal powers there. G. Ceci, "I feudatori napoletani alla fine del secolo XVI," *Archivio storico per le provincie Napoletane,* XXIV (1899), 122–138.

52. In the sixteenth century the theater had gone through the same phases in Naples as in Milan: antagonism from the Church, a temporary ban in 1581 resulting probably from St. Carlo Borromeo's campaign, and in 1588 the imposition of a tax in favor of convents (see Croce, *I teatri di Napoli,* p. 35). But at any court, viceregal or otherwise, these bans were difficult to enforce, as theatrical entertainments had become a standard feature of noble weddings and receptions.

king and his ministers were anxious to arrange.[53] As Don García had
been the uncle of Henry's queen, Marie de' Medici, this choice of her
cousin as ambassador seemed particularly appropriate, though Don Pedro's
haughtiness did not endear him to the French court.[54] The negotia-
tions dragged on, and Don Pedro did not return to Madrid until February, 1609. He almost certainly was entertained by performances of the
company of the Accesi, who, as we have seen, were in France in 1608 from
February until the end of October, with Silvio Fiorillo, Girolamo Salimbeni, and Aniello di Mauro among their number.

Before Don Pedro left Paris, Henry IV gave him two commissions. One
was to choose some horses for the Dauphin (the future Louis XIII, then
only eight years old); the other was to send the King himself some rare
birds, both from Spain and from the Indies, for his newly-built aviary at
Fontainebleau. Such commissions are not likely to be entrusted by a king
except to a fellow-connoisseur, and we know that Don Pedro had already
executed them, at least in part, within a month after his return to
Madrid.[55] It would not be difficult to find good horses in Spain, but that
he should also have found exotic birds in such a short time suggests that
he himself had a collection, or at least had access to a collection, from
which he could dispatch specimens to France.

This interest in rare birds is in all probability a clue to the origin of the
Feather Book. It may also explain why the book contains pictures of a
dodo, South American parrots, and Arctic birds, possibly specimens from

53. F. T. Perrens, *Les Mariages espagnols sous le règne de Henri IV* (Paris, n.d.),
pp. 112 ff.

54. A less happy relationship with the Medici family had been the marriage of
Don Pedro's sister Eleonora to Pietro de' Medici (Marie de' Medici's uncle). After
five years of an unhappy marriage, Pietro had his wife strangled in 1576 on
well-based suspicions of her infidelity. Don Pedro was criticized for having exercised
no control over his sister and for not having reported Pietro's complaints to Don
García. His resentment against the Medici was violent, but he became reconciled to
them and even welcomed Pietro to the Spanish court in 1578. R. Galluzzi, *Istoria del
Granducato di Toscana*, 2d ed. (Florence, 1781), IV, 57–60, 92–93, 114.

55. Perrens, *Les Mariages espagnols*, p. 202. The magnificent *volière* at Fontainebleau, with a great central statuary fountain under a vaulted roof, had been Henry's
own addition to the palace. See Pierre Dan, *Le Trésor de merveilles de la maison
royale de Fontainebleau* (Paris, 1642), Book II, chap. XVIII.

Don Pedro's own collection.[56] It is natural to suppose that Don Pedro should wish to assemble specimens of the birds of Lombardy, and he must have found in his unusually gifted gardener an enthusiastic collector and recorder, who had probably been practicing his unusual art (of which, as we have seen, models already existed in Milan) even before his new employer's arrival.

Dionisio Minaggio's success in designing backgrounds for the specimens of birds may have led him on to the more elaborate compositions which included human figures. The choice of actors for models was a natural one, and Don Pedro may well have been particularly interested in the theater. In 1617 it was he who granted Pietro Maria Cecchini a license to perform in Milan, in answer to a request made in such casual terms that it is obviously confident of a favorable reply.[57] Cecchini must have been presented to Don Pedro in France in 1608, and three members of his troupe of that year are represented in the Feather Book. It is also noticeable how many Neapolitan actors are included, all of whom were probably familiar to Don Pedro from his youth.

The composition of the Feather Book between about 1615 and 1618 may then be taken as established with reasonable certainty, and we know that the actors whom it represents did actually perform in Milan during those years. Don Pedro's sudden removal from office in consequence of his alleged conspiracy against Venice may easily account for the rather surprising omission of his name from the title-page. While Dionisio Minaggio was composing the book Don Pedro de Toledo was indeed Governor of Milan, but by the time it was complete he was so no longer, and the artist was anxious to leave on record his association with the gubernatorial household. The abrupt termination of Don Pedro's residence in Milan might also account for the unfinished condition of the picture on leaf 111. It alone has no tree to enframe the actors, and it alone lacks labels to identify them.

The fortunes of the Feather Book after its completion must remain

56. Wood, "Two . . . Unpublished Pictures. . . ." Dr. Wood is convinced that the artist had used a real dodo as a model, though the feathers with which he depicted it are not dodo feathers.

57. Paglicci Brozzi, 31–32.

unknown. Don Pedro would certainly have taken it back with him to Spain, where he died in 1627, but it is surprising that the most elaborate work ever executed in such an unusual and exquisite medium, a work depicting a range of subjects interesting in so many fields, should have escaped the notice of collectors of curiosities for three hundred years.

Faustus' Damnation Reconsidered

T. W. CRAIK

TWENTY YEARS AGO there appeared W. W. Greg's essay "The Damnation of Faustus."[1] Its importance was recognized at once, and its influence since then has been considerable; it has been recently reprinted,[2] and its conclusions have not (as far as I know) been challenged. Greg's two principal points are: first, that Faustus, through the terms of the infernal compact in which he desired to be "a spirit in form and substance," . . . "has himself taken on the infernal nature, although it is made clear throughout that he still retains his human soul"; and second, that Helen is a spirit, that "in this play a spirit means a devil," that "in making her his paramour Faustus commits the sin of demoniality, that is, bodily intercourse with demons," that by this sin "the nice balance between possible salvation and imminent damnation is upset," and that this is "the central theme of the damnation of Faustus."

The former point, considered in itself, is an academic and theological one rather than a dramatic one, since the possibility of Faustus' repentance and salvation is still manifestly open, even supposing him to have "taken on the infernal nature." However, since it is based on the firm

1. *MLR*, XLI (1946), 97-107.
2. In *Marlowe: Twentieth Century Views*, ed. Clifford Leech (Englewood Cliffs, N.J., 1964).

189

interpretation of "spirit" as "devil," it also underlies the latter point, which
is of great dramatic importance, affecting as it does the climax of the play
—Faustus' sin of demoniality being indeed, if Greg's interpretation holds
good, the climax itself. I do not think his interpretation does hold good,
and I wish accordingly to reexamine the relevant portions of Marlowe's
play, commenting on what I take to be their literal meaning and their
dramatic function. Quotations are from the text of John D. Jump (The
Revels Plays; London, 1962).

I *Faustus as a "Spirit"*

Greg is obviously correct in stating that a usual meaning of "spirit" in
this play is "devil." Yet it is allowable to doubt whether this is always the
meaning. There are times, to take a comparable instance, when "repent"
is used loosely and generally:

> When I behold the heavens, then I repent
> And curse thee, wicked Mephostophilis,
> Because thou hast depriv'd me of those joys
>
> (vi. 1–3)

and other times when it has a precise theological sense:

> If heaven was made for man, 'twas made for me:
> I will renounce this magic and repent.
>
> (vi. 10–11)

The two senses are found here within a dozen lines; the use of "spirit" in
the following five lines seems similarly free:

> GOOD ANGEL
> Faustus, repent; yet God will pity thee.
> BAD ANGEL
> Thou art a spirit; God cannot pity thee.
> FAUSTUS
> Who buzzeth in mine ears I am a spirit?
> Be I a devil, yet God may pity me;
> Yea, God will pity me if I repent.
>
> (vi. 12–16)

Faustus seizes on the word "spirit" and proceeds to put a still more
desperate case: "Be I a devil, yet God may pity me." The rhetorical stress

falls on "devil": it falls here because "spirit" is not repeated (if it were, and only then, could we stress "Be"), and it shows that Faustus is making a distinction, whether or not the Bad Angel would accept it as valid.

Does Faustus think at any time that he is a devil? Greg argues that in the first article of the bond he expressed his wish to be one:

"First, that Faustus may be a spirit in form and substance" (v. 96). He draws attention to "the explicit statement in the *Damnable Life* that Faustus' 'request was none other than [*sic*] to become a devil.'" Now this phrase is not in the bond itself, but is part of the context in which the bond is drawn up:

... this swift flying Spirit appeared to *Faustus*, offering himself with al submissio[n] to his seruice, with ful authority from his Prince to doe what-soeuer he would request, if so be *Faustus* would promise to be his. . . . Doctor *Faustus* gaue him this answere, though faintly (for his soules sake) That his request was none other but to become a Diuel, or at the least a limme of him, and that the Spirit should agree vnto these Articles as followeth.

1 That he might be a Spirite in shape and qualitie.
2 That *Mephostophiles* should be his seruant. . . .[3]

Faustus knew that to obtain his desires he had to join the Devil's party: his "faint" request to become a devil, "or at the least a limme of him," was his acceptance of the Devil's terms ("if so be *Faustus* would promise to be his"), and formed the first article to which he bound himself: "First, that Doctor *Faustus* should giue himselfe to his [i.e. the Spirit's] Lord *Lucifer, body and soule.*"[4] "That he might be a Spirite in shape and qualitie" was, on the other hand, the first of the articles to which he required the Devil to subscribe in return. Greg remarks that critics have strangely neglected this article (when it reappears, insignificantly reworded, in Marlowe's play): "Presumably they have taken it to mean merely that he should be free of the bonds of flesh, so that he may be invisible at will, invulnerable, and able to change his shape, ride on dragons, and so forth." But this is what the article does mean.

Faustus desires to do such things as Ariel was to do in *The Tempest.* Ariel is a spirit and is referred to as such throughout. Shakespeare is not concerned with Ariel's theological position, but evidently the Elizabethans

3. Christopher Marlowe, *Faustus,* ed. John D. Jump (The Revels Plays; London, 1962), Appendix II, p. 125.
4. *Ibid.,* p. 126.

could conceive of some spirits outside both hell and heaven.[5] It is for spiritual powers such as theirs that Faustus is here bargaining.

When Faustus distinguishes between a spirit and a devil, he chooses to interpret the Bad Angel's "spirit" in this neutral sense. He implies that he has not lost his human soul (Who says he is a spirit? He is not a spirit!), and insists that if he had lost it (even if he were so far from grace as to be a devil) he could still get it back by repentance. This is doubtless theological nonsense, but it is dramatic sense, an understandably passionate outcry against the damnation to which he fears he has given himself up by the bond.

II   *Demoniality*

"What is Helen?" asks Greg, and he proceeds: "We are not told in so many words, but the answer is there, if we choose to look for it." The very fact that the Old Man does not explicitly condemn Faustus for demoniality, in the course of his moral comment as Faustus leaves the stage with Helen, is a strong argument against the importance which Greg assigns to Faustus' act. Greg asserts that "the implications of Faustus' action are made plain in the comments of the Old Man and the Angels"; he continues:

Immediately before the Helen episode the Old Man was still calling on Faustus to repent—
    Ah, Doctor Faustus, that I might prevail
    To guide thy steps into the way of life!
(so 1604: 1616 proceeds:)
    Though thou hast now offended like a man,
    Do not persever in it like a devil:
    Yet, yet, thou hast an amiable soul,
    If sin by custom grow not into nature . . .
But with Faustus' union with Helen the nice balance between possible salvation and imminent damnation is upset. The Old Man, who has witnessed the meeting (according to the 1604 version), recognizes the inevitable:
    Accursèd Faustus, miserable man,
    That from thy soul exclud'st the grace of heaven
    And fliest the throne of his tribunal-seat!

5. C. S. Lewis, *English Literature in the Sixteenth Century* (Oxford, 1954), pp. 7–12, discusses the matter in some detail.

The Good Angel does no less:

> O Faustus, if thou hadst given ear to me
> Innumerable joys had followed thee . . .
> Oh, thou hast lost celestial happiness . . .

He quotes also Faustus' words of despair,

> A surfeit of deadly sin, that hath damned both body and soul. . . . Faustus'
> offence can ne'er be pardoned: the Serpent that tempted Eve may be saved, but
> not Faustus

(xix. 37–38, 41–42)

and Mephostophilis' words of triumph,

> Ay, Faustus, now thou hast no hope of heaven!

(xix. 87)

None of these quotations supports his case. The Old Man's call to repent does not immediately precede the Helen episode: it precedes Faustus' attempted suicide, which the Old Man prevents. He is warning Faustus against persisting in his present sinful state, not against committing demoniality in the future (I am not sure whether or not Greg means us to infer the latter when he quotes "Do not persever in it like a devil"), and his present sinful state is what it has always been, unrepentant alienation from God. These words move Faustus, but they move him to despair. The Old Man exclaims,

> O, stay, good Faustus, stay thy desperate steps!
> I see an angel hovers o'er thy head
> And with a vial full of precious grace
> Offers to pour the same into thy soul:
> Then call for mercy, and avoid despair.

(xviii. 60–64)

Faustus is calmed, and asks the Old Man to leave him to ponder on his sins; and the Old Man goes, with forebodings that Faustus will backslide, as, under Mephostophilis' threats, he immediately does. When he reappears, he finds Faustus embracing Helen; and the Old Man's lines show not that Faustus is committing a new and unforgivable sin, but that he is still committing his old one: "the grace of heaven" which he is excluding from his soul is the "vial full of precious grace" which the visionary angel offered to pour into it. It might be objected that since Faustus is obviously unrepentant we need no comment from the Old Man unless some new aspect of the situation is to be shown. To this the first answer is that Marlowe never shrinks from stressing what is important (Faustus too has explained that Helen's "sweet embraces" are to "extinguish" his repentant impulses), and the second is that the three lines beginning "Accursed Faustus, miserable man" bring the Old Man back on stage to resist the assaults of the devils. As for the Good Angel, all that he says (when he appears, more than a hundred lines after Faustus has been seen with Helen) is that Faustus has lost celestial happiness through neglecting his warnings, loving the world, and leaving sweet divinity. He had warned Faustus against magic and against unrepentance, but not against the demoniality which, if we are to believe Greg, is here implied to have damned him. Like Greg's quotations from Faustus himself and from Mephostophilis, the Good Angel's words are pointing not backward to the scene with Helen, but forward to the hero's fate.

In short, all Greg's quotations fashion a connection in his essay which does not exist in Marlowe's play. The same connection is made by Roma Gill (with acknowledgments to Greg) in her "New Mermaid" edition of *Doctor Faustus:*

The kiss signals the ultimate sin, demoniality, the bodily intercourse with spirits. Now the Old Man gives up hope of saving Faustus; the Good Angel leaves him. After such knowledge there is no forgiveness.[6]

The case, reduced to this summary form, is ludicrous. It is as though the Old Man and the Good Angel said, "We're leaving—there's too much demoniality going on round here"; as though their words and deeds were the visible dramatic consequences of Faustus' embracing Helen and taking her for his paramour. They are nothing of the sort.

Suppose we grant that "that heavenly Helen" is a spirit in her form and that to have bodily intercourse with such a spirit is demoniality, what then? Is it the first time that Faustus has committed this sin, "the direst sin of which human flesh is capable" (Greg), after which "there is no forgiveness" (Gill)?

> Marriage is but a ceremonial toy;
> And if thou lov'st me, think no more of it.
> I'll cull thee out the fairest courtesans
> And bring them every morning to thy bed;

6. (London, 1965), Introd., p. xxvi.

> She whom thine eye shall like, thy heart shall have,
> Were she as chaste as was Penelope,
> As wise as Saba, or as beautiful
> As was bright Lucifer before his fall.
>
> (v. 151–158)

In these lines, which everyone agrees to be by Marlowe, Mephostophilis is offering Faustus the magic satisfaction of his desires. If a woman will not consent to be his mistress, he shall enjoy a spirit in her form, which will do just as well:

> She whom thine eye shall like, thy heart shall have,
> Were she as chaste as was Penelope.

"Were she," not "Be she." [7] Faustus could have Penelope if he wanted her, or Helen of Troy. This interpretation of the lines has the *Damnable Life* to back it: at the same point in the story (after Faustus has insisted on a wife and been presented with "an ougly Diuell"), Mephostophilis tells Faustus:

It is no iesting with vs, holde thou that which thou hast vowed, and wee will performe as wee haue promised: and more than that, thou shalt haue thy hearts desire of what woman soeuer thou wilt, bee shee aliue or dead, and so long as thou wilt, thou shalt keepe her by thee. [8]

Are we asked to believe that Faustus never took advantage of this offer until his twenty-four years were up? This would be to interpret "And none but thou shalt be my paramour" literally indeed. [9]

7. Such is the text of 1616; 1604 has "Be she." Greg regards neither reading as preferable (*Marlowe's "Doctor Faustus," 1604–1616* [Oxford, 1950], p. 44), and says: "It is obvious that given two equal grammatical possibilities it would be pure chance which an actor would choose, unless he were far more word-perfect than we have any reason to suppose most Elizabethan actors were" (p. 332). On the other hand, I think it more likely that an actor would substitute "Be she" (to harmonize with the future tenses of the previous line) than that an editor would substitute "Were she" (to conform with "as was Penelope"). In any case, there is no moral distinction between enjoying a spirit in the form of a woman who is dead and enjoying a spirit in the form of a woman who is still alive.

8. Jump, Appendix II, p. 127.

9. The *Damnable Life* makes no doubt of it: "These words pleased *Faustus* wonderfull well, and [he] repented himselfe that hee was so foolish to wish himselfe married, that might haue any woman in the whole Citie brought to him at his command; the which he practised and perseuered in a long time" (quoted by Greg,

It is the literal-mindedness with which it has been invented and applied, and the materialistic view of sin which it implies, that make the theory of Faustus' damning demoniality so repugnant to the whole nature of Marlowe's play. "The direst sin of which human flesh is capable" surely does not count for so much when Faustus is dominated throughout his tragedy by two sins not of the flesh but of the spirit—pride and despair. He that toucheth pitch shall be defiled therewith; by fornicating with a devil, Faustus is damned; so runs the theory. It is never suggested, in the text or by any critic, that Faustus wants to fornicate with a devil.

> I will be Paris, and for love of thee
> Instead of Troy shall Wittenberg be sack'd,
> And I will combat with weak Menelaus
> And wear thy colours on my plumed crest,
> Yea, I will wound Achilles in the heel
> And then return to Helen for a kiss.
>
> (xviii. 106–111)

These lines show that (however unreasonable his belief may be) Faustus believes that he is speaking to Helen herself. So if he is damned for taking this Helen as his paramour, if this is what puts him beyond reach of the divine forgiveness, then he is damned for the act of demoniality without the intention.

What, then, becomes of "Her lips suck forth my soul"? It is true that, if the theory of damning demoniality is discounted, the phrase reverts to metaphor,[10] and cannot bear a literal sense of which Faustus is ironically ignorant. However, the irony of the passage is not impaired (for it is still true that Faustus is turning his back on heaven), while the unity of the passage is improved, by dropping the unnecessary and distracting literal sense.

Marlowe's "Doctor Faustus," p. 332). The implication is surely that he enjoyed spirits in their forms, not the women themselves.

10. Similarly, Spenser describes Acrasia dallying with Verdant:

> And oft inclining downe with kisses light,
> For feare of waking him, his lips bedewd,
> And through his humid eyes did sucke his spright,
> Quite molten into lust and pleasure lewd.
>
> (*The Faerie Queene,* II.xii.73)

Elizabeth I, Jodelle, and Cleopatra

KENNETH MUIR

THE STUDY OF SHAKESPEARE'S SOURCES may sometimes throw some light on the interpretation of his plays. It may, therefore, be worthwhile to consider some previous dramatic treatments of the Cleopatra story and, in particular to put forward the suggestion that Shakespeare knew Jodelle's play *Cléopâtre captive* as well as *Antonie* in the Countess of Pembroke's translation and Daniel's *Cleopatra*.

G. Wilson Knight's chapters in *The Imperial Theme* [1] on "The Transcendental Humanism of *Antony and Cleopatra*" and "The Diadem of Love" are perhaps the most eloquent expression of an attitude to the play which has found a sympathetic response in many readers and critics. Harold S. Wilson, for example, speaks of the "ennoblement for the tragic protagonists" and declares that in their deaths they "affirm for us the supreme value—in this world—of human love . . . the greatest affirmation of this value in the world's literature." [2] John Dover Wilson similarly refers to the play as Shakespeare's "Hymn to Man." [3] But not everyone agrees. Franklin M. Dickey, after discussing the treatment of Cleopatra by

1. (London, 1931).
2. *On the Design of Shakespearian Tragedy* (Toronto, 1957), p. 177.
3. *Antony and Cleopatra,* ed. John Dover Wilson (Cambridge, Eng., 1950).

Shakespeare's many predecessors, concludes that Chaucer alone gives a sympathetic picture of her as one of love's martyrs, and that

Instead of seeing Antony and Cleopatra as patterns of nobility and of a deathless love, the Elizabethan reader must have seen them as patterns of lust, of cruelty, of prodigality, of drunkenness, of vanity, and, in the end, of despair.[4]

Traditionally, he tells us,

Antony and Cleopatra are examples of rulers who threw away a kingdom for lust, and this is how, despite the pity and terror which Shakespeare makes us feel, they appear in his play.[5]

Another critic, L. C. Knights, writing not from a historical but from a critical and moralistic standpoint, comes to a similar conclusion about the play. He sums up what he regards as Shakespeare's attitude in these words:

It is, of course, one of the signs of a great writer that he can afford to evoke sympathy or even admiration for what, in his final judgment, is discarded or condemned. In *Antony and Cleopatra* the sense of potentiality in life's untutored energies is pushed to its limit, and Shakespeare gives the maximum weight to an experience that is finally "placed." It is perhaps this that makes the tragedy so sombre in its realism, so little comforting to the romantic imagination.[6]

To which one can only retort that the play has given comfort and inspiration to the romantic imagination of many poets and critics.

Some, like Bradley, have attempted to steer a middle course between the two extremes; or they have agreed with John F. Danby that Shakespeare objectively presents two opposing points of view, without embracing either;[7] or with Ernest Schanzer, who treats *Antony and Cleopatra* as the greatest of the problem plays;[8] or with Bernard Shaw and L. L. Schücking, that Cleopatra at the end of the play is totally inconsistent with the character depicted in the first three acts.[9] In the first acts, she is a

4. *Not Wisely But Too Well* (San Marino, 1957), pp. 159–160.

5. *Ibid.*, p. 179.

6. *Some Shakespearian Themes* (London, 1959), p. 149.

7. *Poets on Fortune's Hill* (London, 1952), p. 128 ff.

8. *The Problem Plays of Shakespeare* (London, 1963), pp. 133 ff.

9. Bernard Shaw, *Three Plays for Puritans* (London, 1925), p. xxviii; L. L. Schücking, *Character Problems in Shakespeare's Plays* (New York, 1922).

courtesan, rather than a queen. We have "an exhibition of all the arts of harlotry." Another critic declares that "she owes more to a study of prostitutes than to a knowledge of how even the worst queens behave."

One of the scenes which occasioned this verdict is that in which Cleopatra questions the messenger about Octavia, asking him the color of her hair, her height, her voice, her gait, her age, and her face. It so happens that when Mary, Queen of Scots, sent James Melville to the English Court, Elizabeth asked a whole series of questions about her rival:

Who, she asked, was the fairer, Mary or she? a question Melville tried to dodge by declaring that she was the fairest Queen in England and theirs the fairest Queen in Scotland. As Elizabeth was not to be put off, he replied that they were both the fairest ladies of their courts, but the Queen of England was whiter. . . . Next she wanted to know who was the higher. Mary was, answered Melville. Then is she over high, retorted Elizabeth; she herself being neither over high nor over low.[10]

Questions followed about Mary's skill in playing and dancing, and Elizabeth later demonstrated her own skill in both respects. When one considers, too, Elizabeth's occasional acts of violence, one is bound to wonder whether Shakespeare was so ignorant of how queens, good or bad, behave.

Another critic, Daniel Stempel, thinks that "lass unparalleled" is a sign that Cleopatra cannot rise above the vices of her sex; and, in commenting on her self-description—

> a woman, and commanded
> By such poor passion as the maid that milks
> And does the meanest chares—

declares that the lines mean that she is "governed by no specifically noble passion.[11] Once again Elizabeth's own words show that Shakespeare knew better than his critic. In a speech to Parliament in 1576, Elizabeth replied to a petition that she should take a husband:

If I were a milk-maid, with a pail on my arm, whereby my private person might be little set by, I would not forsake that poor and single state to match with the greatest monarch.

It is not, of course, claimed that Shakespeare had heard of Elizabeth's inquiries about her rival, or even that he was echoing her speech to

10. J. E. Neale, *Queen Elizabeth I* (London, 1960), p. 131.
11. "The Transmigration of the Crocodile," *SQ*, VII (1956), 59–72.

Parliament. It is merely suggested that in two scenes where Cleopatra's conduct has been stigmatized as unregal, Shakespeare came uncannily close to contemporary examples of queenly behavior—closer, indeed, than Samuel Daniel did in his statuesque portrait.

We have seen that Professor Dickey has shown that most writers who treated the story of Antony and Cleopatra before Shakespeare used it as an *exemplum* of the destructive effect of lust; but if we were to concentrate on the dramatic treatments of the story a somewhat different picture would emerge. It is now generally accepted that Shakespeare made some use of Daniel's *Cleopatra;*[12] it is probable that he knew the Countess of Pembroke's translation of *Antonie;* and he may even have read one of Daniel's sources, Jodelle's *Cléopâtre captive,* a play which was performed in 1552–53 and published in 1574. This play, like *Gorboduc,* is more interesting as a forerunner of later tragedy than for its intrinsic merits. The verse, apart from the thin stanzaic choruses, is disconcertingly varied: in the prologue it consists of alexandrines; in Act I of alexandrines with exclusively feminine rhymes; in Acts II and III of pentameters; in Act IV of alexandrines again; and in the last act of pentameters. This variety was probably the result not, as Ferdinand Gohin declares,[13] of haste, but rather of uncertainty about the proper medium for tragedy. The characters are flat and wooden. As in all neo-Senecan plays, what action there is takes place off stage, and there is no real dramatic tension. Indeed, the only scene which comes alive is in Act III where there is, at last, a confrontation of Cléopâtre and Octavien.

The plot is even simpler than that of Daniel's play. In Act I the Ghost of Antoine, resentful of the passion which has brought about his ruin, determines to appear to Cléopâtre in a dream and demand that she shall commit suicide, so that he will have a companion in misfortune:

> Pour venir endurer en nostre palle bande,
> Or se faisant compagne en ma peine et tristesse,
> Qui s'est faite long temps compagne en ma liesse.

(p. 31)

12. E.g., *Narrative and Dramatic Sources of Shakespeare,* ed. G. Bullough (London, 1964), V, 231 ff.

13. E. Jodelle, *Cléopâtre captive,* ed. Ferdinand Gohin (Paris, 1925), p. 12. Page references are from this edition.

Cléopâtre, despite the protests of Eras and Charmium, resolves to obey Antoine's commands. In Act II there is a corresponding scene between Octavien and his followers, Proculee and Agrippe, in which he resolves that Cléopâtre shall grace his triumph. In Act III Octavien visits Cléopâtre and pardons her attempted deception about the amount of her treasure; and in Act IV she explains that her submission was feigned in order to save the lives of her children. Eras and Charmium now approve of her resolve to die. In Act V the suicide of the three women is duly described by Proculee.

Jodelle arouses considerable sympathy for Cléopâtre in the course of the play—more, perhaps, than he originally intended, if we may judge from the Prologue and Antoine's opening speech. It is noteworthy, for example, that the Chorus at the end of Act III regards her treatment of Seleuque as a proof of her nobility and resolution:

> Mais or' ce dernier courage
> De ma Roine est un presage,
> S'il faut changer de propos,
> Que la meurdriere Atropos
> Ne souffrira pas qu'on porte
> A Romme ma Roine forte,
> Qui veut de ses propres mains
> S' arracher des fiers Rommains.
>
> (p. 83)

And, at the end of the play, the Chorus praises her for her noble suicide and declares that her fame will never die, "Ayant un cœur plus que d'homme."

It has not been seriously suggested that Shakespeare was acquainted with Jodelle's play, although M. W. MacCallum has called attention to the lines in Act III where Cléopâtre admits she has not declared all her possessions:

> Hé! si j'avois retenu des joyaux,
> Et quelque part de mes habits royaux.
>
> (p. 77)

But this is part of his argument that Cleopatra, in her scene with Octavius, is anxious to retain her royal robes so that she can adorn herself for her death scene.[14] The objection to this theory is that it is nowhere supported by Shakespeare's text, or even by Plutarch.

There are, however, a number of resemblances between Jodelle's play and Shakespeare's. Cléopâtre's motive for suicide—"Plutost qu'estre dans Romme en triomphe portee"—is, of course, that of Shakespeare's heroine; but it is a feature of all versions of the story. Charmium's fear that

> ceste douce contree
> Il nous faudra laisser, pour à Romme menees,
> Donner un beau spectacle à leurs effeminees

(p. 86)

may be compared with Cleopatra's fear of becoming a spectacle to "the shouting varletry / Of censuring Rome"; of being staged extemporally by "the quick comedians"; and of seeing "Some squeaking Cleopatra boy my greatness / I' th' posture of a whore." But both dramatists could have developed these ideas independently from the hints given by Plutarch.

More significant, perhaps, are the resemblances between the third act of Jodelle's play and the corresponding scene in Shakespeare's. Jodelle, Daniel, and Shakespeare all follow Plutarch fairly closely. Daniel is the only one of the four writers who does not suggest that Cleopatra deliberately underestimated the amount of her treasure so that Caesar, on discovering the truth, would believe that she did not intend to commit suicide. In Jodelle, Cléopâtre confesses afterwards that her motive was to save her children. It is the liveliest scene in *Cléopâtre captive,* and Jodelle conveys, as Shakespeare does, the theatrical violence of his heroine's behavior.

Plutarch describes how Cleopatra flew upon Seleucus, "and tooke him by the heare of the head, and boxed him wellfavoredly." She then addresses Cæsar:

Alas, said she, O Cæsar: is not this a great shame and reproche, that thou having vouchesaved to take the pains to come unto me, and hast done me this honor, poore wretche, and caitife creature, brought into this pitiful and miserable estate: and that mine owne servaunts should come now to accuse me, though it may be I have reserved some juells and trifles meete for women, but not for me (poore soule) to set out my selfe withall, but meaning to geve some pretie presents and gifts unto Octavia and Livia, that they making meanes and

---

14. *Shakespeare's Roman Plays* (London, 1935), p. 435.

intercession for me to thee, thou mightest yet extend thy favor and mercie upon me? [15]

Cæsar takes his leave, "supposing he had deceived her, but in deede he was deceived him selfe."

This is the corresponding passage in Daniel's play: [16]

CLEOPATRA
What, vile ungrateful wretch, dar'st thou controule
Thy Queene and soveraigne, caitife as thou art.

CAESAR
Holde, holde; a poore revenge can worke so feeble hands.

CLEOPATRA
Ah *Cæsar*, what a great indignitie
Is this, that here my vassal subject stands
T'accuse me to my Lord of trecherie?
If I reserv'd some certaine womens toyes,
Alas it was not for my selfe (God knowes,)
Poore miserable soule, that little joyes
In trifling ornaments in outwards showes.
But what I kept, I kept to make my way
Unto thy *Livia* and *Octavias* grace,
That thereby in compassion mooved, they
Might mediate thy favour in my case.

(ll. 681–694)

The corresponding passage in Jodelle's play [17] is as follows:

CLEOPATRE
A! faux meurdrier! a! faux traistre! arraché
Sera le poil de ta teste cruelle.
Que pleust aux Dieux que ce fust ta cervelle!
Tien, traistre, tien.

SELEUQUE
O Dieux!

CLEOPATRE
O chose detestable!
Un serf, un serf!

OCTAVIEN
Mais chose émerveillable
D'un cœur terrible!

15. Ed. Ridley, p. 283.
16. Grosart edition (1885).
17. Cf. Joan Rees, "Samuel Daniel's *Cleopatra* and 'Two French Plays,'" *MLR*, XLVII (1952), 1–10, for an account of Daniel's debt to Jodelle.

CLEOPATRE
Et quoy, m'accuses tu?
Me pensois tu veufve de ma vertu
Comme d'Antoine? a a! traistre.
SELEUQUE
Retiens la,
Puissant Cesar, retiens la doncq.
CLEOPATRE
Voila
Tous mes biensfaits. Hou! le dueil qui m'efforce
Donne à mon cœur langoureux telle force,
Que je pourrois, ce me semble, froisser
Du poing tes os, et tes flances crevasser
A coups de pied.
OCTAVIEN
O quel grinsant courage!
Mais rien n'est plus furieux que la rage
D'un cœur de femme. Et bien, quoy, Cleopatre?
Estes vous point ja saoule de le battre!
Fuy t'en, ami, fuy t'en.
CLEOPATRE
Mais quoy, mais quoy?
Mon Empereur, est-il un tel esmoy
Au monde encor que ce paillard me donne?
Sa lacheté ton esprit mesme estonne,
Comme je croy, quand moy, Roine d'ici,
De mon vassal suis accusee ainsi,
Que toy, Cesar, as daigné visiter,
Et par ta voix à repos inciter,
Hé! si j'avois retenu des joyaux,
Et quelque part de mes habits royaux,
L'aurois-je fait pour moy, las, malheureuse!
Moy, qui de moy ne suis plus curieuse?
Mais telle estoit ceste esperance mienne
Qu'à ta Livie et ton Octavienne
De ces joyaux le present je feroy,
Et leurs pitiez ainsi pourchasseroy
Pour (n'estant point de mes presens ingrates)
Envers Cesar estre mes advocates.

(pp. 75–77)

Daniel reduces the violence of Cleopatra's attack on her treasurer and
disposes of it in three lines; the epithet "ungrateful," though a natural
addition to Plutarch's words, could have been suggested by "Voila / Tous

mes biensfaits"; he uses Jodelle's word, "vassal"; and he follows him in inverting Plutarch's "unto Octavia and Livia":

> à ta Livie et ton Octavienne . . .
> Unto thy *Livia* and *Octavias* grace. . . .

Shakespeare, in the corresponding scene, follows North's translation closely. He transfers Cleopatra's physical violence to another scene (II.v) where she maltreats the messenger from Rome. But the verbal parallels with North are sufficiently obvious: *shame* (l. 159), *vouchesaved / vouchsaving* (l. 160), *mine own servants* (l. 162), *trifles* (l. 165), *reserved* (l. 165). Shakespeare also echoes two of Daniel's words—*toys* (l. 166), *mediate/mediation* (l. 170)—and he, like Daniel and Jodelle, stresses the ingratitude of Seleucus.

In one respect Shakespeare is closer to Jodelle than he is to North or Daniel. North does not put any abusive language into Cleopatra's mouth; Daniel's Cleopatra calls Seleucus a "vile, ungrateful wretch," a "vassal," and a "caitife"—the last is transferred from Cleopatra's words about herself. But Jodelle's heroine calls Seleuque a variety of names—*"faux meurdrier . . . faux traistre . . . un serf . . . ce paillard"*—and she refers to his *lacheté.* So Shakespeare's Cleopatra says:

> O slave, of no more trust
> Than love that's hir'd!
> slave, soulless villain, dog!
> O rarely base!
>
>   (V. ii. 152–153, 156–157)

This discussion of Jodelle's play—whether Shakespeare read it or not—will at least have shown that, despite the conventional condemnation of the lovers, and despite Cléopâtre's rage, we are left with an impression of her nobility and courage. In the play she does not appear as an evil temptress, except in the speech of the ghost of Antoine. The Countess of Pembroke's *Antonie,* as Ernest Schanzer has pointed out, gives a remarkably sympathetic portrait of the Queen;[18] and Daniel's Cleopatra, despite the moralizing of his chorus, is shown in an entirely favorable light. The Victorian lady's comment on Shakespeare's Cleopatra—"How unlike the life of our own dear Queen!"—could not be applied to Daniel's.

Professor Dickey's account of the traditional portrayal of the story of

18. Schanzer, *Problem Plays of Shakespeare,* p. 151.

Antony and Cleopatra seems to overlook the ambivalence in the plays before Shakespeare's. Of course she was an adultress; of course she was the cause of Antony's ruin; but (they seem to say) how magnificent she was, and what a noble end she made! We cannot, therefore, assume that the moral of *Antony and Cleopatra* was simple and unambiguous, especially if we acknowledge that in the last act the heroine is "changed, changed utterly," so that "a terrible beauty is born." It may well be that "transcendental humanism" is a more accurate label for the play than Morley's (and Quiller-Couch's) "All for Lust."

Discussion

French Renaissance Tragedy and Its Critics: A Reply to Donald Stone, Jr.

ELLIOTT FORSYTH

I

IN RECENT YEARS, renewed efforts have been made by scholars to bring to more general notice certain neglected French Renaissance writers and to achieve a reassessment of others whose work has long been treated as inferior. Such efforts are, of course, part of the normal routine of literary scholarship, and lately they have brought forth a considerable number of critical editions of hitherto inaccessible texts and a good many historical and critical studies. In some of these studies, however, we find a tendency to assume that progress in scholarship can only be made by denigrating the work of other scholars, especially those who came earlier to the field, even where these scholars have carried out indispensable basic research. As this denigration is commonly based on an inaccurate representation of the other scholars' views, it tends to lead to research conclusions of doubtful validity.

Recent examples of this procedure are to be found in an article by Donald Stone, Jr. published in *Renaissance Drama*, IX (1966) under the title "An Approach to French Renaissance Drama," and in a section of Enea Balmas' important book on Jodelle,[1] which Professor Stone quotes,

1. *Un Poeta del Rinascimento Francese: Etienne Jodelle—La sua vita—Il suo tempo* (Florence, 1962).

and from which he appears to have derived at least one of his main themes.

In his chapter on Jodelle as a dramatist,[2] Professor Balmas protests at the ironical remarks made about Jodelle's tragedy *Cléopâtre captive* by Henri Chamard in his *Histoire de la Pléiade*[3] and says:

> Ma il rimprovero mosso dallo Chamard a Jodelle—che è sostanzialmente quello di Lanson e della sua scuola—di non essere abbastanza «regolare» e cioè di non costruire la sua tragedia in base a precetti—o preconcetti—critici che saranno di moda solo un secolo più tardi, è assai inconsistente. È gratuito supporre che Jodelle abbia voluto scrivere una tragedia «regolare», e non vi sia riuscito; ed è sterile accusarlo di essersi mostrato maldestro in un'impresa alla quale egli si è certo accinto con criteri diversi da quelli che gli si vorrebbero attribuire.
>
> (p. 309)

In support of this criticism, Professor Balmas gives footnote references to Chamard's *Histoire,* to an important article by Gustave Lanson ("L'Idée de la tragédie en France avant Jodelle"[4]), and to the works of Raymond Lebègue, in particular *La Tragédie française de la Renaissance*[5] and one article.[6] Now if we check these references, we find that while Chamard is severe in his criticism of Jodelle's play, he makes no mention of any lack of "regularity" in it and does not refer to any precepts peculiar to a later age. There is a similar lack of such comments in Lanson's article: indeed Lanson, in this article, makes no comment at all about Jodelle, whose name is used simply to represent a date. Only Lebègue uses the word "régularité"[7] but it is clear from the context that he is using the word to refer not to a seventeenth-century norm, but to the norm accepted by Jodelle and his humanist contemporaries. This usage is consistent with that of Lanson, who, in his *Esquisse d'une histoire de la tragédie française,*[8] uses and defines the word in exactly this sense (p. 32): for Lanson it is a matter of contrasting the "tragédie régulière" of the Renaissance

2. *Ibid.,* chap. V.

3. Henri Chamard, *Histoire de la Pléiade,* 2d ed. (Paris, 1961), II, 22–23.

4. *Revue d'histoire littéraire de la France,* XI (1904), 541–585.

5. 1st ed. (Brussels, 1944); 2d ed. (Brussels, 1954).

6. "La Tragédie shakespearienne en France," *Revue des cours et des conferences,* XXXVIII (1937), 385 ff.

7. *La Tragédie française de la Renaissance,* 2d ed., p. 36.

8. 1st ed. (New York, 1920); 2d ed. (Paris, 1954).

with the medieval theater (p. 25) and with the "tragédies irrégulières" of the late sixteenth century (pp. 36–41), which are now more commonly classified as "tragédies baroques."

If anyone has misjudged the tragedies of Jodelle in the way alleged by Professor Balmas, it is certainly not the scholars he has named, and indeed the view attributed to Lanson and his "school" is one explicitly condemned by Lanson in his *Esquisse:*

> Erreur de considérer la tragédie de la Renaissance comme une tragédie classique mal faite, procédant de la même conception que celle de Racine et de Corneille, et n'ayant besoin que d'être améliorée.
>
> (p. 16)

II

In his article on "An Approach to French Renaissance Drama," which is partly an attempt to rehabilitate Jodelle's reputation as a dramatist, Professor Stone refers to the latter part of the passage quoted above from Balmas' book and also cites in a footnote the statement by Lanson. But he accepts Balmas' contention quite uncritically and even with warm praise as "the first recent voice of protest," failing to note the obvious contradiction between the two. Furthermore, he sets out to extend the list of scholars who have subjected Jodelle to this "prejudicial treatment."

The whole section of Professor Stone's article dealing with past studies of Renaissance drama is in fact written in highly tendentious terms. He begins: "It is hard to conceive of an aspect of the French Renaissance that has been more systematically neglected than the drama. Yet total neglect might have been preferable to the prejudicial treatment the genre has received in the past and continues to receive today." One wonders what "system" has been applied to produce this neglect. He continues: "At the present time a student interested in French Renaissance drama will have little success in finding a satisfactory survey of the genre or an unbiased evaluation of its accomplishments" (p. 279). He then lists four general works, none of which he finds satisfactory: R. Lebègue's *La Tragédie française de la Renaissance* is dismissed because it "contains a bare 109 pages"; two books by Rigal [9] (dated 1901 and 1911 respectively, and long

9. *Le Théâtre français avant la période classique* (Paris, 1901), which combines material from two earlier books; and *De Jodelle à Molière* (Paris, 1911).

since considered outmoded by specialists) are rejected because they say little about the sixteenth century; and a book by myself, which is set aside because it considers the development of tragedy from the standpoint of a particular theme.[10] He quotes at length two student manuals (both of which say simply that Jodelle's *Cléopâtre* lacks dramatic action) and accuses them, along with the other writers, of neglect and prejudice.

Several comments need to be made on these criticisms. First, they are based on the assumption that the absence of a large-scale survey of a genre necessarily implies neglect. It would be hard to find a large-scale scholarly study of French classical tragedy as a whole, but I am not aware that the field has been in any way neglected. In both cases there exist a reasonable number of studies on individual authors and aspects of the theater. For sixteenth-century tragedy, I have listed in my own book some twenty-five books and articles and a considerable number of modern editions of texts, and since its publication at least two new theses have appeared. All this, I should add, is to cover a total output of about eighty plays, good, bad, and indifferent, written from 1550 to 1600.

Secondly, to dismiss Professor Lebègue's short survey of Renaissance tragedy because of its small size is hardly a fair assessment of the work of a scholar who had devoted about a thousand published pages to the theater of the sixteenth century before this book was written, and who has contributed more than any other to our knowledge of this field. Professor Lebègue's book, written under the difficulties of the German occupation, is intended as an introduction for the student and general reader and forms part of a collection of a standard size. It is nonetheless a concise, well-documented and authoritative survey, which specialists continue to use for reference. Professor Stone makes no mention of Lebègue's major

10. E. C. Forsyth, *La Tragédie française de Jodelle à Corneille* (*1553–1640*): *le thème de la vengeance* (Paris, 1962); Professor Stone dismisses this book as "a long enumeration of Renaissance plays where the theme of vengeance appears" (p. 280). Obviously the author is predisposed in favor of his own work, but he would have imagined that, as a complement to Lebègue's book, it would be of considerable use to Professor Stone's hypothetical student, for the revenge theme has a place of major importance in the development of French tragedy; furthermore, the book contains, in addition to a detailed literary and historical analysis of a large number of tragedies, a 140-page preliminary study of the social, religious, and literary traditions concerned with the theme, and, as an appendix, a complete bibliographical list of the tragedies of the period.

single contribution to the study of the Renaissance theater, *La Tragédie religieuse en France: les débuts (1514-1573)*,[11] which covers much of the ground Stone discusses later in his article. Nor does he mention Lebègue's partially completed edition of the works of Garnier.

This does not mean that there is no further room for research, but it does mean that any further research must take into account the significant results already achieved. We must also consider the fact that the field is small: 81 extant tragedies for the period 1550–1600 as against 187 for 1601–1640. And of these, as one would expect, only a small minority are of any real literary interest. Whatever the merits of individual plays, anyone who has read the whole range is forced to admit that in France the sixteenth century, the great age of lyric poetry, was not the age of great drama.

III

Professor Stone's second objection is more fundamental, as it is concerned with aesthetic judgments. He declares that "the prejudicial treatment of French Renaissance drama is in many ways related to a general tendency among French critics to glorify their classical period. The brilliant success of the seventeenth-century theater has tended to close their eyes to all other efforts with tragedy. They can accept or approve only what conforms to Aristotle and resembles Corneille and Racine" (p. 281). In support of this damning statement, Stone quotes phrases from Lebègue and myself, into which he reads the following implications: (1) "And naturally, since Renaissance drama looks like classical tragedy, it can be judged as such"; (2) "In both cases the judgment is clearly based on a comparison with the classical tragedy of Corneille and Racine" (pp. 281–282).

Even wrenched out of their context as they are, it is difficult to find in the phrases quoted by Stone any of the implications attributed to them. Rereading the full text of the quotation taken from Lebègue's book, I am unable to find any hint of a critical evaluation which sets out to judge the tragedies of Jodelle as though they were classical tragedies. Nor can I find any such statement or implication in my own writing on the subject. Comparisons with plays of other ages and traditions can certainly be

11. (Paris, 1929).

found: comparisons with Greek and Senecan tragedy, with Italian and English tragedy, with the theater of the Middle Ages, and more rarely with the classical theater. Such factual comparisons and contrasts are indispensable to an informed study of any play, especially one written in an unfamiliar idiom. But they do not necessarily imply value judgments based on any one of them. When Lebègue says of Jodelle's *Cléopâtre captive:* "Pas d'incertitude, pas un conflit intérieur. Rien n'est plus vide," he is referring to characteristics of tragedy which are commonly found in the works of the Greeks, the English dramatists, and even some of Jodelle's French contemporaries: they are in no way peculiar to the French classical theater. To say, as I have done, that Jodelle's *Didon se sacrifiant* is "une pièce élégiaque, sans action," would seem to be a fairly objective statement: if one made a similar comment about, say, T. S. Eliot's *Murder in the Cathedral,* one could hardly be accused of judging it in terms of French classical tragedy, or even according to the norms of the Elizabethan theater.

In a footnote on p. 281, Stone quotes with approval the comment given above from Lanson's *Esquisse d'une histoire de la tragédie française* and claims that the words were "not heeded." We should note that the remark was addressed to an American audience at Columbia in 1916–17 and published primarily for American readers at a time when little was available on the tragedy of the sixteenth century apart from the works of Faguet and Rigal, whose weaknesses had already been shown by Lanson himself in a number of articles. It is also worth noting that in the same section of his notes (5° Leçon, I), Lanson refers to the tragedies of Jodelle and others in the following terms: "Absence de psychologie, de conflit dramatique, et d'action (intrigue); rares et fortuites apparitions de ces trois intérêts." As this comment is very similar to those criticized by Stone, one is tempted to ask if this proves that Lanson was unable to heed his own words.

On p. 282, H. W. Lawton's comments about the "important and lamentable development" [12] which followed the choice of Seneca as the model for tragedy are dismissed in the following terms:

Nevertheless, his ultimate judgment leaves us with the same impression: French humanists were not of the same stature as their classical successors.

12. *Handbook of French Renaissance Dramatic Theory* (Manchester, 1949), p. xxi.

They betrayed the nature of tragedy. They betrayed that antiquity whose aesthetics Aristotle had so conveniently codified and, by inference, the seventeenth century had so carefully followed. There is no escaping the dominance of the classical moment here; it even represents the very historical point ("le théâtre avant Corneille") from which we set out to judge Renaissance drama.

I am unable to find any evidence whatever in Professor Lawton's book for this series of accusations and inferences, least of all for the idea of "betrayal": the most I can find is a statement that "the subjects of tragedy . . . were selected and treated in such a way as to emphasize the pathetic rather than the tragic" (p. xxii), which I consider to be a fairly neutral and factual remark.

Throughout the second and third parts of his article, Stone refers to these supposed critical views and extends them:

To compare the love theme of *Didon se sacrifiant* and *Phèdre* with the intention of proving that Racine was the better psychologist contorts entirely the function of love in the Renaissance play (p. 286).

Racine's portrait of love has vastly more in common with Vergil's analysis of Dido than does *Didon se sacrifiant*. Yet Jodelle was easily as proficient a Latinist as Racine, and the ugly charge of a betrayal of antiquity inevitably returns (p. 287).

In short, by insisting that the differences between a Jodelle and a Racine are distinctions of talent and intelligence rather than chronology and tradition, critics merely accuse Renaissance dramatists of not doing what in fact they never intended to do, and at the same time pursue comparisons that rarely lead to the essential differences which divide the two centuries as well as their literatures (p. 289).

Who, one may ask, are the critics who make these fruitless detailed comparisons between Jodelle and Racine and who make "the ugly charge of a betrayal of antiquity" against Jodelle? Certainly not those mentioned earlier by Stone, who offers no references for the passages just quoted. For my own part, I know of no serious critical work written in this vein in the last fifty years.[13] I am forced to conclude that the critics concerned either wrote more than fifty years ago or are entirely hypothetical.

13. Since I live in Australia, I cannot of course answer for the whole range of American publications, especially doctoral theses, but I doubt if they fall into such errors. Nor have I seen, at the time of writing, M. Valency, *The Flower and the Castle* (New York, 1963), quoted by Stone, or Stone's own edition of *Four Renaissance Tragedies* (Cambridge, Mass., 1966).

IV

Professor Stone's own approach to French Renaissance drama is based, in his article, almost entirely on an examination of two tragedies: Buchanan's *Jephthes* (written by the Scottish humanist in Latin about 1539–44) and Jodelle's *Didon se sacrifiant* (written 1554–73). There is no mention of comedy or tragicomedy, nor is there any mention of the two major writers of French Renaissance tragedy, Robert Garnier and Jean de La Taille. Stone sets out to show that humanist tragedy attempts a moral lesson on Man's destiny, and that, since the medieval theater also had a didactic purpose, medieval influences on the Renaissance theater must have been strong.

Professor Lebègue has made an exhaustive examination, in the books mentioned above, of the transition from the medieval to the Renaissance theater, especially in the field of religious drama. He has pointed out various common elements,[14] has shown clearly how some classical features penetrated into the Latin mystery plays of the early sixteenth century, how the neo-Latin tragedies of Buchanan and Muret did much to foster the development of tragedy in France, and how the medieval theater continued its performances, especially in the provinces, until the end of the century. There is thus no question of a sudden change from medieval to Renaissance genres in the French theater as a whole.

The individual humanist playwrights, on the other hand, especially those who were members of the Pléiade or espoused its ideals, were highly critical of the medieval theater and would have strongly denied any medieval influence, believing that they had severed all contact with the medieval theater:

Seulement vous adviseray-je, qu'autant de Tragedies et Comedies, de Farces, et Moralitez (où bien souvent n'y a sens ny raison, mais des paroles ridicules avec quelque badinage) et autres jeux qui ne sont faicts selon le vray art, et au moule des vieux, comme d'un Sophocle, Euripide et Seneque, ne peuvent estre que choses ignorantes, malfaites, indignes d'en faire cas, et qui ne deussent servir de passetemps qu'aux varlets et menu populaire, et non aux personnes graves . . .[15]

14. See, for example, *La Tragédie religieuse,* pp. 24–26 and 453–455. Cf. *La Tragédie française de la Renaissance,* pp. 9–10.

15. Jean de La Taille, *De l'art de la tragedie* (Paris, 1572), fol. 4. Cf. Du Bellay, *Deffence et illustration de la langue françoyse* (Paris, 1549), Vol. II, chap. IV.

Hence Lebègue's statement: "Comme ses successeurs, Jodelle rompt complètement avec le théâtre médiéval . . . ,"[16] which Stone wrongly transcribes as "Jodelle 'rompt complètement avec le moyen âge'" and misinterprets as a consequence (p. 285). This, of course, does not necessarily prove that there was no such influence. But if we examine the humanist tradition, we find that the idea of tragedy as a play with a moral purpose was also present in the teachings of those ancients from whom they derived their concept: if it remains only implicit in Donatus and Diomedes, it is quite explicit in Horace (*Ars poetica,* 343–344). It is thus unnecessary to assume that the idea of a didactic purpose in tragedy must be due to medieval influence.[17]

The moral and didactic orientation of Renaissance tragedy has, of course, been emphasized by the critics whose work Stone rejects, and it has been shown that even in biblical plays the influence of Seneca is not limited to dramatic form but extends to the moral lesson as a result of the fusion of Christian and stoic moral ideas.[18] The image of the "wheel of Fortune," as Stone has to acknowledge, is a Senecan image[19] and is only one of many which fill the choruses and the *sententiae* of Jodelle and his contemporaries. Seneca's tragedies themselves were written as illustrated lessons in stoic moral philosophy, and as they were much more readily accessible even to the humanists than the plays of the Greeks and thus became the standard models for all playwrights, it is easy to see how Renaissance tragedy acquired this kind of moral orientation. The exhaustive research done by Lebègue has shown that, apart from the plays of the Protestant writers Théodore de Bèze and Louis Desmasures, whose biblical plays were addressed to a popular audience, we find little in the texts that can be attributed to direct medieval influences rather than classical influences and humanist aspirations.[20] At most we can say that, at this

16. *La Tragédie française de la Renaissance,* 2d ed., p. 33.

17. In commenting on this point, Stone gives the date of Lazare de Baïf's translation of Sophocles' *Electra* as 1551. The correct date is 1537 (see Lebègue, *La Tragédie religieuse,* p. 114). It is clear that in the definition given in his preface, Baïf uses *moralité* to mean "a serious play with a moral purpose": his definition is addressed to readers whose experience of the theater is limited to medieval genres.

18. Forsyth, pp. 100–115, 176–181, 210–215.

19. *Thyestes,* 614–621.

20. *La Tragédie française,* pp. 9–10, and personal correspondence.

moment of transition, the humanist ideas on the didactic purpose of tragedy fell on receptive ears prepared by the medieval tradition.

One further point should be mentioned. It would be a mistake to assume that the didactic orientation of Renaissance tragedy always followed the same pattern. In fact, it underwent quite a complex series of changes ranging from humanist teaching on stoic principles and Protestant biblical lessons to bitter politico-religious propaganda linked with the Wars of Religion and the strange distortions of Senecan techniques which mark the "horror" tragedy of the end of the century.[21]

V

From his examination of Buchanan's *Jephthes* and Jodelle's *Didon se sacrifiant,* Professor Stone concludes, in part III of his article, that the playwrights of the sixteenth century were not interested in creating dramatic action. Indeed, he seems to believe that Corneille, justifying the introduction of several scenes of violence in his *Clitandre* in 1631, is the first to show concern for the element of action. It may be true that Jodelle is lacking in such interest, although even he seems to make an attempt to put action into Act III of *Cléopâtre* when he has the queen seize a servant by the hair and beat him in the presence of the Emperor Octavian, a scene which my "prejudiced" mind can only describe as curiously out of key with the dignified humanist idea of tragedy. But the sample is in any case too small, and to assume that all writers lack this interest is to ignore the lesson of the main body of plays and the theoretical writings of their authors.

Even a slow-moving play like Garnier's *Les Juives* (1583) shows a real concern for the development of dramatic tension, for the element of suspense is exploited by the use of verbal ambiguity (l. 1194), and where Seneca, in the revenge plays which Garnier used as models, brought his opposing parties face to face in the third act, Garnier goes a stage further and brings them together three times (Amital and the queen; Amital and Nebuchadnezzar; Nebuchadnezzar and Zedekiah), thus greatly increasing the tension before the catastrophe.[22]

21. Forsyth, chaps. V–VIII.
22. *Ibid.,* pp. 210–215.

But more important is the example of Jean de La Taille, who, in his essay *De l'art de la tragedie* (1572), speaks of dramatic structure in terms that indicate a demand for action through the use of peripeteia:

Or c'est le principal point d'une Tragedie de la sçavoir bien disposer, bien bastir, et la deduire de sorte qu'elle change, transforme, manie, et tourne l'esprit des escoutans deça delà, et faire qu'ils voyent maintenant une joye tournee tout soudain en tristesse, et maintenant au rebours, à l'exemple des choses humaines.

(fol. 3ᵛ)

If the meaning of this theoretical statement were in doubt, it would be sufficient to look at La Taille's first tragedy, *Saül le furieux* (1572),[23] for which the essay serves as a preface. Instead of beginning his play with a tedious prologue, in the tradition established by Jodelle, he starts *in medias res* with a scene in which King Saul, in a fit of madness, attempts to kill his sons, whom he takes for Philistine enemies, and shows us the sons trying to cope with a critical military situation at a time when their commander is unfit to direct operations. The model for the mad scene is found in Seneca's *Hercules furens* (Act IV), but instead of making it the climax of his play as Seneca did, La Taille places it right at the beginning, thus giving his tragedy a vigorous start by the immediate creation of dramatic tension and arousing interest and curiosity before the presentation of the historical exposition in Act II. The tension builds up to the scene where Saul persuades the witch of Endor to conjure up the spirit of Samuel and learns, trembling, from the shade of the prophet the terrible verdict of his inevitable doom—undoubtedly the most dramatic scene in the French theater before Tristan's *Mariane* (1637).

Although Jean de La Taille made less impact on his contemporaries than Garnier, who was obviously a better poet and rhetorician, it is clear that he was a playwright who made a conscious and successful attempt to introduce both dramatic action and psychological content into tragedy— and this before Jodelle's *Didon* was published. Perhaps La Taille's contemporaries would have seen the significance of his innovations if his *Saül* had been performed at court as the author wished.

Alongside the authentic tragedy of La Taille and Garnier, who develop in rather different ways the humanist tradition of the Pléiade, we must

23. These points are discussed more fully in the introduction to my edition of La Taille, *Saül le furieux; la Famine, ou les Gabeonites* (Paris, 1968).

note the attempts to create dramatic action in the baroque tragedies of the end of the century: here, in dramas reminiscent of the Elizabethan "tragedy of blood," we encounter gory spectacles far removed from the elegiac tragedies of lamentation written by Jodelle (Poullet, *Charite,* 1595; Hays, *Cammate,* 1598; Heudon, *Pyrrhe,* 1598, etc.).[24] The fact that these plays were written and in some cases definitely performed suggests that a real need was felt for movement as well as lamentation on the stage long before Corneille.

VI

One other paragraph of Professor Stone's article calls for comment. On p. 288 he begins: "Although the form of humanist tragedy is nearly that of seventeenth-century drama, the development of theater from the Pléiade to Corneille is not a simple linear progression." The second part of this statement has, of course, been acknowledged as true since G. Lanson formulated it in almost identical terms in 1920.[25] But the first part can only be considered true at a very superficial level: the prologues and choruses of Renaissance tragedy are rare in seventeenth-century classical tragedy, and while some Senecan elements remain, the structure of a classical tragedy is far removed from the Senecan form so predominant in the Renaissance theater.

Professor Stone declares, in the same paragraph, that psychological drama began in the 1630's, when Mairet and the Academy restored tragedy after its temporary eclipse by the pastoral and tragicomedy of the early 1600's, and when "the salons of the *précieuses* demanded a literature that pleased, not preached," seeking their inspiration in the theme of love as revealed by Ariosto and Tasso. This is again misleading, for we do not have to wait until 1630 before the theme of love in psychological drama enters French tragedy. The earliest clearly identifiable play in which we find these elements combined is Chrestien des Croix's *Rosemonde, ou la Vengeance* (1603),[26] a horror tragedy in which we see the heroine, whose

24. See Forsyth, chap. VIII.

25. "Erreur de croire au développement continu et rectiligne de la tragédie, de *Cléopâtre* à *Athalie* (Faguet)" (*Esquisse,* 5ᵉ leçon).

26. See Forsyth, pp. 267–282.

character develops in the course of the action, caught in a dilemma in which love for her husband and the duty to take revenge on him struggle for supremacy. It is possible that A. Hardy's play *Mariamne* (published only in 1625), in which we find a similar psychological conflict, was performed even before 1603.[27] In any case, Corneille acknowledges his debt to Hardy in the *Examen* of his first play, *Mélite* (1629), in which he makes use of the dilemma as a dramatic motif in much the same way as he does several years later in his first tragedy *Médée* (performed 1634–35).[28] More important still, both the subject and the essential psychological conflict of Hardy's play were taken up again and developed with more skill by Tristan L'Hermite in 1636–37 (*La Mariane*), shortly before *Le Cid* was performed.[29]

VII

What conclusions can we draw from this rather confused picture? Firstly, we must be aware—and here Professor Stone is quite right—that the concept of tragedy undergoes some profound changes in the course of its evolution from the Renaissance to the classical forms. Envisaged first as a conscious imitation of the ancient genre, it was concerned essentially with the presentation of an exemplary spectacle of human suffering drawn from ancient history, mythology, or the Bible, in which the elegiac and didactic elements were paramount. But as the religious wars gathered momentum, tragedy became more and more the vehicle, not merely of general moral lessons on the instability of human fortunes, but of specific lessons on contemporary issues and then of politico-religious propaganda. Even within this context we see the emergence of a desire for dramatic action and character study in the work of Jean de La Taille, whose *Saül le furieux* is the most dramatic play produced by the French Renaissance. But the achievement of La Taille was overshadowed by the works of Robert Garnier, who continued to write in a rhetorical style, and whose last play, *Les Juives*, in which the deep religious concern of the author is revealed in a conflict between disobedient Man and a just, avenging God,

27. *Ibid.*, pp. 341–345.
28. *Ibid.*, pp. 383–389.
29. *Ibid.*, pp. 362–370.

is probably the only great tragedy of the sixteenth century. The desire for action and excitement appeared, however, in a cruder form towards the end of the century in a series of plays presenting physical violence and death on the stage, sometimes with an ostensibly didactic intention. While the majority of these plays are only curiosities, we find that it is within the context of this horror and violence that a fundamental concept of the seventeenth-century theater first appears: the inner conflict or tragic dilemma. Revealed to Tristan L'Hermite and Corneille by the professional playwright Alexandre Hardy, this new concept of tragedy as a psychological conflict enacted within the soul of the protagonist enabled these men of genius, at a point in time when a new interest in tragedy was emerging, to transform completely the idiom of the French theater.

Secondly, we must be aware that, while the contribution of playwrights like Buchanan and Jodelle to this development was a real one, the intrinsic value of their works must not be overrated. It may be that we have done some injustice to Jodelle in the past and that there is room for a more appreciative assessment of the kind proposed by Balmas. Jodelle's works undoubtedly fulfilled the immediate aspirations of those about him, who had little experience of tragedy as a stage presentation and whose concept of tragedy was therefore still limited. But that does not automatically make them great works, and any reassessment of a Renaissance playwright must be based on a wide acquaintance with this theater as a whole and on an accurate and objective reading of both the texts and the writings of critics and historians. The mere denigration of previous critical work on the basis of a misreading or a hazy recollection and an inadequate coverage does nothing to advance scholarship. And unless positive reasons for admiring the plays of Jodelle, based on analysis of the texts within the context of the Renaissance theater as a whole, can be advanced, their interest, especially compared with that of authors like Garnier and La Taille, will remain mainly historical.

Professor Stone Replies

Professor Forsyth has presented his ideas with such clarity that the points which divide us are immediately evident. Naturally he knows best what he meant when writing about Jodelle, and it is true that Lawton does not speak of a "betrayal" in his remarks on French Renaissance tragedy; still there is no doubting the negative quality of their judgments: "*sans* action," "lyrical or rhetorical *rather than* dramatic" (italics mine). Were the second element in the comparison French Classicism or not, we are offered a comparison according to which we must appreciate in essence wherein this theater failed. I do believe that Lanson did not heed his own advice, for seeing differences between Renaissance and Classical drama did not keep him from offering the same negative definition we find in the manuals, which by linking the two say more than that Jodelle's *Cléopâtre* lacks dramatic action. From the word "approach" in my title to the close of my article, I wished to call attention to the negative quality of these judgments and to outline a more positive orientation toward the subject. This intent explains why I referred to the older school of criticism as "prejudiced" and why I felt its work hindered further study. That Professor Forsyth chooses to see in my remarks a denigration of this judgment gives to my words a sinister quality that was never intended. The article never says that, contrary to Forsyth's words, there is action in *Didon* or that, contrary to Lawton's views, Renaissance drama is dramatic, not lyrical. Similarly, I am surprised to learn that part of my article is construed as an attempt to rehabilitate Jodelle's reputation. At no point do I speak of his plays as great works of art. They are not. I speak of them as "rich" with respect to what they can teach us about the period, after having sketched a procedure for understanding why their author wrote as he did in preference to repeating why the plays fail to resemble other schools of drama. This is my approach to French Renaissance drama, one that leads me to doubt Lebègue's dictum about Jodelle and medieval theater, which is correctly cited on p. 281. Also, quoting Jean de La Taille on medieval theater cannot establish norms for dramatists who lived some decades before, and it is incorrect to suggest that I base medieval influence on Buchanan or Jodelle on didactic purpose alone.

A second area of misunderstanding appears in Professor Forsyth's discussion of dramatic action. Even while recognizing that there is tension in *Les Juives* and that there may be drama in certain scenes such as Saul's madness, I still do not believe that humanist tragedy sought to be dramatic in the fashion outlined by Corneille in 1631. It abounds in *récits,*

now called "ennuyeux" and does so out of respect for those classical
dramatists now associated with "incommodités." Whether La Taille or
Garnier sought primarily to "divertir les yeux" is a very moot point.

I am not unaware of the existence of the "blood tragedies" at the end of
the sixteenth century, but as this movement is recognized to signal a
breakdown in the humanist technique I had just discussed, I moved on to
the moment when regular drama was about to reappear (as the paragraph
preceding the quotation from Corneille states). At this point my article is
admittedly very general; it was intended to be. I am grateful to Professor
Forsyth for his additional information and for his admission that on one
major point my ideas were correct.

Reviews

SALERNO, HENRY F., translator and editor. *Scenarios of the Commedia dell'Arte: Flaminio Scala's* IL TEATRO DELLE FAVOLE RAPPRESENTATIVE. With a Foreword by Kenneth McKee. New York: New York University Press; London: University of London Press Limited, 1967. Pp. xxxiii, 413. $9.75.

FLAMINIO SCALA's *Teatro,* the only collection of scenari to be published in the seventeenth century, has never been reprinted in full since its first appearance in 1611, though Vito Pandolfi, in *La Commedia dell' Arte* (Florence, 1957–61), published numbers 1–5, 18, 25, 36, and 42, and gave the table of contents of the whole work (II, 213–223). He also gave summaries of all the plays (V, 213–223). Only two scenari, *The Faithful Friend* (29) and *The Portrait* (39, translated by Professor Salerno as *The Picture*) have formerly appeared in English, according to Eric Bentley in his *The Genius of the Italian Theater* (New York, 1964), pp. 566–567.

Students of the English drama, then, should welcome Professor Salerno's translation of the complete series of fifty plays. Their debt would be even greater if the work had been executed in a more scholarly fashion. The foreword by Professor Kenneth McKee gives a brief and not always accurate account of the commedia dell'arte and its relation to the theater outside Italy. The volume has no bibliography, and in the eight footnotes

223

to the foreword no work published later than 1934 is cited. It is surprising to find no reference to Allardyce Nicoll's *The World of Harlequin* (Cambridge University Press, 1963).

Neither Professor McKee nor Professor Salerno (who in a fifteen-page appendix relates some of the scenari to English and French plays) attempts to identify Flaminio Scala, or to give any account of his work. Yet the author of so unusual a collection surely deserves some notice. It is true that little is known of his life outside the theater; even the dates of his birth and death remain obscure. His name does not appear in the list of the members of the company of the Gelosi, led by Francesco and Isabella Andreini; yet he was their close friend, and their names, as well as his own stage name Flavio (he played the part of a lover), appear in the dramatis personae of almost all his scenari. Francesco is Captain Spavento, the braggart and butt of innumerable plots.

In 1597 Scala became the leader of the Desiosi troupe, and in 1601 he joined the Accesi, with whom he went to France, possibly in the company of the great Arlecchino, Tristano Martinelli, more probably with Pier Maria Cecchini, the comedian known as Frittellino. The company entertained Henri IV in Paris, and Scala also went to Lyons with Cecchini. In 1606 he performed before the Duke of Mantua, and may have entered the Duke's service then. Scala was still employed in Mantua when he published *Il Teatro,* but in the same year, 1611, he became director of the second Confidenti company under the patronage of Don Giovanni de' Medici, a post which he still held when he performed in Venice in 1620. His relationship with the Andreini induced him to assist Francesco in publishing the literary remains of Isabella (who had died in 1604) in Turin in 1621. This is the last known record of his name. His one regular play, *Il finto marito,* based on his ninth scenario, was published in Venice in 1619.

It has been conjectured that the names used in his scenari do not refer to the members of one company alone, but include reminiscences of actors and actresses in several of the companies with which he had been associated. His Pantalone was probably Giulio Pasquati, his Franceschina Silvia Roncagli, both of the Gelosi. His Pedrolino may have been Giovanni Pellesini, of the Uniti and the first company of the Confidenti. These figures appear constantly, while others occur in only one or two plays. Vittoria, who figures occasionally, may have been Vittoria Amorevoli, or, more probably, Antonia Bajardi, who used that name on the stage. Piombino (Girolamo Salimbene) appears with Vittoria, and they both play themselves in *Il Ritratto* (39), an interesting and early play about the acting profession. Both Piombino and Ricciolina (Angela Lucchesi), of scenario 38, were members of the Accesi company. Zanobio (8) is Scala's own creation of a Pantalone figure with a new name.

The scenari themselves were probably not all Scala's original compositions but were collected by him and enlarged into a coherent readable form, with long prefatory explanations of the situation and the interrelations of the characters. The subjects range from farce to tragedy to pastoral, thus giving some conception of the scope and repertory of the commedia dell'arte companies of the time. As their properties and sometimes their scenes are listed it is evident what a wide variety of staging they must have required: some are very simple, some indicate a need for the elaborate machines which had already become so popular in noble theaters and which Niccolò Sabbattini was designing with such imaginative skill. The settings include the street scene traditional to comedy, the Temple of Pan in Arcadia (46), the throne room of the King of Poland (50), and the courtyard of the Viceroy's palace in Naples (36). Turkish scenes or characters appear in many of the scenari. Musicians are listed in so many plays that it is evident what a large part music held in these entertainments.

Strange though it is that Scala is mentioned only cursorily by Professor Salerno and Professor McKee, his fate at the former's hands is even more remarkable. The translator's knowledge of Italian is reasonably adequate to deal with the almost telegraphic simplicity of the scenari, though even there mistakes are not infrequent—*ruffiano*, for instance, does not mean *ruffian*. But formal seventeenth-century prose and verse are quite beyond his powers, and the translation of all the prefatory material is not merely inaccurate, it is wildly, unbelievably, at variance with the original. One or two examples will suffice to demonstrate this.

According to the translation, Flaminio Scala begins his Dedication thus:

That virtue which renders men amiable is disastrous to our souls. Nobility is a quality worthy of esteem: in loving others, we bring greatness out of obscurity and sound the trumpet of fame in praise of others to a world beyond our own. Who will admire your most illustrious self, whose virtue is equal to nobility and magnanimity appearing in all the nobility, if I yield to my compulsion to dedicate these fifty dramatic outlines to you?

(p. xxv)

This makes so little sense that the reader is perplexed; and with good reason, for the Italian is:

> La Virtù, che rende gli huomini amabili, è una calamita de gli animi nostri, la Nobiltà è un ornamento riguardevole, ch'innamorando l'altrui volere si rende soggetti ancora i non conosciuti giamai; la Magnanimità è la Tromba della Fama, che rende sonore l'altrui lodi fra gente un Mondo lontano dal nostro Mondo. Qual maraviglia sarà dunque se ritrovandosi in V.S. Illustriss. virtù eguale alla nobiltà, e magnanimità pari alla nobiltà, io sia stato violentato dalla volontà mia a dedicarle questi Cinquanta Soggetti per opere Drammatiche?

A reasonably literal rendering might be:

> Virtue, which makes men worthy of love, is a lodestone to our minds. Nobility is an admirable ornament which, kindling the will to love, subjects even those who are unknown. Magnanimity is the trumpet of Fame, which sounds forth the praise of its possessors among peoples a world away from our world. What wonder can it be then, since in your Lordship there exists virtue to equal your nobility, and magnanimity equal to your nobility, if my will has compelled me to dedicate to you these fifty subjects for dramatic works?

The mangled verse is better left unexamined; but the close of Francesco Andreini's address to the readers contains an interesting point that writers on Scala have not noticed, and that is obscured in the present translation. Andreini urges the readers to give Scala's plays the applause they deserve, "difendendole il più che potrete da chiunque volesse, o per malignità, o per mera ignoranza biasimarle, che ciò facendo li porgerete ardire di metter fuora la seconda parte delle sue opere Sceniche e rappresentative"— a graceful reference to the title of the book—"non punto inferiore a questa prima." This is translated: "give them [his works] the applause they merit. Resist, as much as you are able, whatever compulsion you feel to find fault with them. In this way you will strengthen your resolve to continue into the following, his representative stage works, not a whit inferior to this opening" (p. xxxii). It should rather be rendered: "defending them to the best of your powers from anyone who might wish, through malice or pure ignorance, to criticize them adversely; and if you do so you will give him courage to put forth the second part of his stage works intended for performance, in no wise inferior to this first one."

This suggests that Scala had in readiness fifty more scenari; and he may have been discouraged from publishing them by the failure of the first part to reach a second edition. For it is true that, except to the scholar or the author looking for plots, scenari are arid reading; and those who are lured into buying this volume by its sensational dust jacket will be disappointed.

Andreini's preface also offers an example of a curious inconsistency in the translation of proper names. Roscio, Socrate, Cicerone, are translated (p. xxxi) as Roscius, Socrates, Cicero; but Lisippo, Tito, and Varo are left in Italian, though Lysippus, Titus, and Varus would be more familiar to English readers. In three scenari a merchant of Lyons figures, a reference both to Scala's visit to that city and to the long-established connection between Lyons and Italy; but this may not be recognized by the general reader, as the name is left as Lione.

Professor Salerno's book, then, will be useful but also dangerous to the English scholar who knows no Italian. It is disturbing that a work of such dubious merits should be sponsored by two university presses.

BEATRICE CORRIGAN

McDONALD, CHARLES OSBORNE. *The Rhetoric of Tragedy: Form in Stuart Drama.* Amherst: University of Massachusetts Press, 1966. Pp. viii + 360. $7.50.

THIS LARGE and handsome-looking book seems to contain a rehandling of material presented in 1959 as a Ph.D. thesis, under the direction of Eugene Waith. It is important to know this, for Professor Waith's interest in the relationship of formal rhetorical exercises and dramatic exercises is obviously the starting point of Mr. McDonald's work.

Mr. Waith, however, centered his work on direct use of the *controversiae* by Beaumont and Fletcher and modestly confined his observations to one particular set of dramatic effects. Mr. McDonald attempts nothing less than "an intensive study of the effects of antilogistic rhetoric upon the form of Stuart dramatic literature." Even this is not really grandiose enough as a statement: he attempts to expose the whole history of "Stuart tragedy" from the point of view of rhetoric.

Mr. McDonald attempts to give shape and meaning to his various observations by loading them with historical significance. Unfortunately Mr. McDonald's view of history is rather elementary. The only authorities he quotes are Tawney, L. C. Knights, and Leo Salingar (especially the last). *The Pelican Guide* is a useful little book, and Mr. Salingar's essay is a handy brief compendium (I'm sure he would not claim any more); but it is too cursory to support the weight of generalization that Mr. McDonald imposes on it. The whole "scrutiny" view of the cultural history of the seventeenth century is doubtful, even in the subtle and sensitive shadings of L. C. Knights. How much more suspect must it appear clothed in the "gaudiness and inane phraseology" of Mr. McDonald:

> The story is an old one told in all the histories of the period—what had started in the Sixteenth Century as a dramatic venture in the enlarging of all the horizons of human existence, suddenly, in the first decade of the Seventeenth seemed to dilate into a vista of anarchy, of chaos, of the void itself. Wrenched successively adrift from their moorings in the placid harbors of medieval and contractual society, the "body politic," the theocratic and benevolent (in theory at least) economic commonweal, and the powerfully authoritarian Queen, driven from the havens of religion by ever more fractuous winds of schism, from the old notions of the hierarchical order of Nature and the universe under God, blasted loose in the roadsteads of science from the sheet-anchors of Ptolemy and Galen by the "new learning," the minds and spirits of Renaissance Englishmen at first tried hard to beat back upwind into the shelters they were now denied, but as the century progressed that recourse became obviously impossible, and they resorted more and more to scudding under bare poles before the gales of new learning, new opinion, new action, retaining but nostalgic (and even quite unrealistically ideal) memories of old ports, quieter waters, and sunnier climes of youth and tradition. Yet, even in the moments before the seas of civil war overwhelmed them, there were still voices, though now plaintive, telling of a vanished heroic age. The spectrum of mentality Stuart men exhibit is, in short, that of a progression from optimistic faith to pessimistic despair, or, what is even more poignant, to a pseudo-optimistic whistling in the dark.

Mr. McDonald's concern is with "Stuart drama"—Marston, Chapman, Tourneur, Webster, Ford—presumably because of the limitations that have to be placed on a thesis. But it is a very odd book that jumps straight from Seneca to Marston (after a brief glance at *Hamlet*). The rhetoric of the Stuart dramatists was derived primarily from the rhetoric of the Tudor dramatists; and *The Spanish Tragedy* (not to mention *Horestes*) is of more immediate importance than the *Medea* of Euripides. But Mr. McDonald seems to think that having mentioned the relationship between Euripides (good) and Seneca (bad) he can assume a similar relationship between Elizabethans and Jacobeans, so that the *Medea* might be thought to stand for *The Spanish Tragedy;* but this will hardly do.

Given Mr. McDonald's simplified historical view of the period it is to be expected that the Tudor drama should serve only to indicate a vaguely conceived Golden Age of un-disassociated sensibilities, an ideal from which most seventeenth-century drama must be a falling-away. But in a book devoted to the uses of rhetoric it is strange to find that the good and the bad drama are represented in terms of character ("good") and rhetoric ("bad"). This dichotomy is most obvious in the lamentable essay on Webster, which defines the limitations of Mr. McDonald's sympathies as bounded (in spite of his new-look rhetorical vocabulary) by the good old concepts of well-made plotting and realistic characterization. The method of the essay on Webster is to look at each major character in turn, discovering (in turn) that each is lacking in power as a central tragic figure. We are told that motivation is inadequate, that there are too many coincidences in the plot, that evil is too prominent. It needs no circuitous route from Abdera to reach charges that Archer could derive equally plausibly and more immediately from a love of Ibsen.

In the usual "Scrutiny" manner, Mr. McDonald uses Tourneur as a stick to beat Webster. It is a measure, I suppose, of his simplifying historical view that he does not use the other usual stick—*The Changeling*. Being written in 1622 *The Changeling* ought to be an example of decadence, if decadence derives, as Mr. McDonald implies, from decades. It is assumed (on very inadequate evidence) that Webster is trying to copy *The Revenger's Tragedy,* and Mr. McDonald finds (naturally enough) that Webster fails in this. Flamineo, it is true, prostitutes his sister to the duke; and Vindice acts as duke's pander to *his* sister. So we have a common motif. But the idea that courtly advancement is an enemy to family loyalties is the mainspring to much Jacobean drama—*The Malcontent, Women Beware Women, Westward-Ho* come immediately to mind. And what Webster makes of the motif is quite distinct from what Tourneur makes of it.

I trust I need not labor the point that Castiza is a very different figure from Vittoria.

The final charge against Webster is that he steals so many of his lines from other people; Mr. McDonald supposes that this prevents him from exercising a proper artistic control over his material. I would have expected a student of rhetoric to be better acquainted than this implies with the theory of *imitatio* (not mentioned in this connection). If we disallow the license for "originality" allowed by *imitatio*, what becomes of *Sejanus, Astrophel and Stella, Euphues,* even *Coriolanus?* Mr. McDonald does not answer, does not indeed even raise, this question.

The essay on Webster marks the nadir of the book, and it would be improper to stop with remarks on this as if on a final judgment. Where Mr. McDonald's sympathies and understanding are better aligned, as in the essays on Chapman and Tourneur, he is a much better critic. But even in these essays the need to support a thesis about rhetorical forms gets in his way. Talk of the opposition between appearance and reality in *The Revenger's Tragedy* as an antilogy seems unnecessarily labored. There is a thematic opposition in the play, supported by the tendency of drama to set up opposed speeches; and this is as obvious in *The Dance of Death* as in *The Revenger's Tragedy*. Need any more be said?

One final point: before the University of Massachusetts Press sets up another book spattered with words in Greek it would be well advised to secure compositors or proofreaders who can recognize the need for accents and breathers.

G. K. Hunter

Notes on Contributors

JOHN CANUTESON teaches in the English department at the Marathon County Center of the University of Wisconsin. He has articles on medieval poetry and *Volpone* awaiting publication.

MAURICE CHARNEY is Professor of English at Rutgers University. His publications include *Shakespeare's Roman Plays* (1961) and *"Hamlet Without Words"* (1965). He is currently working on Elizabethan dramatic form.

BEATRICE CORRIGAN, Professor of Italian at The University of Toronto, has published *A Catalogue of Italian Plays, 1500–1700, in The Library of The University of Toronto* (1961) and has previously contributed to *Renaissance Drama*.

T. W. CRAIK is Senior Lecturer in English at the University of Aberdeen. He has written *The Tudor Interlude* (1958) and *The Comic Tales of Chaucer* (1964) and has edited works by Sidney, Massinger, and Marlowe.

E. C. FORSYTH is Foundation Professor of French at La Trobe University,

Melbourne, Australia. He has written on "The Tragic Dilemma in Horace" (1965) and edited Jean de La Taille.

O. B. HARDISON, Professor of English at the University of North Carolina, is an editor of *The Encyclopedia of Poetry and Poetics* (1965) and the author of *The Enduring Monument* (1962) and *Christian Rite and Christian Drama in the Middle Ages* (1965).

G. K. HUNTER, Professor of English Literature at the University of Warwick, has edited *All's Well That Ends Well* and is the author of *John Lyly: The Humanist as Courtier* (1962).

JOEL H. KAPLAN of the University of Western Ontario has produced and directed Elizabethan plays.

RICHARD LEVIN is Professor of English at The State University of New York at Stony Brook. He has published a number of articles on plot structure in Elizabethan drama.

JULIET SUTTON McMASTER, Assistant Professor of English at The University of Alberta, has written articles on "Thackeray's Mother-in-law" (1965) and "Ford's Use of Burton's Imagery" (1963). She is currently working on articles on Henry James and Jane Austen.

MICHAEL MANHEIM is Professor of English and chairman of the department at the University of Toledo and has published articles on the plays of Thomas Dekker in various journals.

DIETER MEHL is Professor of English at the University of Bonn. His publications include *The Elizabethan Dumb Show* (1965), *The Middle English Romances of the Thirteenth and Fourteenth Centuries* (1968), and numerous translations and articles.

KENNETH MUIR, who is King Alfred Professor of English Literature at the University of Liverpool, is editor of *Shakespeare Survey*. He has edited *King Lear* for the New Arden Shakespeare and is the author of *Shakespeare's Sources* (1957).

PETER MULLANY, Assistant Professor of English at Marquette University, is writing a book on Caroline drama.

MOODY PRIOR, Professor of English at Northwestern University, is the author of *The Language of Tragedy* (1947).

Books Received

The listing of a book does not preclude its subsequent review in *Renaissance Drama*.

Anglo-Polish Renaissance Texts, For the Use of Shakespeare Students, ed. WITOLD CHWALEWIK. The Neophilological Committee of Polish Academy of Sciences. Warsaw: PWN—Polish Scientific Publishers, 1968. Pp. 262. 70 zlotys.

BEAUMONT, FRANCIS. *The Knight of the Burning Pestle,* ed. JOHN DOEBLER. Regents Renaissance Drama. Lincoln: University of Nebraska Press, 1967. Pp. xxiv + 145. $4.75 (paper, $1.65).

———. *The Knight of the Burning Pestle,* ed. ANDREW GURR. The Fountainwell Drama Texts. Edinburgh: Oliver & Boyd, 1968. Pp. 123. 10s 6d (paper).

BROME, RICHARD. *A Jovial Crew,* ed. ANN HAAKER. Regents Renaissance Drama. Lincoln: University of Nebraska Press, 1968. Pp. xxi + 144. $4.75 (paper, $1.65).

CHAPMAN, GEORGE. *All Fools,* ed. FRANK MANLEY. Regents Renaissance Drama. Lincoln: University of Nebraska Press, 1968. Pp. xx + 103. $4.75 (paper, $1.65).

CIBBER, COLLEY. *An Apology for the Life of Colley Cibber, With an Historical View of the Stage During His Own Time, Written by Himself*, ed. B. R. S. FONE. Ann Arbor: The University of Michigan Press, 1968. Pp. xxxii + 372. $9.75.

CRAIG, HARDIN. *The Literature of the English Renaissance 1485–1600*. Volume II in *A History of English Literature*, gen. ed. HARDIN CRAIG. New York: Collier Books, 1966. Pp. 290. $.95 (paper).

DEKKER, THOMAS. *The Shoemakers' Holiday*, ed. PAUL C. DAVIES. The Fountainwell Drama Texts. Edinburgh: Oliver & Boyd, 1968. Pp. 111. 10s 6d.

DRYDEN, JOHN. *All For Love: Or, the World Well Lost*, ed. JOHN J. ENCK. Crofts Classics. New York: Appleton-Century-Crofts, 1966. Pp. xxxix + 86. $.50 (paper).

DUCHARTRE, PIERRE LOUIS. *The Italian Comedy*, translated from the French by RANDOLPH T. WEAVER. New York: Dover Publications, Inc., 1966. Pp. 367. $3.00 (paper).

Elizabethan Love Stories, ed. T. J. B. SPENCER. Baltimore: Penguin Books, 1968. Pp. 215. $1.25 (paper).

Evidence for Authorship: Essays on Problems of Attribution, ed. DAVID V. ERDMAN and EPHIM G. FOGEL. Ithaca: Cornell University Press, 1966. Pp. xiv + 559.

FORD, JOHN. *The Broken Heart*, ed. DONALD K. ANDERSON, JR. Regents Renaissance Drama. Lincoln: University of Nebraska Press, 1968. Pp. xxiii + 117. $4.75 (paper, $1.65).

HEYWOOD, THOMAS. *The Fair Maid of the West*, Parts I and II, ed. ROBERT K. TURNER, JR. Regents Renaissance Drama. Lincoln: University of Nebraska Press, 1968. Pp. xx + 213. $4.75 (paper, $1.65).

JONSON, BEN. *The Alchemist*, ed. S. MUSGROVE. The Fountainwell Drama Texts. Edinburgh: Oliver & Boyd, 1968. Pp. 163. 12s 6d (paper).

———. *Volpone*, ed. JAY L. HALIO. The Fountainwell Drama Texts. Edinburgh: Oliver & Boyd, 1968. Pp. 170. 12s 6d (paper).

KYD, THOMAS. *The Spanish Tragedy*, ed. THOMAS W. ROSS. The Fountainwell Drama Texts. Edinburgh: Oliver & Boyd, 1968. Pp. 128. 10s 6d (paper).

LAWLESS, DONALD S. *Philip Massinger and His Associates*. Ball State Monograph Number Ten (Publications in English, No. 6). Muncie: Ball State University, 1967. Pp. ix + 67 (paper).

Literary Criticism and Historical Understanding: Selected Papers from the English Institute, ed. PHILIP DAMON. New York & London: Columbia University Press, 1967. Pp. vii + 190. $5.50.

McDONALD, CHARLES OSBORNE. *The Rhetoric of Tragedy: Form in Stuart*

Drama. Amherst: The University of Massachusetts Press, 1966. Pp. vii + 360. $7.50.

MARLOWE, CHRISTOPHER. *Tamburlaine the Great, Parts I and II,* ed. JOHN D. JUMP. Regents Renaissance Drama. Lincoln: University of Nebraska Press, 1967. Pp. xxvi + 205. $4.75 (paper, $1.65).

MARSTON, JOHN. *The Dutch Courtesan,* ed. PETER DAVISON. The Fountainwell Drama Texts. Edinburgh: Oliver & Boyd, 1968. Pp. 115. 10s 6d (paper).

MIDDLETON, THOMAS. *A Trick to Catch the Old One,* ed. CHARLES BARBER. The Fountainwell Drama Texts. Edinburgh: Oliver & Boyd, 1968. Pp. 109. 10s 6d (paper).

MUIR, KENNETH. *Introduction to Elizabethan Literature.* Random House Studies in Language and Literature. New York: Random House, 1967. Pp. 207. $1.95 (paper).

PRICE, JOSEPH G. *The Unfortunate Comedy. A Study of* All's Well that Ends Well *and Its Critics.* Toronto: University of Toronto Press, 1968. Pp. viii + 197. $7.25.

RIGHTER, ANNE. *Shakespeare and the Idea of the Play.* Penguin Shakespeare Library. Baltimore: Penguin Books, 1967. Pp. 200. $1.65 (paper).

SCALA, FLAMINIO. *Scenarios of the* Commedia dell'Arte: *Flaminio Scala's* Il Teatro delle favole rappresentative, *trans. and ed. HENRY F. SALERNO. With a foreword by Kenneth McKee. New York: New York University Press, 1967. Pp. xxxii + 413. $9.75.

Shakespeare Jahrbuch, v. 103, ed. ANSELM SCHLÖSSER and ARMIN-GERD KUCKHOFF. Deutsche Shakespeare-Gesellschaft. Weimar: Hermann Böhlaus Nachfolger, 1967. Pp. 302.

Shakespeare Jahrbuch. Supplement zu v. 103, ed. ANSELM SCHLÖSSER and ARMIN-GERD KUCKHOFF. Deutsche Shakespeare-Gesellschaft. Weimar: Hermann Böhlaus Nachfolger, 1967. Pp. 157.

Shakespeare Jahrbuch, v. 104, ed. ANSELM SCHLÖSSER and ARMIN-GERD KUCKHOFF. Deutsche Shakespeare-Gesellschaft. Weimar: Hermann Böhlaus Nachfolger, 1968. Pp. 432.

Shakespeare's Comedies: An Anthology of Modern Criticism, ed. LAURENCE LERNER. Penguin Shakespeare Library. Baltimore: Penguin Books, 1967. Pp. 346. $1.65 (paper).

SPINGARN, J. E. *A History of Literary Criticism in the Renaissance,* with a new introduction by BERNARD WEINBERG. New York and Burlingame: Harcourt, Brace & World, Inc., 1963. Pp. xxi + 227. $2.25 (paper).

STAVIG, MARK. *John Ford and the Traditional Moral Order.* Madison, Milwaukee, and London: The University of Wisconsin Press, 1968. Pp. xx + 225. $6.95.

STYAN, J. L. *Shakespeare's Stagecraft.* Cambridge, Eng.: Cambridge University Press, 1967. Pp. viii + 244. $7.95 (paper, $2.45).

Twentieth Century Interpretations of The Duchess of Malfi: *A Collection of Critical Essays,* ed. NORMAN RABKIN. Englewood Cliffs, N.J.: Prentice-Hall, Inc., 1968. Pp. viii + 120. $1.25 (paper).

Twentieth Century Interpretations of Hamlet: *A Collection of Critical Essays,* ed. DAVID BEVINGTON. Englewood Cliffs, N.J.: Prentice-Hall, Inc., 1968. Pp. viii + 120. $3.95 (paper, $1.25).

VELZ, JOHN W. *Shakespeare and the Classical Tradition: A Critical Guide to Commentary, 1660–1960.* Minneapolis: University of Minnesota Press, 1968. Pp. xvii + 459. $17.50.

WAGER, W. *The Longer Thou Livest* and *Enough Is as Good as a Feast,* ed. R. MARK BENBOW. Regents Renaissance Drama. Lincoln: University of Nebraska Press, 1967. Pp. xxii + 156. $4.75 (paper, $1.65).

WEIMANN, ROBERT. *Shakespeare und die Tradition des Volkstheaters: Soziologie, Dramaturgie, Gestaltung.* Berlin: Henschelverlag, 1967. Pp. 552. DM 27.50.

YOUNG, DAVID P. *Something of Great Constancy: The Art of "A Midsummer Night's Dream."* Yale Studies in English, vol. 164. New Haven & London: Yale University Press, 1966. Pp. xii + 190. $5.00.

Corrigendum

IN THE PROCESS OF PRINTING "Inigo Jones and the Jonsonian Masque," by Stephen Orgel, in *Renaissance Drama,* New Series I, 1968, Figure 3 (page 136) was printed as a line engraving rather than as a halftone. This resulted in the unfortunate loss of the perspective lines which should be clearly visible through the central arch, to which Mr. Orgel referred on page 135.